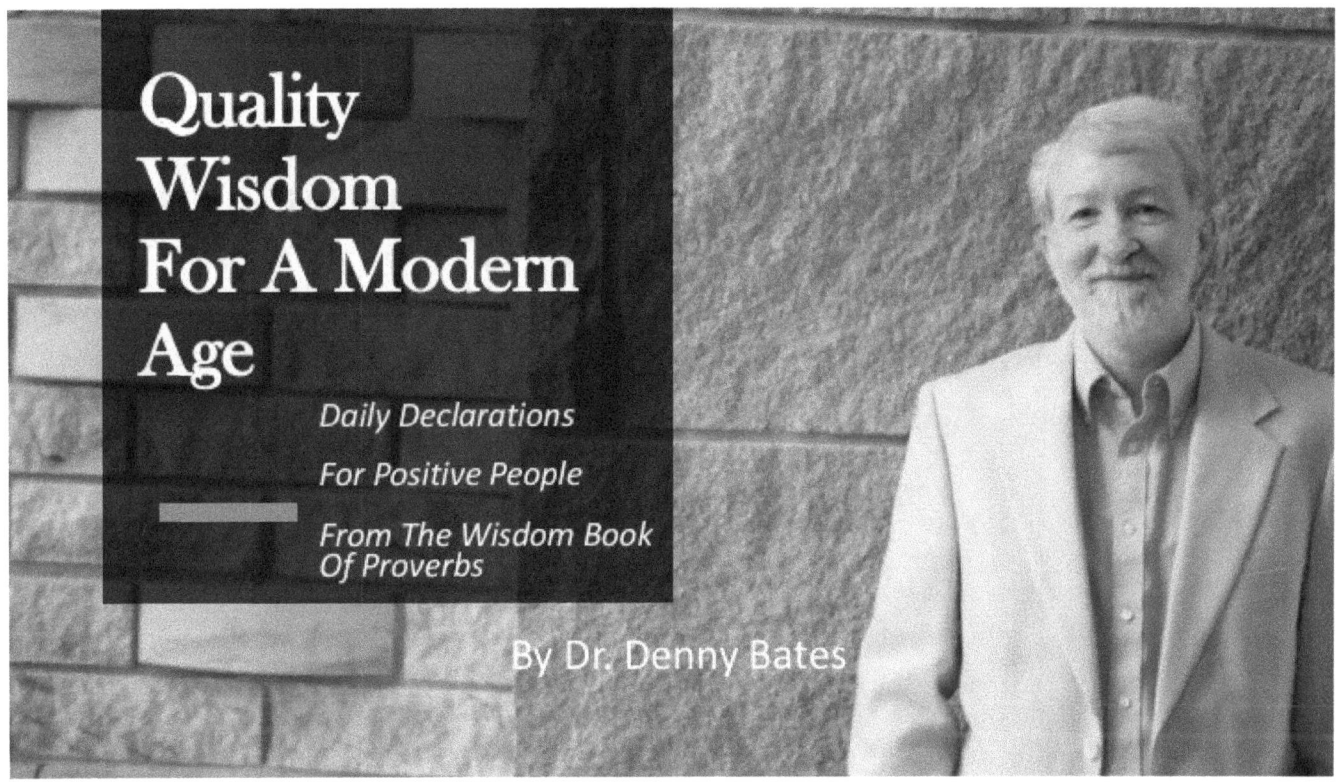

Quality Wisdom For A Modern Age:
Daily Declarations For Positive People

Based On, Today May You In Proverbs:
The Quality Leader's Essential Guidebook For
Personal, Professional, and Spiritual Growth

By Dr. Denny Bates

Quality Wisdom For A Modern Age

Quality Wisdom For A Modern Age:
Daily Declarations For Positive People

Today May You In Proverbs
The Quality Leader's Essential Guidebook For
Personal, Professional, and Spiritual Growth

Copyright © 2019 by
Dr. Denny Bates and Something New Christian Publishers

Scripture quotations marked (NLT) are taken from the Holy Bible, New Living Translation, copyright © 1996, 2004, 2007 by Tyndale House Foundation. Used by permission of Tyndale House Publishers, Inc., Carol Stream, Illinois 60188. All rights reserved.

All other Bible study and reference tools, Copyright © 2019
by Dr. Denny Bates, The Quality Disciple, and Something New Christian Publishers

ISBN-978-0-578-61417-5

All Rights Reserved. No part of this publication may be reproduced, stored in a retrieval system, or transmitted in any form or by any means—electronic, mechanical, photocopy, recording, or any other—except brief quotations in printed reviews, without the prior permission of the author.

Quality Wisdom For A Modern Age: Daily Declarations For Positive People is written as a tool for the people of God to use in order to grow in their faith and then to pass it on to other believers. The purpose of the copyright is to prevent the reproduction, misuse, and abuse of the material. Please address all requests for information or permission to:

Something New Christian Publishers
E-Mail dennybates@gmail.com
On the Web: www.dennybates.com

You can "friend" me on Facebook at www.facebook.com/denny.bates
or follow me on Twitter @dennybates

www.TheQualityDisciple.com

Daily Declarations For Positive People

Table Of Contents

SPECIAL FEATURES	vi
DEDICATION AND ACKNOWLEDGEMENTS	vii
FOREWORD	viii
ABOUT THE BOOK OF PROVERBS	ix
QUALITY QUOTES FOR THE QUALITY LEADER WHO DESIRES TO GROW	x
INTRODUCTION TO SECTION ONE	xi
HOW TO USE THIS RESOURCE	xii
Section One: **"GROWING IN GREATNESS"** (Proverbs 1:1-5:14)	Page 1
Section Two: **"LEGACY LIVING"** (Proverbs 6:1-11:11)	Page 20
Section Three: **"EMPOWERED TO ENCOURAGE"** (Proverbs 11:13-13:14)	Page 40
Section Four: **"INTENTIONAL INFLUENCE"** (Proverbs 13:16-15:17)	Page 59
Section Five: **"DISCIPLINED FOR DESTINY"** (Proverbs 15:22-17:17)	Page 75
Section Six: **"STRATEGIC SELF-AWARENESS"** (Proverbs 17:18-20:13)	Page 90
Section Seven: **"PURSUING THE PROMISES"** (Proverbs 20:15-23:11)	Page 108
Section Eight: **"COMMITTED TO THE CALL"** (Proverbs 23:17-28:2)	Page 128
Section Nine: **"LOVING TO LEAD"** (Proverbs 28:3-31:30)	Page 148
My Quality Life Mission Statement Manifesto based upon Proverbs 3:5-6	Page 168
RESOURCES FOR THE QUALITY LEADER	Page 169

My Quality Life Plan	Page 170
The Balanced Triad of Biblical Discipleship	Page 171
How You Can Have A Relationship With Jesus	Page 172
Subject Index	Page 173
Scripture Index	Page 286
Topical Bibliography For The Quality Disciple	Page 296
Quality Leadership and Spiritual Growth Resources	Page 299
Help Me Write My Story	Page 301
Quality Leadership Consultants	Page 304
Something New / The Quality Disciple / Disciple-Making Ministry	Page 306
Testimonials	Page 307
About Dr. Denny Bates	Page 309
Praise For Quality Wisdom For A Modern Age	Page 310

Daily Declarations For Positive People

SPECIAL FEATURES OF
"QUALITY WISDOM FOR A MODERN AGE"

"Quality Wisdom For A Modern Age" Is A Book For . . .

❖ Busy People!	❖ Business Leaders	❖ Parents
❖ Students	❖ Pastors	❖ Teachers
❖ Small Group Leaders	❖ Civic Leaders	❖ Government Leaders
❖ Counselors	❖ Doctors	❖ Lawyers
❖ The New Christian	❖ The Seasoned Christian	❖ The Not Sure

- ❖ Nine full sessions, with thirty-one days of devotions in each session that are easy to read and practically apply to one's life in five minutes or less.
- ❖ Positive declarations of prayer that will seal each devotional truth in one's heart.
- ❖ Nine full Bible study lessons for each of the nine sessions.
- ❖ 279 daily devotions designed to move the reader to experience a transformational life change.
- ❖ At the end of this book there is a 112-page subject index where one can choose between over 500 major subjects and thousands of subpoints that can be used as a topical Bible study for living the victorious Christian life.
- ❖ Each passage of Scripture written out, using the modern, easy to understand and read, New Living Translation (NLT).
- ❖ Formatted in a convenient workbook size that gives the reader plenty of space for taking notes.
- ❖ Strategically designed for use in small groups and as sermon prep and classroom studies.
- ❖ The perfect gift for the person who loves the Book of Proverbs.

Dedication and Acknowledgements

Friendship. Relationship. Fellowship. Mentorship. Discipleship. Leadership. Partnership. Stewardship. Workmanship. All nine of these descriptive terms pretty well sum up what I've come to experience in doing life with my cherished friend Hank "Hammer" "Bubba" Anderson going on now for about 45 years and counting.

The path of life presents to all of us, often it seems at times, a very curious journey where we meet the people we are meant to meet and where we are then led to experience extraordinary incredible memories with them. The older I become, I've begun to appreciate the people who have crossed my path. By looking back, I have a much better appreciation for how rich I've become when it comes to the relational treasures the Lord has so graciously given to me. One of those treasures is Hank.

We first met when he was a young boy. His dad and I had met and quickly formed a bond that is still impacting my life today. Morris, Hank's dad, was my mentor when I was transitioning from being a teenager to crossing over into adulthood into my twenties. Dr. Anderson was a pivotal mentor that God used to set me on the course I am today. And as Morris was mentoring me, I was doing the same with his son, Hank.

I marvel at where Hank and I are today. As we have both progressed through the years, when many relationships come and go and are only meant for a season, we've seen our friendship not only continue but to actually grow even deeper. For us, what began as a friendship has developed over time into a priority meeting that goes on the "repeat event" calendar of weekly events. Rarely do we miss our weekly meeting.

In making this commitment of time, we have both personally experienced a deeper layer of **Friendship** (Iron does sharpen iron). **Relationship** (We matter to each other, and it shows). **Fellowship** (There are few things any sweeter in life than to have a trustworthy person to talk with about the challenges; And, just as important, the blessings of life). **Mentorship** (I'm honored to have been Hank's confidant for years and have been able, by God's grace, to guide him through personal, professional, and spiritual growth opportunities). **Discipleship** (There are far few joys for the believer than to be a DiscipleMaker4Jesus). **Leadership** (The great leaders are doers. I've seen Hank make the necessary sacrifices to become one of the most respected attorneys in his field of specialty). **Partnership** (I have no greater supporter in what I do than Hank. The Lord has used him when I needed a boost of encouragement as I pursued my dream job of writing and coaching). **Stewardship** (Time is our greatest investment. We have been willing to spend the time to meet and then to grow). **Workmanship** (God is at work in both of us. We are both in process and are thankful to be created by Him for good works).

When I began to take this book from the creative storage bin in my mind and get into the flow of writing, I knew to whom I would dedicate *Quality Wisdom for a Modern Age* was an important decision. My criteria were pretty clear and concise: I needed to have a significant history with them, and this person needed to be a living example of how to live life based upon the wisdom of Proverbs. After praying, who I needed to dedicate this transformational book to became obvious. Having a friendship that began in the previous century and has spanned over four decades, Hank Anderson is not only extremely faithful and loyal, my personal attorney, my brother in Christ, but even more humbling is that he honors me by calling me his friend.

So, I dedicate this book to my friend Hank. But I dedicate it to you also, my dear reader. If you commit to become a Person of the Proverbs, your life will never be the same again. That is my prayer for Hank, for you, and for me: Daily, Today May We all be transformed by the practical and ageless principles given in *Quality Wisdom For A Modern Age*.

Dr. Denny Bates

November 20, 2019

"May you experience the love of Christ, though it is too great to understand fully. Then you will be made complete with all the fullness of life and power that comes from God. Now all glory to God, who is able, through his mighty power at work within us, to accomplish infinitely more than we might ask or think."
Ephesians 3:19-20 NLT

Acknowledgements

My books are so much better because of those who willingly volunteer their time to read through the sample proof and make sure, first and foremost, that the contents speak to the heart first and then to the mind. They are also people of good grammar and watch out for those pesky typos that get by me, but not them. I am grateful to Bryan Braddock, Amy Watts, Reeves Cannon, Dick Brown, Tamara Rhodes, Lisa Ray, Traci McCombs, Amy Clark, Ron Lyles, Wick Jackson, Patty Smith, Leslie Rutten, Laura Harris, Cleo Corey, Carol Mabe, and Kirby King.

FOREWORD

There are a very select few people that you will find in life that are just as passionate about your success as you are. Usually your greatest support team will be you mother, father, spouse, grand-parent or a very close childhood friend. Seldom if ever do you come across someone later in life that sees something in you that you no longer see in yourself and will come along side of you as your biggest cheerleader. That miracle someone came in my life in the form of Denny Bates. At a time when my mother and greatest cheerleader had just passed away, my father-in-law had passed away and my wife, Tracey, and I were doing the best we could to prop each other up during our time of grief is when I met Dr. Denny Bates.

I remember vividly meeting our first time in person at Panera Bread for lunch. Because of some mutual friends we had become connected on Facebook, so we had a little knowledge of each other via the Facebook filtered lens. We all know that Facebook is a promotional tool for the best parts of our life and the life we want everyone to think we live. So, through this lens I knew Denny as the local encouraging Rockstar from Aisle 31 at the local hardware store. This guy had his picture taken with every local in town who was a celebrity in the city of Florence, SC. Preachers, local politicians, community movers and shakers as well as the longtime community legacies in our small city were displayed in hundreds of pictures with Dr. Denny Bates. I had to meet this guy and see if he was the real deal. It didn't take me long in our conversation to see his genuineness. He was transparent, humble, aware of his failures yet sure of his calling. That calling is to help and encourage others. I sensed an immediate connection and brotherhood with Denny. I knew that we would be lifelong friends. He was what we all need in life. Someone that will listen to us, connect with us and passionately encourage us. There is no lack of people that will tell you what you can't do in life but few that will not only support what you think you can do while encouraging you that you can achieve far more.

Denny has helped me in many ways. We have enjoyed fellowship over a meal, been in Bible studies together and worked on projects together. He is great at one on one and that connection is what he brings to his book "Quality Wisdom for A Modern Age." You will get to know Dr. Denny Bates personally as he takes you through a spiritual growth process using the greatest book on wisdom ever written. Denny presents the biblical truths of the book of Proverbs to help you believe in you and he encourages you all along the way. Even non-believers use the principles of Proverbs in their self-help books, but they don't understand the true power of these principles and that is having a relationship with Jesus Christ. Denny makes sure that he doesn't leave you believing that applying these principles may work for others. He makes sure you believe that they will work for you and encourages you every step of the way. I have been blessed to come to know Denny and call him my friend. I am certain that you will be blessed to get to know him through this book and that you too will find a lifelong friend in Dr. Denny Bates.

Proverbs 18:24 "A man that hath friends must shew himself friendly: and there is a friend that sticketh closer than a brother."

Bryan A. Braddock
Executive Director of the House of Hope

Forward Focused LLC
www.forwardfocusedllc.com

Quality Wisdom For A Modern Age

What Notable Theologians Say About the Book of Proverbs

Charles Spurgeon on The Book of Proverbs:

"The Proverbs appear at first sight to be thrown together without connection, but it is not so: when you come to close reading you will discover that they are threaded pearls, and that they are in proper position with regard to each other."

Billy Graham on the Book of Proverbs:

"The Psalms tell us how to get along with God, and the Proverbs tell us how to get along with our fellow man."

Nate Pickowicz on the Book of Proverbs:

"The beautiful thing about the wisdom of Proverbs is that it's timeless. While textbooks often need updating, Proverbs hasn't had a 2nd edition in three millennia!"

The Book of Proverbs *is* the pathway towards Growing in Greatness!

> [5] Trust in the LORD with all your heart; do not depend on your own understanding.
> [6] Seek his will in all you do, and he will show you which path to take. **Proverbs 3:5-6 (NLT)**

"God does not give us everything we want, but He does fulfill His promises, leading us along the best and straightest paths to Himself." – **Dietrich Bonhoeffer**

This wonderful and timeless book of Proverbs will be the path that will, as Bonhoeffer says, lead us along the best and straightest paths to Himself.

Daily Declarations For Positive People

QUALITY QUOTES FOR THE QUALITY LEADER
WHO DESIRES TO GROW:

"Transformation is not five minutes from now; it's a present activity. In this moment you can make a different choice, and it's these small choices and successes that build up over time to help cultivate a healthy self-image and self-esteem." —*Jillian Michaels*

"Transformation literally means going beyond your form." —*Wayne Dyer*

"Transformation is a process, and as life happens there are tons of ups and downs. It's a journey of discovery." —*Rick Warren*

"Income seldom exceeds personal development." —*Jim Rohn*

"You cannot dream yourself into a character; you must hammer and forge yourself one."
—*Henry David Thoreau*

"Personal development is a major time-saver. The better you become, the less time it takes you to achieve your goals." —*Brian Tracy*

"The only person you are destined to become is the person you decide to be." —*Ralph Waldo Emerson*

"There is nothing noble in being superior to your fellow man; true nobility is being superior to your former self." —*Ernest Hemingway*

"When we are no longer able to change a situation, we are challenged to change ourselves."
—*Viktor E. Frankl*

"Of course motivation is not permanent. But then, neither is bathing; but it is something you should do on a regular basis." – *Zig Ziglar*

"As the physically weak man can make himself strong by careful and patient training, so the man of weak thoughts can make them strong by exercising himself in right thinking." – *James Allen*

"Growth is the great separator between those who succeed and those who do not. When I see a person beginning to separate themselves from the pack, it's almost always due to personal growth."
—*John C. Maxwell*

'And I am certain that God, who began the good work within you, will continue his work until it is finally finished on the day when Christ Jesus returns.' (Philippians 1:6 NLT) –*The Apostle Paul*

'But if you remain in me and my words remain in you, you may ask for anything you want, and it will be granted! When you produce much fruit, you are my true disciples. This brings great glory to my Father.' (John 15:7-8 NLT)—*Jesus*

Introduction To Section One:
"GROWING IN GREATNESS" (Proverbs 1:1-5:14)

Growing In Greatness Is To Be Every Leader's Goal

That is a noble goal. But what does it really mean to grow in greatness? Does it mean to become great at the expense of others? Does it mean that one allows just being "good enough" and to just settle for an average life? I do not believe so. In this case I align my thinking with the words of Jesus when it comes to greatness. He said,

[42] And calling them to Himself, Jesus said to them, "You know that those who are recognized as rulers of the Gentiles lord it over them; and their great men exercise authority over them. [43] "But it is not so among you, but whoever wishes to become great among you shall be your servant; [44] and whoever wishes to be first among you shall be slave of all. [45] "For even the Son of Man did not come to be served, but to serve, and to give His life a ransom for many." **Mark 10:42-45 (NASB77)**

Or as a modern translation puts it . . .

[43] But among you it will be different. Whoever wants to be a leader among you must be your servant, [44] and whoever wants to be first among you must be the slave of everyone else. [45] For even the Son of Man came not to be served but to serve others and to give his life as a ransom for many." **Mark 10:43-45 (NLT)**

If you are serious about growing in greatness then you are going to have to be serious in growing as a leader in three strategic areas of your life: Your Personal growth, your Professional growth, and your Spiritual growth. What is the key to experiencing monumental and measurable growth in all three? Having the heart of a servant kind of leader! How do you get there? The timeless Book of Proverbs will show you the way!

Before you jump in, I want to share with you a few ideas on how you can maximize your use of *Quality Wisdom For A Modern Age*.

Some Suggestions On How To Use Quality Wisdom For A Modern Age:

- You can use this spiritual growth resource as a daily devotion. It is designed as a tool you can use as a devotion and a Bible study: You can use it in the morning before you begin your day and at night, at the end of your day. *You can also customize this resource and turn it into a small group study!*
- Contained in each devotional entry is The Day, The Title of The Devotion, The Proverb, The Positive Confession of "Today May You," and then the Declaration Of Quality Wisdom written as a Prayer Of Commitment.
- Though each one of the nine sections are set up as a thirty-one-day exercise, it can be adapted to your lifestyle. In other words, use what you need and then set aside the rest for another time. Your goal is not speed. Your goal needs to be spiritual growth.
- At the end there is a 112 page subject index where you can choose between over 500 major subjects and thousands of subpoints that can be used as a topical Bible study.

If you decide you want to take the daily approach, here is what you will experience:

- A passage of Scripture you can read and then let it set your spiritual framework for the rest of the day. Look for <u>key words</u> and <u>phrases</u> that you can mull over.
- For each daily Scripture there also is a *"Declaration Of Quality Wisdom"* which is your declaration for the day. It may help you better grasp the power of what you are reading by reading it aloud several times at the beginning and throughout the day.
- After you read the declaration you will be invited to personalize your declaration by offering it as a prayer. It might help you to also read this prayer aloud. Resist the temptation to rush through this spiritual experience. Words have meaning. Ponder each one of these precious words as you pray over each one.
- If you want to go deeper in your study, refer to the Subject Index at the back of the book.

Okay! Let's begin your journey into living out the great promises of *Quality Wisdom For A Modern Age!* Your next step towards spiritual growth begins on the next page.

Quality Wisdom For A Modern Age

"GROWING IN GREATNESS"
(Proverbs 1:1-5:14)

DAY ONE: "A Life Of Influence"

Today May You . . . have a heart that is open to wisdom, a mind that is willing to be disciplined, and have an unswerving commitment to do what is right, just, and fair.

These are the proverbs of Solomon, David's son, king of Israel.

Their purpose is to teach people wisdom and discipline,

to help them understand the insights of the wise.

Their purpose is to teach people to live disciplined and successful lives, to help them do what is right, just, and fair. (Proverbs 1:1-3 NLT).

Turn your *Declaration Of Quality Wisdom* into this prayer of commitment:

> *Lord Jesus, **Today May I** have a heart that is open to wisdom, a mind that is willing to be disciplined, and have an unswerving commitment to do what is right, just, and fair.*

DAY TWO: "Always The Student"

Today May You . . . ALWAYS be in a posture of learning where the more you learn the less you know, thus the need to keep on learning more and more!

These proverbs will give insight to the simple,

knowledge and discernment to the young.

Let the wise listen to these proverbs and become even wiser.

Let those with understanding receive guidance

by exploring the meaning in these proverbs and parables,

the words of the wise and their riddles. (Proverbs 1:4-6 NLT).

Turn your *Declaration Of Quality Wisdom* into this prayer of commitment:

> *Lord Jesus, **Today May I** ALWAYS be in a posture of learning where the more I learn the less I know, thus the need to keep on learning more and more!*

DAY THREE: "Awesome Living"

Today May You . . . have an AWESOME respect for an AWESOME Lord and set your heart in place to learn from Him.

Fear of the Lord is the foundation of true knowledge,
but fools despise wisdom and discipline. (Proverbs 1:7 NLT).

Turn your *Declaration Of Quality Wisdom* into this prayer of commitment:

> *Lord Jesus, **Today May I** have an AWESOME respect for an AWESOME Lord and set my heart in place to learn from Him.*

DAY FOUR: "The No Greed Zone"

Today May You . . . be CONTENT with what your PROVIDER provides and not be GREEDY in what only you can PROVIDE.

If a bird sees a trap being set,
it knows to stay away.
But these people set an ambush for themselves;
they are trying to get themselves killed.

Such is the fate of all who are greedy for money;

it robs them of life. (Proverbs 1:17-19 NLT).

Turn your *Declaration Of Quality Wisdom* into this prayer of commitment:

> Lord Jesus, ***Today May I*** be CONTENT with what my PROVIDER provides and not be GREEDY in what only I can PROVIDE.

DAY FIVE: "Guiding Wisdom"

Today May You . . . allow the Wisdom of the Lord guide you in everything you BELIEVE, THINK and DO.

Come and listen to my counsel.

I'll share my heart with you

and make you wise. (Proverbs 1:23 NLT).

Turn your *Declaration Of Quality Wisdom* into this prayer of commitment:

> Lord Jesus, ***Today May I*** allow the Wisdom of the Lord guide me in everything I BELIEVE, THINK and DO.

DAY SIX: "Listen And Do"

Today May You . . . set your ear to LISTEN to wisdom and not only hear what she has to say to you, but to do it as well.

But all who listen to me will live in peace,

untroubled by fear of harm." (Proverbs 1:33 NLT).

Turn your *Declaration Of Quality Wisdom* into this prayer of commitment:

*Lord Jesus, **Today May I** set my ear to LISTEN to wisdom and not only hear what she (wisdom) has to say to me, but to do it as well.*

DAY SEVEN: "High Value Wisdom"

Today May You . . . place a HIGH VALUE on the Lord's wisdom and the grace He gives for you to understand what to do with His wisdom.

My child, listen to what I say,

and treasure my commands.

Tune your ears to wisdom,

and concentrate on understanding.

Cry out for insight,

and ask for understanding.

Search for them as you would for silver;

seek them like hidden treasures.

Then you will understand what it means to fear the Lord,

and you will gain knowledge of God. (Proverbs 2:1-5 NLT).

Turn your *Declaration Of Quality Wisdom* into this prayer of commitment:

*Lord Jesus, **Today May I** place a HIGH VALUE on the Lord's wisdom and the grace He gives for me to understand what to do with His wisdom.*

DAY EIGHT: "The Common Sense Life"

Today May You . . . RECEIVE His wisdom and LISTEN closely to the knowledge and understanding that come from His mouth to your heart and then you will experience common sense and integrity.

For the Lord grants wisdom!
From his mouth come knowledge and understanding.
He grants a treasure of common sense to the honest.
He is a shield to those who walk with integrity. (Proverbs 2:6-7 NLT).

Turn your *Declaration Of Quality Wisdom* into this prayer of commitment:

> *Lord Jesus,* **Today May** *I RECEIVE Your wisdom and LISTEN closely to the knowledge and understanding that come from Your mouth to my heart and then I will experience common sense and integrity.*

DAY NINE: "A Wisdom That Fills You With Joy"

Today May You . . . be a "wise guy" or "wise gal" as His wisdom fills your heart and may the knowledge of His incredible love for you fill you with joy.

For wisdom will enter your heart,
and knowledge will fill you with joy. (Proverbs 2:10 NLT).

Turn your *Declaration Of Quality Wisdom* into this prayer of commitment:

> *Lord Jesus,* **Today May** *I be a "wise guy" or "wise gal" as Your wisdom fills my heart and may the knowledge of Your incredible love for me fill me with joy.*

DAY TEN: "The Wisdom Of Thinking Before You Speak"

Today May You . . . THINK before you ACT and UNDERSTAND what you want to SAY before you SPEAK.

Wise choices will watch over you.
Understanding will keep you safe. (Proverbs 2:11 NLT).

Turn your *Declaration Of Quality Wisdom* into this prayer of commitment:

> *Lord Jesus, **Today May I** THINK before I ACT and UNDERSTAND what I want to SAY before I SPEAK.*

DAY ELEVEN: "The Wisdom Of Avoiding Negative People"

Today May You . . . be on your guard and not become entangled with the kind of people who want to pull you down with their NEGATIVE WORDS and DESTRUCTIVE DEEDS.

Wisdom will save you from evil people,
from those whose words are twisted.
These men turn from the right way
to walk down dark paths.
They take pleasure in doing wrong,
and they enjoy the twisted ways of evil.
Their actions are crooked,
and their ways are wrong. (Proverbs 2:12-15 NLT).

Turn your *Declaration Of Quality Wisdom* into this prayer of commitment:

> Lord Jesus, **Today May I** be on my guard and not become entangled with the kind of people who want to pull me down with their NEGATIVE WORDS and DESTRUCTIVE DEEDS.

DAY TWELVE: "The Path Of Right Living"

Today May You . . . take a walk down the path of PROMISE, PROSPERITY, and PASSION so you may think right, speak right, and do right.

So follow the steps of the good,
and stay on the paths of the righteous.
For only the godly will live in the land,
and those with integrity will remain in it. (Proverbs 2:20-21 NLT).

Turn your *Declaration Of Quality Wisdom* into this prayer of commitment:

> Lord Jesus, **Today May I** take a walk down the path of PROMISE, PROSPERITY, and PASSION so I may think right, speak right, and do right.

DAY THIRTEEN: "Heart Resources"

Today May You . . . put enough of God's Word in your heart so that you will have plenty of spiritual resources to draw from, not just for now but for the future too.

My child, never forget the things I have taught you.
Store my commands in your heart.

If you do this, you will live many years,

and your life will be satisfying. (Proverbs 3:1-2 NLT).

Turn your *Declaration Of Quality Wisdom* into this prayer of commitment:

> *Lord Jesus, **Today May I** put enough of God's Word in my heart so that I will have plenty of spiritual resources to draw from, not just for now but for the future too.*

DAY FOURTEEN: "The Best Kind Of Life"

Today May You . . . set it to be your goal to be the most LOYAL and KIND person you know.

Never let loyalty and kindness leave you!

Tie them around your neck as a reminder.

Write them deep within your heart.

Then you will find favor with both God and people,

and you will earn a good reputation. (Proverbs 3:3-4 NLT).

Turn your *Declaration Of Quality Wisdom* into this prayer of commitment:

> *Lord Jesus, **Today May I** set it to be my goal to be the most LOYAL and KIND person I know.*

DAY FIFTEEN: "The Keys To A Wildly Successful Life"

Today May You . . . TRUST Him with everything you've got instead of TRUSTING you with everything you have, and as you live your life, TRUST His will to take you where you need to go.

Trust in the Lord with all your heart;

do not depend on your own understanding.

Seek his will in all you do,

and he will show you which path to take. (Proverbs 3:5-6 NLT).

Turn your *Declaration Of Quality Wisdom* into this prayer of commitment:

Lord Jesus, **Today May I** *TRUST You with everything I've got instead of TRUSTING me with everything I have, and as I live my life, I will TRUST Your will to take me where I need to go.*

DAY SIXTEEN: "Wisdom That Heals And Strengthens"

Today May You . . . protect yourself from taking your own advice and not His.

Don't be impressed with your own wisdom.

Instead, fear the Lord and turn away from evil.

Then you will have healing for your body

and strength for your bones. (Proverbs 3:7-8 NLT).

Turn your *Declaration Of Quality Wisdom* into this prayer of commitment:

Lord Jesus, **Today May I** *protect myself from taking my own advice and not Yours.*

DAY SEVENTEEN: "The Secret To Experiencing An Abundant Life"

Today May You . . . give back to God what He has already given to you and ENJOY the abundant fruit of His blessing.

Honor the Lord with your wealth

and with the best part of everything you produce.

Then he will fill your barns with grain,

and your vats will overflow with good wine. (Proverbs 3:9-10 NLT).

Turn your *Declaration Of Quality Wisdom* into this prayer of commitment:

> *Lord Jesus, **Today May I** give back to You what You has already given to me and ENJOY the abundant fruit of Your blessing.*

DAY EIGHTEEN: "How To Know God Really Loves You"

Today May You . . . be willing to check your heart and be humble and be open to the Lord's loving correction--and experience an ABUNDANT LIFE.

My child, don't reject the Lord's discipline,

and don't be upset when he corrects you.

For the Lord corrects those he loves,

just as a father corrects a child in whom he delights. (Proverbs 3:11-12 NLT).

Turn your *Declaration Of Quality Wisdom* into this prayer of commitment:

> *Lord Jesus, **Today May I** be willing to check my heart and be humble and be open to the Your loving correction--and experience an ABUNDANT LIFE.*

DAY NINETEEN: "Joyful Wisdom"

Today May You . . . be a person of JOY because you are finding wisdom in everything you THINK and DO.

Joyful is the person who finds wisdom,

the one who gains understanding.

For wisdom is more profitable than silver,

and her wages are better than gold.

Wisdom is more precious than rubies;

nothing you desire can compare with her. (Proverbs 3:13-15 NLT).

Turn your *Declaration Of Quality Wisdom* into this prayer of commitment:

> *Lord Jesus,* ***Today May I*** *be a person of JOY because I am finding wisdom in everything I THINK and DO.*

DAY TWENTY: "The Astounding Benefits Of Embracing God's Wisdom"

Today May You . . . have a deep and abiding relationship with God's wisdom and enjoy LONG LIFE, RICHES and HONOR, and a HAPPY and SATISFIED LIFE.

She [wisdom] offers you long life in her right hand,

and riches and honor in her left.

She will guide you down delightful paths;

all her ways are satisfying.

Wisdom is a tree of life to those who embrace her;

happy are those who hold her tightly. (Proverbs 3:16-18 NLT).

Turn your *Declaration Of Quality Wisdom* into this prayer of commitment:

*Lord Jesus, **Today May I** have a deep and abiding relationship with God's wisdom and enjoy LONG LIFE, RICHES and HONOR, and a HAPPY and SATISFIED LIFE.*

DAY TWENTY-ONE: "The Great Value Of Embracing Common Sense And Discernment"

Today May You . . . place great value on embracing common sense and discernment and do everything in your power to make them an essential part of your day.

My child, don't lose sight of common sense and discernment.

Hang on to them,

for they will refresh your soul.

They are like jewels on a necklace.

They keep you safe on your way,

and your feet will not stumble.

You can go to bed without fear;

you will lie down and sleep soundly.

You need not be afraid of sudden disaster

or the destruction that comes upon the wicked,

for the Lord is your security.

He will keep your foot from being caught in a trap. (Proverbs 3:21-26 NLT).

Turn your *Declaration Of Quality Wisdom* into this prayer of commitment:

*Lord Jesus, **Today May I** place great value on embracing common sense and discernment and do everything in my power to make them an essential part of my day.*

DAY TWENTY-TWO: "Won't You Be My Neighbor?"

Today May You . . . do the kinds of things that will make you the kind of neighbor you want your neighbor to be to you.

Do not withhold good from those who deserve it
when it's in your power to help them.
If you can help your neighbor now, don't say,
"Come back tomorrow, and then I'll help you."
Don't plot harm against your neighbor,
for those who live nearby trust you.
Don't pick a fight without reason,
when no one has done you harm. (Proverbs 3:27-30 NLT).

Turn your *Declaration Of Quality Wisdom* into this prayer of commitment:

> *Lord Jesus, **Today May I** do the kinds of things that will make me the kind of neighbor I want my neighbor to be for me.*

DAY TWENTY-THREE: "Fork In The Road Living"

Today May You . . . ALWAYS make the right decisions when you come to the Fork in The Road between living a life for Jesus or a life for you.

Don't envy violent people
or copy their ways.
Such wicked people are detestable to the Lord,
but he offers his friendship to the godly.
The Lord curses the house of the wicked,
but he blesses the home of the upright.

The Lord mocks the mockers

but is gracious to the humble.

The wise inherit honor,

but fools are put to shame! (Proverbs 3:31-35 NLT).

Turn your *Declaration Of Quality Wisdom* into this prayer of commitment:

*Lord Jesus, **Today May I** ALWAYS make the right decisions when I come to the Fork in The Road between living a life for Jesus or a life for myself.*

DAY TWENTY-FOUR: "Get Wisdom While You Can"

Today May You . . . GET WISDOM before foolishness gets you.

Get wisdom; develop good judgment.

Don't forget my words or turn away from them.

Don't turn your back on wisdom, for she will protect you.

Love her, and she will guard you.

Getting wisdom is the wisest thing you can do!

And whatever else you do, develop good judgment.

If you prize wisdom, she will make you great.

Embrace her, and she will honor you.

She will place a lovely wreath on your head;

she will present you with a beautiful crown." (Proverbs 4:5-9 NLT).

Turn your *Declaration Of Quality Wisdom* into this prayer of commitment:

*Lord Jesus, **Today May I** GET WISDOM before foolishness gets me.*

DAY TWENTY-FIVE: "Making Sure My Walk Matches My Talk"

Today May You . . . make a commitment to have your WALK match your TALK.

My child, listen to me and do as I say,

and you will have a long, good life.

I will teach you wisdom's ways

and lead you in straight paths.

When you walk, you won't be held back;

when you run, you won't stumble.

Take hold of my instructions; don't let them go.

Guard them, for they are the key to life. (Proverbs 4:10-13 NLT).

Turn your *Declaration Of Quality Wisdom* into this prayer of commitment:

> *Lord Jesus,* ***Today May I*** *make a commitment to have my WALK match my TALK.*

DAY TWENTY-SIX: "The Word-Centered Believer"

Today May You . . . be laser focused upon His Words and not give any attention to the words that seek to tear you down.

My child, pay attention to what I say.

Listen carefully to my words.

Don't lose sight of them.

Let them penetrate deep into your heart,

for they bring life to those who find them,

and healing to their whole body. (Proverbs 4:20-22 NLT).

Turn your *Declaration Of Quality Wisdom* into this prayer of commitment:

> *Lord Jesus, **Today May I** be laser focused upon Your Words and not give any attention to the words that seek to tear me down.*

DAY TWENTY-SEVEN: "Heart Guard"

Today May You . . . GUARD, PROTECT, DEFEND, WATCH, SECURE, TAKE VERY GOOD CARE of your heart and set the course for a SUCCESSFUL life.

Guard your heart above all else,
for it determines the course of your life. (Proverbs 4:23 NLT).

Turn your *Declaration Of Quality Wisdom* into this prayer of commitment:

> *Lord Jesus, **Today May I** GUARD, PROTECT, DEFEND, WATCH, SECURE, TAKE VERY GOOD CARE of my heart and set the course for a SUCCESSFUL life.*

DAY TWENTY-EIGHT: "Mums The Word!"

Today May You . . . watch WHAT you say before you SAY IT.

Avoid all perverse talk;
stay away from corrupt speech. (Proverbs 4:24 NLT).

Turn your *Declaration Of Quality Wisdom* into this prayer of commitment:

Lord Jesus, Today May I watch WHAT I say before I SAY IT.

DAY TWENTY-NINE: "On Purpose Living That Keeps You Right"

Today May You . . . be ON PURPOSE in what you are THINKING and what you are DOING.

Look straight ahead,

and fix your eyes on what lies before you.

Mark out a straight path for your feet;

stay on the safe path.

Don't get sidetracked;

keep your feet from following evil. (Proverbs 4:25-27 NLT).

Turn your *Declaration Of Quality Wisdom* into this prayer of commitment:

Lord Jesus, Today May I be ON PURPOSE in what I am THINKING and what I am DOING.

DAY THIRTY: "Look Up Living"

Today May You . . . look UP before you look DOWN and stay out of sexual trouble.

So now, my sons, listen to me.

Never stray from what I am about to say:

Stay away from her!

Don't go near the door of her house!

If you do, you will lose your honor

and will lose to merciless people all you have achieved.

Strangers will consume your wealth,

and someone else will enjoy the fruit of your labor.

In the end you will groan in anguish

when disease consumes your body.

You will say, "How I hated discipline!

If only I had not ignored all the warnings!

Oh, why didn't I listen to my teachers?

Why didn't I pay attention to my instructors?

I have come to the brink of utter ruin,

and now I must face public disgrace." (Proverbs 5:7-14 NLT).

Turn your *Declaration Of Quality Wisdom* into this prayer of commitment:

> *Lord Jesus, Today May I LOOK UP before I LOOK DOWN so that I may STAY OUT OF TROUBLE.*

DAY THIRTY-ONE: "Focusing Your Passion To Keep Your Purity"

Today May You . . . focus your PASSION to keep your PURITY.

So now, my sons, listen to me.

Never stray from what I am about to say:

Stay away from her!

Don't go near the door of her house!

If you do, you will lose your honor

and will lose to merciless people all you have achieved.

Strangers will consume your wealth,

and someone else will enjoy the fruit of your labor.

In the end you will groan in anguish

when disease consumes your body.

You will say, "How I hated discipline!

If only I had not ignored all the warnings!

Oh, why didn't I listen to my teachers?

Why didn't I pay attention to my instructors?

I have come to the brink of utter ruin,

and now I must face public disgrace." (Proverbs 5:7-14 NLT).

Turn your *Declaration Of Quality Wisdom* into this prayer of commitment:

---

*Lord Jesus, **Today May I** focus my PASSION to keep my PURITY.*

Introduction To Section Two:
"LEGACY LIVING" (Proverbs 6:1-11:11)

Living A Legacy Is A Daily Decision,

Not A Decision You Make At The End Of Your Life

What is the power of *a* legacy? What if the greatest contribution of your life would be to give to others a tangible gift that would be *priceless*? This is exactly what the Apostle Paul did for his mentorees:
Keep putting into practice all you learned and received from me—everything you heard from me and saw me doing. Then the God of peace will be with you. (Philippians 4:9 NLT).

How about THAT for a legacy? Those who follow in your steps after you will experience God's peace as a lifestyle. It's hard to improve on that!

There is a familiar phrase that is quoted often as gospel truth and it's this: "experience is the best teacher." I do not agree. I believe that "Guided" experience is the best teacher. Please don't only tell me *how* to do it *but* show me how its best done because you've done it before.

I've always had a deep appreciation for the mentor/mentoree relationship. I'll never forget the time I reached out to two men who were seasoned leaders in their organizations. One of them was the CEO of the largest company in the county. We are both the same age and since I have a passion for all things leadership, what better person from which I could learn.

The other one was a religious leader who had years of experience in the ministry and had probably seen it all. He was gray. He was seasoned. And I thought he was mature. I was mistaken about that one. I fully expected both of them to agree to meet with me one day a month so I could learn from them. In my view, it was a win/win for both of us. I was shocked when they both said, "We don't have time in our schedules (or to the heart of the matter, we have absolutely no interest) to do it."

Once I got over the hurt and rejection, I made a commitment in my heart that I would never give that response to anyone who was serious about growing in their personal, professional and spiritual life. As a matter of fact, it was at that moment where my focus upon discipleship (mentoring) became a focal point of all that I do now and with intentionality for the rest of my days.

It's pretty audacious of Paul to offer his life to those he is mentoring. Remember where he is writing this letter. It's not a local coffee shop. He's under arrest, bound to the Praetorian guard and in spite of those "inconveniences" he is modeling his faith and leading others to experience the peace of God. That is the power of making a commitment to mentoring others. If you are serious about legacy living, there are five principles in this Scripture that validate the benefits of mentorship.

> Five key phrases for why mentorship matters:
> ◊ Keep putting into practice
> ◊ All you learned
> ◊ Received from me
> ◊ Everything you heard from me and saw me doing
> ◊ Then the God of peace will be with you

A secure individual, a secure leader, is always looking for ways to pass on the baton to those who can go where he or she cannot go and do things that only the mentoree can do.

Moses was blessed with a full life. We know he was not perfect (had some serious battles with self-doubt and worth as well some anger issues too) but God still used his life to prepare the next man up. Here's a clear illustration of why legacy matters. All of the years Moses and Joshua spent together paid off:

[1] Now it came about after the death of Moses the servant of the LORD, that the LORD spoke to Joshua the son of Nun, Moses' servant, saying, [2] "Moses My servant is dead; now therefore arise, cross this Jordan, you and all this people, to the land which I am giving to them, to the sons of Israel. [3] "Every place on which the sole of your foot treads, I have given it to you, just as I spoke to Moses. [4] "From the wilderness and this Lebanon, even as far as the great river, the river Euphrates, all the land of the Hittites, and as far as the Great Sea toward the setting of the sun will be your territory. [5] "No man will *be able to* stand before you all the days of your life. Just as I have been with Moses, I will be with you; I will not fail you or forsake you. [6] "Be strong and courageous, for you shall give this people possession of the land which I swore to their fathers to give them. [7] "Only be strong and very courageous; be careful to do according to all the law which Moses My servant commanded you; do not turn from it to the right or to

the left, so that you may have success wherever you go. ⁸ "This book of the law shall not depart from your mouth, but you shall meditate on it day and night, so that you may be careful to do according to all that is written in it; for then you will make your way prosperous, and then you will have success. ⁹ "Have I not commanded you? Be strong and courageous! Do not tremble or be dismayed, for the LORD your God is with you wherever you go." **Joshua 1:1-9**

My mentor John Maxwell says that, *"The best leaders lead today with tomorrow in mind by making sure they invest in leaders who will carry their legacy forward. Why? Because a leader's lasting value is measured by succession.*

Here is the take-a-way for the leader who desires to leave a legacy How is it done? What does a Quality Leader have to do in order to empower others to lead beyond his or her time? Here are a few suggestions:

1. Be sober and humble. It's not all about you.
2. Be intentional. Look for those who take the baton from you and win.
3. Be courageous. It's hard to let go of control and power. It takes courage to pass on the baton to others you have trained.

Does your legacy matter? When you do it well, you are . . .

Making a Difference. Making a Life. Making a Leader Who Succeeds You (and does better)

Now, let's continue our 31-day journey of Legacy Living through this next session of Proverbs.

Quality Wisdom For A Modern Age

"LEGACY LIVING"
(Proverbs 6:1-11:11)

DAY ONE: "Encouragers Are Essential"

Today May You . . . seek to be an ENCOURAGER and not an ENABLER

My child, if you have put up security for a friend's debt

or agreed to guarantee the debt of a stranger—

if you have trapped yourself by your agreement

and are caught by what you said—

follow my advice and save yourself,

for you have placed yourself at your friend's mercy.

Now swallow your pride;

go and beg to have your name erased.

Don't put it off; do it now!

Don't rest until you do. (Proverbs 6:1-4 NLT).

Turn your *Declaration Of Quality Wisdom* into this prayer of commitment:

> Lord Jesus, ***Today May I*** have the kind of heart that will help me be an ENCOURAGER and not an ENABLER.

DAY TWO: "Right On!"

Today May You . . . be diligent in doing the RIGHT things in the RIGHT way for the RIGHT reasons, RIGHT now.

Take a lesson from the ants, you lazybones.

Learn from their ways and become wise!

Though they have no prince

or governor or ruler to make them work,

they labor hard all summer,

gathering food for the winter.

But you, lazybones, how long will you sleep?

When will you wake up?

A little extra sleep, a little more slumber,

a little folding of the hands to rest—

then poverty will pounce on you like a bandit;

scarcity will attack you like an armed robber. (Proverbs 6:6-11 NLT).

Turn your *Declaration Of Quality Wisdom* into this prayer of commitment:

> *Lord Jesus, **Today May I** be diligent in doing the RIGHT things in the RIGHT way for the RIGHT reasons, RIGHT now.*

DAY THREE: "The Stay Away Life"

Today May You . . . embrace the things the Lord likes and stay far away from doing the things He detests.

There are six things the Lord hates—

no, seven things he detests:

haughty eyes,

a lying tongue,

hands that kill the innocent,

a heart that plots evil,

feet that race to do wrong,

a false witness who pours out lies,

a person who sows discord in a family. (Proverbs 6:16-19 NLT).

Turn your *Declaration Of Quality Wisdom* into this prayer of commitment:

> *Lord Jesus, **Today May I** embrace the things You like and stay far away from doing the things You detest.*

DAY FOUR: "Embracing The Mentored Life"

Today May You . . . embrace the life teachings from your spiritual parents (Mentors) and live a life marked by success.

My son, obey your father's commands,

and don't neglect your mother's instruction.

Keep their words always in your heart.

Tie them around your neck.

When you walk, their counsel will lead you.

When you sleep, they will protect you.

When you wake up, they will advise you.

For their command is a lamp

and their instruction a light;

their corrective discipline

is the way to life. (Proverbs 6:20-23 NLT).

Turn your *Declaration Of Quality Wisdom* into this prayer of commitment:

> *Lord Jesus, **Today May I** embrace the life teachings from my spiritual parents (Mentors) and live a life marked by success.*

DAY FIVE: "The Prize-Driven Life"

Today May You . . . do whatever it takes to keep your eyes on the PRIZE of experiencing the abundant life and keep yourself from stumbling into the PIT of despair.

Follow my advice, my son;

always treasure my commands.

Obey my commands and live!

Guard my instructions as you guard your own eyes.

Tie them on your fingers as a reminder.

Write them deep within your heart. (Proverbs 7:1-3 NLT).

Turn your *Declaration Of Quality Wisdom* into this prayer of commitment:

> *Lord Jesus, **Today May I** do whatever it takes to keep my eyes on the PRIZE of experiencing the abundant life and keep myself from stumbling into the PIT of despair.*

DAY SIX: "Wisdom Works"

Today May You . . . have a keen awareness of the influence Wisdom wants to have in every decision you make and in every relationship you have.

Listen as Wisdom calls out!

Hear as understanding raises her voice!

On the hilltop along the road,

she takes her stand at the crossroads.

By the gates at the entrance to the town,

on the road leading in, she cries aloud,

"I call to you, to all of you!

I raise my voice to all people.

You simple people, use good judgment.

You foolish people, show some understanding.

Listen to me! For I have important things to tell you.

Everything I say is right,

for I speak the truth

and detest every kind of deception. (Proverbs 8:1-7 NLT).

Turn your *Declaration Of Quality Wisdom* into this prayer of commitment:

> *Lord Jesus, **Today May I** have a keen awareness of the influence Wisdom wants to have in every decision I make and in every relationship I have.*

DAY SEVEN: "Wisdom Matters"

Today May You . . . cling to every bit of wisdom you can collect . . . and use it.

My advice is wholesome.

There is nothing devious or crooked in it.

My words are plain to anyone with understanding,

clear to those with knowledge.

Choose my instruction rather than silver,

and knowledge rather than pure gold.

For wisdom is far more valuable than rubies.

Nothing you desire can compare with it. (Proverbs 8:8-11 NLT).

Turn your *Declaration Of Quality Wisdom* into this prayer of commitment:

> *Lord Jesus, **Today May I** cling to every bit of wisdom I can collect . . . and use it.*

DAY EIGHT: "Thinking For Success"

Today May You . . . commit yourself to thinking wise THOUGHTS that will help you to create wise PLANS so that you may make wise DECISIONS and live a rich LIFE.

"I love all who love me.

Those who search will surely find me.

I have riches and honor,

as well as enduring wealth and justice.

My gifts are better than gold, even the purest gold,

my wages better than sterling silver!

I walk in righteousness,

in paths of justice.

Those who love me inherit wealth.

I will fill their treasuries. (Proverbs 8:17-21 NLT).

Turn your *Declaration Of Quality Wisdom* into this prayer of commitment:

> Lord Jesus, *Today May I* commit myself to thinking wise THOUGHTS that will help me to create wise PLANS so that I may make wise DECISIONS and live a rich LIFE.

DAY NINE: "Joyful Wisdom, Joyful Life"

Today May You . . . experience a JOYFUL day as you embrace God's wisdom in everything you do and say.

"And so, my children, listen to me,

for all who follow my ways are joyful.

Listen to my instruction and be wise.

Don't ignore it.

Joyful are those who listen to me,

watching for me daily at my gates,

waiting for me outside my home!

For whoever finds me finds life

and receives favor from the Lord. (Proverbs 8:32-35 NLT).

Turn your *Declaration Of Quality Wisdom* into this prayer of commitment:

> *Lord Jesus, **Today May I** experience a JOYFUL day as I embrace God's wisdom in everything I do and say.*

DAY TEN: "Time Investment"

Today May You . . . make an intentional investment in people who are serious about becoming an even better version of themselves.

Anyone who rebukes a mocker will get an insult in return.

Anyone who corrects the wicked will get hurt.

So don't bother correcting mockers;

they will only hate you.

But correct the wise,

and they will love you.

Instruct the wise,

and they will be even wiser.

Teach the righteous,

and they will learn even more. (Proverbs 9:7-9 NLT).

Turn your *Declaration Of Quality Wisdom* into this prayer of commitment:

> *Lord Jesus, **Today May I** make an intentional investment in people who are serious about becoming an even better version of themselves.*

DAY ELEVEN: "Why Wisdom Is A Stewardship"

Today May You . . . make wise decisions that will benefit you and those you love.

Fear of the Lord is the foundation of wisdom.

Knowledge of the Holy One results in good judgment.

Wisdom will multiply your days

and add years to your life.

If you become wise, you will be the one to benefit.

If you scorn wisdom, you will be the one to suffer. (Proverbs 9:10-12 NLT).

Turn your *Declaration Of Quality Wisdom* into this prayer of commitment:

> *Lord Jesus, **Today May I** make wise decisions that will benefit me and those I love.*

DAY TWELVE: "Business Issues"

Today May You . . . make it your goal not to be a "Christian" businessman or businesswoman but to be a businessman or businesswoman who TRUSTS God, who LIVES for God, who LOVES like God, and who is BLESSED by God.

Tainted wealth has no lasting value,

but right living can save your life. (Proverbs 10:2 NLT).

Turn your *Declaration Of Quality Wisdom* into this prayer of commitment:

> *Lord Jesus, **Today May I** make it my goal not to be a "Christian" businessman or businesswoman but to be a businessman or businesswoman who TRUSTS God, who LIVES for God, who LOVES like God, and who is BLESSED by God.*

DAY THIRTEEN: "A Promise Made Is A Promise Kept"

Today May You . . . hold to the promises God makes to the godly and with gratitude receive His blessings.

The Lord will not let the godly go hungry,

but he refuses to satisfy the craving of the wicked.

Lazy people are soon poor;

hard workers get rich.

A wise youth harvests in the summer,

but one who sleeps during harvest is a disgrace.

The godly are showered with blessings;

the words of the wicked conceal violent intentions. (Proverbs 10:3-6 NLT).

Turn your *Declaration Of Quality Wisdom* into this prayer of commitment:

> *Lord Jesus, **Today May I** hold to the promises God makes to the godly and with gratitude receive His blessings.*

DAY FOURTEEN: "Never Ending Lessons Of Life"

Today May You . . . make it your decision to learn more about the Lord, more about the people you know, and more about who you really are.

The wise are glad to be instructed,

but babbling fools fall flat on their faces. (Proverbs 10:8 NLT).

Turn your *Declaration Of Quality Wisdom* into this prayer of commitment:

> *Lord Jesus, **Today May I** make it my decision to learn more about the Lord, more about the people I know, and more about who I really am.*

DAY FIFTEEN: "Integrity Impacts Your Influence"

Today May You . . . make decisions that will add value to others and credibility to your legacy.

People with integrity walk safely,

but those who follow crooked paths will be exposed. (Proverbs 10:9 NLT).

Turn your *Declaration Of Quality Wisdom* into this prayer of commitment:

> *Lord Jesus, **Today May I** make decisions that will add value to others and credibility to my legacy.*

DAY SIXTEEN: "Courage In Your Core"

Today May You . . . have the kind of INNER courage to SAY what is RIGHT and SAY what is WRONG.

People who wink at wrong cause trouble,

but a bold reproof promotes peace.

The words of the godly are a life-giving fountain;

the words of the wicked conceal violent intentions. (Proverbs 10:10-11 NLT).

Turn your *Declaration Of Quality Wisdom* into this prayer of commitment:

> *Lord Jesus, **Today May I** have the kind of INNER courage to SAY what is RIGHT and SAY what is WRONG.*

DAY SEVENTEEN: "Lover, Not A Hater"

Today May You . . . be a LOVER not a HATER.

Hatred stirs up quarrels,

but love makes up for all offenses. (Proverbs 10:12 NLT).

Turn your *Declaration Of Quality Wisdom* into this prayer of commitment:

*Lord Jesus, **Today May I** be a LOVER not a HATER.*

DAY EIGHTEEN: "Why Right Words Matter"

Today May You . . . use words that prove you know what you are talking about.

Wise words come from the lips of people with understanding,

but those lacking sense will be beaten with a rod.

Wise people treasure knowledge,

but the babbling of a fool invites disaster. (Proverbs 10:13-14 NLT).

Turn your *Declaration Of Quality Wisdom* into this prayer of commitment:

*Lord Jesus, **Today May I** use words that prove I know what I am talking about.*

DAY NINETEEN: "Managing What You Do Not Own"

Today May You . . . treat everything you OWN as if God OWNS everything you OWN, because He does.

The earnings of the godly enhance their lives,

but evil people squander their money on sin. (Proverbs 10:16 NLT).

Turn your *Declaration Of Quality Wisdom* into this prayer of commitment:

> *Lord Jesus, **Today May I** treat everything I OWN as if God OWNS everything I OWN, because He does.*

DAY TWENTY: "Why It's Important To Have The Ability To Adjust And Go"

Today May You . . . learn to ADJUST and GO.

People who accept discipline are on the pathway to life,

but those who ignore correction will go astray. (Proverbs 10:17 NLT).

Turn your *Declaration Of Quality Wisdom* into this prayer of commitment:

> *Lord Jesus, **Today May I** learn to ADJUST and GO.*

DAY TWENTY ONE: "The Power Of A Positive Message"

Today May You . . . be INTENTIONAL and use your WORDS for GOOD.

Hiding hatred makes you a liar;

slandering others makes you a fool.

Too much talk leads to sin.

Be sensible and keep your mouth shut.

The words of the godly are like sterling silver;

the heart of a fool is worthless.

The words of the godly encourage many,

but fools are destroyed by their lack of common sense. (Proverbs 10:18-21 NLT).

Turn your *Declaration Of Quality Wisdom* into this prayer of commitment:

*Lord Jesus, **Today May I** be INTENTIONAL and use my WORDS for GOOD.*

DAY TWENTY TWO: "Too Blessed To Be Stressed"

Today May You . . . live your life in the FAVOR of GOD.

The blessing of the Lord makes a person rich,

and he adds no sorrow with it. (Proverbs 10:22 NLT).

Turn your *Declaration Of Quality Wisdom* into this prayer of commitment:

*Lord Jesus, **Today May I** live my life in the FAVOR of GOD.*

DAY TWENTY THREE: "The Key To Building Your Life On A Firm Foundation"

Today May You . . . HANG ON as you PRESS ON as He HOLDS ON to you when your storms of life come.

When the storms of life come, the wicked are whirled away,

but the godly have a lasting foundation. (Proverbs 10:25 NLT).

Turn your *Declaration Of Quality Wisdom* into this prayer of commitment:

*Lord Jesus, **Today May I** HANG ON as I PRESS ON as You HOLD ON to me when my storms of life come.*

DAY TWENTY FOUR: "Experiencing A Supernatural High"

Today May You . . . HAVE HIGH HOPES that will make you HAPPY.

The hopes of the godly result in happiness,

but the expectations of the wicked come to nothing. (Proverbs 10:28 NLT).

Turn your *Declaration Of Quality Wisdom* into this prayer of commitment:

> *Lord Jesus, Today May I HAVE HIGH HOPES that will make me HAPPY.*

DAY TWENTY FIVE: "The Gift Of Your Personal Integrity"

Today May You . . . let YOUR PERSONAL INTEGRITY be the greatest gift you give everyone you meet.

The way of the Lord is a stronghold to those with integrity,

but it destroys the wicked. (Proverbs 10:29 NLT).

Turn your *Declaration Of Quality Wisdom* into this prayer of commitment:

> *Lord Jesus, Today May I let MY PERSONAL INTEGRITY be the greatest gift I give everyone I meet.*

DAY TWENTY SIX: "Word Gifts"

Today May You . . . offer your words as a GIFT that build up, not words that DEPLETE and DESTROY.

The mouth of the godly person gives wise advice,

but the tongue that deceives will be cut off.

The lips of the godly speak helpful words,

but the mouth of the wicked speaks perverse words. (Proverbs 10:31-32 NLT).

Turn your *Declaration Of Quality Wisdom* into this prayer of commitment:

> *Lord Jesus, **Today May I** offer my words as a GIFT that build up, not words that DEPLETE and DESTROY.*

DAY TWENTY SEVEN: "God's GPS For You"

Today May You . . . make sure your moral compass is true in every business and personal relationship transaction you make.

The Lord detests the use of dishonest scales,

but he delights in accurate weights. (Proverbs 11:1 NLT).

Turn your *Declaration Of Quality Wisdom* into this prayer of commitment:

> *Lord Jesus, **Today May I** make sure my moral compass is true in every business and personal relationship transaction I make.*

DAY TWENTY EIGHT: "Don't Be Proud Of Your Humility"

Today May You . . . guard your heart from being proud of your humility.

Pride leads to disgrace,

but with humility comes wisdom. (Proverbs 11:2 NLT).

Turn your *Declaration Of Quality Wisdom* into this prayer of commitment:

> *Lord Jesus, **Today May I** guard my heart from being proud of my humility.*

DAY TWENTY NINE: "The Be Honest Life"

Today May You . . . be HONEST to others, HONEST to yourself, and above all, HONEST to God.

Honesty guides good people;

dishonesty destroys treacherous people. (Proverbs 11:3 NLT).

Turn your *Declaration Of Quality Wisdom* into this prayer of commitment:

> *Lord Jesus, **Today May I** be HONEST to others, HONEST to myself, and above all, HONEST to God.*

DAY THIRTY: "The Benefits Of A Life Driven By Integrity"

Today May You . . . live like your PERSONAL INTEGRITY is the greatest gift you will give someone.

The godly are directed by honesty;

the wicked fall beneath their load of sin.

The godliness of good people rescues them;

the ambition of treacherous people traps them. (Proverbs 11:5-6 NLT).

Turn your *Declaration Of Quality Wisdom* into this prayer of commitment:

> *Lord Jesus, **Today May I** live like my PERSONAL INTEGRITY is the greatest gift I will give someone.*

DAY THIRTY ONE: "Citizenship By The Book"

Today May You . . . add value to your community by living a godly life and by living as an upright citizen.

The whole city celebrates when the godly succeed;

they shout for joy when the wicked die.

Upright citizens are good for a city and make it prosper,

but the talk of the wicked tears it apart. (Proverbs 11:10-11 NLT).

Turn your *Declaration Of Quality Wisdom* into this prayer of commitment:

> *Lord Jesus, **Today May I** add value to my community by living a godly life and by living as an upright citizen.*

Introduction To Section Three:

"EMPOWERED TO ENCOURAGE" (Proverbs 11:13-13:14)

"The only person you are destined to become is the person you decide to be."
—Ralph Waldo Emerson

Encouragement. We all like it. If we are honest with ourselves, we need it too. And if we have set some life goals for ourselves, we can use all of the encouragement we can get. This is such an important aspect in the Christian life that the Lord named a man whose very name means "Encouragement." His name?

The Son Of Encouragement

Barnabas is mentioned 29 times in the New Testament

*His real name was Joseph
*His nick name was Barnabas
*He was a generous man

36 And Joseph, a Levite of Cyprian birth, who was also called Barnabas by the apostles (which translated means, Son of Encouragement), 37 and who owned a tract of land, sold it and brought the money and laid it at the apostles' feet. **Acts 4:36-37**

*He was called by God

And while they were ministering to the Lord and fasting, the Holy Spirit said, "Set apart for Me Barnabas and Saul for the work to which I have called them." **Acts 13:2**

*He was teaching and preaching (emphasizing the Good News)

But Paul and Barnabas stayed in Antioch, teaching and preaching, with many others also, the word of the Lord. **Acts 15:35**

*He was beloved or dear (one of our best)

It seemed good to us, having become of one mind, to select men to send to you with our beloved Barnabas and Paul, **Acts 15:25**

*Barnabas—A Mentor In Action

And when he had come to Jerusalem, he was trying to associate with the disciples; and they were all afraid of him, not believing that he was a disciple. But Barnabas took hold of him and brought him to the apostles and described to them how he had seen the Lord on the road, and that He had talked to him, and how at Damascus he had spoken out boldly in the name of Jesus. **Acts 9:26-27**

*What qualities did Barnabas demonstrate?

> Courage
>
> Saw potential in Paul
>
> Exhortation that was needed (Sponsorship) vs. 27

*Barnabas—A Man of Character

22And the news about them reached the ears of the church at Jerusalem, and they sent Barnabas off to Antioch. 23Then when he had come and witnessed the grace of God, he rejoiced and *began* to encourage them all with resolute heart to remain *true* to the Lord; 24for he was a good man, and full of the Holy Spirit and of faith. And considerable numbers were brought to the Lord. 25And he left for Tarsus to look for Saul; 26and when he had found him, he brought him to Antioch. And it came about that for an entire year they met with the church, and taught considerable numbers; and the disciples were first called Christians in Antioch. **Acts 11:22-26**

*Was a good man

*Was an encourager

*Was willing to be sent out

*Was full of the Holy Spirit and faith

*Was evangelistic

*Was a networker

*Was a shepherd

Encouraging each other is not only a good idea; it's a clear command from Scripture: A little bit of encouragement goes a long way in helping another person to take another step, or make it another day. Scripture gives us clear instructions on how we are to encourage a quality disciple of the Lord.

> 1. We are to bear the burdens of the weak.

We who are strong ought to bear with the failings of the weak and not to please ourselves. **Romans 15:1 (NIV)**

> 2. We are to encourage one another and build each other up.

Therefore encourage one another and build each other up, just as in fact you are doing. **1 Thess. 5:11 (NIV)**

> 3. We are to build up and encourage our neighbor.

Each of us should please his neighbor for his good, to build him up. **Romans 15:2 (NIV)**

4.   We are to encourage with our words.

Do not let any unwholesome talk come out of your mouths, but only what is helpful for building others up according to their needs, that it may benefit those who listen. **Ephes. 4:29 (NIV)**

5.   We are to build others up with love.

Now about food sacrificed to idols: We know that we all possess knowledge. Knowledge puffs up, but love builds up. **1 Cor. 8:1 (NIV)**

Mentoring or discipling another believer involves taking upon the burdens of another and giving hope and encouragement. Being a part of a vibrant Christian community with other believers is never accomplished when encouragement cannot be found. The quality disciple is a direct product of an edified relationship, and an edified disciple is a soul-winning disciple.

I really believe that "encouragement" is not only a spiritual gift the Lord gives to the Body of Christ, but it is also an intentional act of kindness that ANYONE who loves the Lord can do. All of us need to learn how to be an encouragement to those who need a boost. We need to be an encourager—but how? You can formulate a strategy, have a strategic plan of encouragement. A little bit of encouragement goes a long, long way in helping a person make it to the next day. Scripture brings this point home.

Moreover David was greatly distressed because the people spoke of stoning him, for all the people were embittered, each one because of his sons and his daughters. But David strengthened [or **encouraged--KJV**] himself in the Lord his God. **1 Samuel 30:6 [NASB]**

Encourage the exhausted, and strengthen the feeble. **Isaiah 35:3 [NASB]**

And Joseph, a Levite of Cyprian birth, who was also called Barnabas by the apostles (which translated means, Son of **Encouragement**), **Acts 4:36 [NASB]**

Then when he had come and witnessed the grace of God, he rejoiced and *began* to **encourage** them all with resolute heart to remain *true* to the Lord; **Acts 11:23 [NASB]**

31And when they had read it, they rejoiced because of its encouragement. 32And Judas and Silas, also being prophets themselves, **encouraged** and strengthened the brethren with a lengthy message. **Acts 15:31-32 [NASB]**

And they went out of the prison and entered *the house of* Lydia, and when they saw the brethren, they **encouraged** them and departed. **Acts 16:40 [NASB]**

And when he wanted to go across to Achaia, the brethren **encouraged** him and wrote to the disciples to welcome him; and when he had arrived, he helped greatly those who had believed through grace; **Acts 18:27** [NASB]

For whatever was written in earlier times was written for our instruction, that through perseverance and the **encouragement** of the Scriptures we might have hope. **Romans 15:4** [NASB]

Now may the God who gives perseverance and **encouragement** grant you to be of the same mind with one another according to Christ Jesus; **Romans 15:5** [NASB]

If therefore there is any **encouragement** in Christ, if there is any consolation of love, if there is any fellowship of the Spirit, if any affection and compassion, **Philip. 2:1** [NASB]

that their hearts may be **encouraged**, having been knit together in love, and *attaining* to all the wealth that comes from the full assurance of understanding, *resulting* in a true knowledge of God's mystery, *that is,* Christ *Himself*, **Col. 2:2** [NASB]

For I have sent him to you for this very purpose, that you may know *about* our circumstances and that he may **encourage** your hearts; **Col. 4:8** [NASB]

and *also* Jesus who is called Justus; these are the only fellow workers for the kingdom of God who are from the circumcision; and they have proved to be an **encouragement** to me. **Col. 4:11** [NASB]

and we sent Timothy, our brother and God's fellow worker in the gospel of Christ, to strengthen and **encourage** you as to your faith, **1 Thess. 3:2** [NASB]

Therefore **encourage** one another, and build up one another, just as you also are doing. **1 Thess. 5:11** [NASB]

And we urge you, brethren, admonish the unruly, **encourage** the fainthearted, help the weak, be patient with all men. **1 Thess. 5:14** [NASB]

that they may **encourage** the young women to love their husbands, to love their children, **Titus 2:4** [NASB]

But **encourage** one another day after day, as long as it is *still* called "Today," lest any one of you be hardened by the deceitfulness of sin. **Hebrews 3:13** [NASB]

in order that by two unchangeable things, in which it is impossible for God to lie, we may have strong **encouragement**, we who have fled for refuge in laying hold of the hope set before us. **Hebrews 6:18** [NASB]

Here are a few practical tools of encouragement:

- A phone call
- Email
- Snail mail

- Personal Visits
- A meal or coffee break
- Prayer—and ask God who needs to hear from you
- Keeping a list of contacts—a record of your ministry and the results. Why do this?

For two reasons:
- It will keep you focused.
- It will be an encouragement to you.

We do not have to muster up the power to encourage. God will give you everything you need. He will, because of His grace and Spirit, allow you to be "Empowered To Encourage."

Quality Wisdom For A Modern Age

EMPOWERED TO ENCOURAGE
(Proverbs 11:13-13:14)

DAY ONE: "The Value Of Keeping A Secret"

Today May You . . . assure those who trust you that they can be CONFIDENT in your COMPETENCE to keep a CONFIDENCE.

A gossip goes around telling secrets,

but those who are trustworthy can keep a confidence. (Proverbs 11:13 NLT).

Turn your *Declaration Of Quality Wisdom* into this prayer of commitment:

> *Lord Jesus, **Today May I** assure those who trust me that they can be CONFIDENT in my COMPETENCE to keep a CONFIDENCE.*

DAY TWO: "When Leaders Depend Upon You"

Today May You . . . PRAY for our leaders so they may be wise in who they listen to and what they do.

Without wise leadership, a nation falls;

there is safety in having many advisers. (Proverbs 11:14 NLT).

Turn your *Declaration Of Quality Wisdom* into this prayer of commitment:

> *Lord Jesus, **Today May I** PRAY for our leaders so they may be wise in who they listen to and what they do.*

DAY THREE: "Using Wisdom With Your Wealth"

Today May You . . . become a good steward of the money God entrusts to you and be careful to learn the balance between using your head and your heart.

There's danger in putting up security for a stranger's debt;

it's safer not to guarantee another person's debt. (Proverbs 11:15 NLT).

Turn your *Declaration Of Quality Wisdom* into this prayer of commitment:

> *Lord Jesus, **Today May I** become a good steward of the money God entrusts to me and be careful to learn the balance between using my head and my heart.*

DAY FOUR: "Kindness As An Investment"

Today May You . . . be the KIND of person who intentionally does KIND things for people who need to experience your KINDNESS.

Your kindness will reward you,

but your cruelty will destroy you. (Proverbs 11:17 NLT).

Turn your *Declaration Of Quality Wisdom* into this prayer of commitment:

> *Lord Jesus, **Today May I** be the KIND of person who intentionally does KIND things for people who need to experience my KINDNESS.*

DAY FIVE: "Rewards That Last"

Today May You . . . make the right kinds of LIFE investments that will pay off in dividends not only NOW but well into the FUTURE.

Evil people get rich for the moment,
but the reward of the godly will last. (Proverbs 11:18 NLT).

Turn your *Declaration Of Quality Wisdom* into this prayer of commitment:

> *Lord Jesus, **Today May I** make the right kinds of LIFE investments that will pay off in dividends not only NOW but well into the FUTURE.*

DAY SIX: "The Real Deal"

Today May You . . . set in your heart to be THE REAL DEAL in your CHARACTER with those who are depending upon you to be HONEST and TRUE.

The Lord detests people with crooked hearts,
but he delights in those with integrity. (Proverbs 11:20 NLT).

Turn your *Declaration Of Quality Wisdom* into this prayer of commitment:

> *Lord Jesus, **Today May I** set in my heart to be THE REAL DEAL in my CHARACTER with those who are depending upon me to be HONEST and TRUE.*

DAY SEVEN: "Choosing An Abundant Mindset For Life"

Today May You . . . live your life with an ABUNDANCE mindset; always ENOUGH money, always ENOUGH time and always ENOUGH of what you NEED to have in order to be a blessing to others who NEED what you HAVE.

Give freely and become more wealthy;
be stingy and lose everything. (Proverbs 11:24 NLT).

Turn your *Declaration Of Quality Wisdom* into this prayer of commitment:

> Lord Jesus, *Today May I* live my life with an ABUNDANCE mindset; always ENOUGH money, always ENOUGH time and always ENOUGH of what I NEED to have in order to be a blessing to others who NEED what I HAVE.

DAY EIGHT: "The Fine Art Of Giving Away What You Cannot Save"

Today May You . . . give your life away so that you can get it back even better.

The generous will prosper;
those who refresh others will themselves be refreshed. (Proverbs 11:25 NLT).

Turn your *Declaration Of Quality Wisdom* into this prayer of commitment:

> Lord Jesus, *Today May I* give my life away so that I can get it back even better.

DAY NINE: "Life Investments"

Today May You . . . SPEND your life on things that really MATTER and SPEND your money to FUND the things that really MATTER.

Trust in your money and down you go!
But the godly flourish like leaves in spring. (Proverbs 11:28 NLT).

Turn your *Declaration Of Quality Wisdom* into this prayer of commitment:

> Lord Jesus, *Today May I* SPEND my life on things that really MATTER and SPEND my money to FUND the things that really MATTER.

DAY TEN: "Winning Friendships"

Today May You . . . make it your goal to ADD VALUE to everyone you meet.

The seeds of good deeds become a tree of life;
a wise person wins friends. (Proverbs 11:30 NLT).

Turn your *Declaration Of Quality Wisdom* into this prayer of commitment:

> Lord Jesus, *Today May I* make it my goal to ADD VALUE to everyone I meet.

DAY ELEVEN: "Love What Matters"

Today May You . . . LOVE humility so that you may embrace discipline and correction and LEARN.

To learn, you must love discipline;

it is stupid to hate correction. (Proverbs 12:1 NLT).

Turn your *Declaration Of Quality Wisdom* into this prayer of commitment:

> *Lord Jesus, **Today May I** LOVE humility so that I may embrace discipline and correction and LEARN.*

DAY TWELVE: "Live The Life You Believe"

Today May You . . . THINK good thoughts, do good DEEDS, and make a good CONTRIBUTION to your community.

The Lord approves of those who are good,

but he condemns those who plan wickedness.

Wickedness never brings stability,

but the godly have deep roots. (Proverbs 12:2-3 NLT).

Turn your *Declaration Of Quality Wisdom* into this prayer of commitment:

> *Lord Jesus, **Today May I** THINK good thoughts, do good DEEDS, and make a good CONTRIBUTION to my community.*

DAY THIRTEEN: "Harnessing The Power Of Your Plans And Your Words"

Today May You . . . add value to others by how you PLAN and by what you SAY.

The plans of the godly are just;

the advice of the wicked is treacherous.

The words of the wicked are like a murderous ambush,

but the words of the godly save lives. (Proverbs 12:5-6 NLT).

Turn your *Declaration Of Quality Wisdom* into this prayer of commitment:

*Lord Jesus, **Today May I** add value to others by how I PLAN and by what I SAY.*

DAY FOURTEEN: "The Results Of Choosing To Live An Intentional Life"

Today May You . . . be INTENTIONAL on using wise words and working hard so you may be SUCCESSFUL.

Wise words bring many benefits,

and hard work brings rewards. (Proverbs 12:14 NLT).

Turn your *Declaration Of Quality Wisdom* into this prayer of commitment:

*Lord Jesus, **Today May I** be INTENTIONAL on using wise words and working hard so I may be SUCCESSFUL.*

DAY FIFTEEN: "Listen 2 Others"

Today May You . . . get advice that is much better than yours.

Fools think their own way is right,

but the wise listen to others. (Proverbs 12:15 NLT).

Turn your *Declaration Of Quality Wisdom* into this prayer of commitment:

> *Lord Jesus, **Today May I** get advice that is much better than mine.*

DAY SIXTEEN: "Free Grace"

Today May You . . . give grace to those who do not deserve it.

A fool is quick-tempered,

but a wise person stays calm when insulted. (Proverbs 12:16 NLT).

Turn your *Declaration Of Quality Wisdom* into this prayer of commitment:

> *Lord Jesus, **Today May I** give grace to those who do not deserve it.*

DAY SEVENTEEN: "Healing Words That Last"

Today May You . . . be intentional on using words that are TRUTHFUL, that are HEALING, and that STAND THE TEST OF TIME.

An honest witness tells the truth;

a false witness tells lies.

Some people make cutting remarks,

but the words of the wise bring healing.

Truthful words stand the test of time,

but lies are soon exposed. (Proverbs 12:17-19 NLT).

Turn your *Declaration Of Quality Wisdom* into this prayer of commitment:

> Lord Jesus, **Today May I** be intentional on using words that are TRUTHFUL, that are HEALING, and that STAND THE TEST OF TIME.

DAY EIGHTEEN: "Truth Is A Verb, An Adjective, And A Noun"

Today May You . . . speak the TRUTH, the whole TRUTH, and nothing but the TRUTH, so help you God.

The Lord detests lying lips,

but he delights in those who tell the truth. (Proverbs 12:22 NLT).

Turn your *Declaration Of Quality Wisdom* into this prayer of commitment:

> Lord Jesus, **Today May I** speak the TRUTH, the whole TRUTH, and nothing but the TRUTH, so help me God.

DAY NINETEEN: "Live Your Life And When Necessary Use Words"

Today May You . . . don't IMPRESS others by WHAT YOU KNOW but by WHAT YOU DO.

The wise don't make a show of their knowledge,

but fools broadcast their foolishness. (Proverbs 12:23 NLT).

Turn your *Declaration Of Quality Wisdom* into this prayer of commitment:

> Lord Jesus, *Today May I* don't IMPRESS others by WHAT I KNOW but by WHAT I DO.

DAY TWENTY: "Lead By Example"

Today May You . . . lead by example and be a good steward of your time by working harder and smarter.

Work hard and become a leader;

be lazy and become a slave. (Proverbs 12:24 NLT).

Turn your *Declaration Of Quality Wisdom* into this prayer of commitment:

> Lord Jesus, *Today May I* lead by example and be a good steward of my time by working harder and smarter.

DAY 21: "Worry-Free Zone. Admit Positive Words Only"

Today May You . . . save your energy on worrying about things you can't control and spend that energy building up someone who needs some encouragement.

Worry weighs a person down;

an encouraging word cheers a person up. (Proverbs 12:25 NLT).

Turn your *Declaration Of Quality Wisdom* into this prayer of commitment:

> Lord Jesus, *Today May I* save my energy on worrying about things I can't control and spend that energy building up someone who needs some encouragement.

DAY TWENTY TWO: "The Blessing Of Passing On Good Advice"

Today May You . . . be willing to SPEAK the truth and ENCOURAGE your friends to make the kinds of choices that will add great VALUE to them.

The godly give good advice to their friends; the wicked lead them astray. (Proverbs 12:26 NLT).

Turn your *Declaration Of Quality Wisdom* into this prayer of commitment:

> *Lord Jesus, **Today May I** be willing to SPEAK the truth and ENCOURAGE my friends to make the kinds of choices that will add great VALUE to them.*

DAY TWENTY THREE: "The Path Of True Prosperity"

Today May You . . . make every decision a life-producing path for you and for those you love.

"The way of the godly leads to life; that path does not lead to death." (Proverbs 12:28 NLT).

Turn your *Declaration Of Quality Wisdom* into this prayer of commitment:

> *Lord Jesus, **Today May I** make every decision a life-producing path for me and for those I love.*

DAY TWENTY FOUR: "Tongue Twisters"

Today May You . . . watch what you say so you will not have to eat your words.

Those who control their tongue will have a long life;
opening your mouth can ruin everything. (Proverbs 13:3 NLT).

Turn your *Declaration Of Quality Wisdom* into this prayer of commitment:

> *Lord Jesus, **Today May I** watch what I say so I will not have to eat my words.*

DAY TWENTY FIVE: "If You Want It, Go Get It"

Today May You . . . do whatever it TAKES to get whatever you WANT to do with whatever you WISH as long as you do it for the RIGHT reasons.

Lazy people want much but get little,

but those who work hard will prosper. (Proverbs 13:4 NLT).

Turn your *Declaration Of Quality Wisdom* into this prayer of commitment:

> *Lord Jesus, **Today May I** do whatever it TAKES to get whatever I WANT to do with whatever I WISH as long as I do it for the RIGHT reasons.*

DAY TWENTY SIX: "Light Shine"

Today May You . . . let your little light shine and bring an infectious joy to everyone you meet.

"The life of the godly is full of light and joy, but the light of the wicked will be snuffed out." (Proverbs 13:9 NLT).

Turn your *Declaration Of Quality Wisdom* into this prayer of commitment:

> *Lord Jesus, **Today May I** let my little light shine and bring an infectious joy to everyone I meet.*

DAY TWENTY SEVEN: "How To Win The Battle And The War"

Today May You . . . have the reputation of being a wise guy or wise gal.

Pride leads to conflict;

those who take advice are wise. (Proverbs 13:10 NLT).

Turn your *Declaration Of Quality Wisdom* into this prayer of commitment:

*Lord Jesus, **Today May I** have the reputation of being a wise guy or wise gal.*

DAY TWENTY EIGHT: "The Real Reason For Creating Wealth"

Today May You . . . work SMARTER and HARDER so you can EARN MORE to GIVE AWAY.

Wealth from get-rich-quick schemes quickly disappears;

wealth from hard work grows over time. (Proverbs 13:11 NLT).

Turn your *Declaration Of Quality Wisdom* into this prayer of commitment:

*Lord Jesus, **Today May I** work SMARTER and HARDER so I can EARN MORE to GIVE AWAY.*

DAY TWENTY NINE: "Discovering The Hope That Fuels Your Dreams"

Today May You . . . keep your hope alive and DARE to DREAM for dreams that only God can answer.

Hope deferred makes the heart sick,

but a dream fulfilled is a tree of life. (Proverbs 13:12 NLT).

Turn your *Declaration Of Quality Wisdom* into this prayer of commitment:

> *Lord Jesus, **Today May I** keep my hope alive and DARE to DREAM for dreams that only You can answer.*

DAY THIRTY: "The Blessing Of Having A Humble Heart"

Today May You . . . have a HEART of HUMILITY that will be open to ADVICE so you can SUCCEED.

People who despise advice are asking for trouble;

those who respect a command will succeed. (Proverbs 13:13 NLT).

Turn your *Declaration Of Quality Wisdom* into this prayer of commitment:

> *Lord Jesus, **Today May I** have a HEART of HUMILITY that will be open to ADVICE So that I can SUCCEED.*

DAY THIRTY ONE: "Why Wisdom Works"

Today May You . . . be WISE enough to listen to the advice of WISE people and make WISE decisions that will be a blessing to you.

The instruction of the wise is like a life-giving fountain;

those who accept it avoid the snares of death. (Proverbs 13:14 NLT).

Turn your *Declaration Of Quality Wisdom* into this prayer of commitment:

> *Lord Jesus, **Today May I** be WISE enough to listen to the advice of WISE people and make WISE decisions that will be a blessing to me.*

Introduction To Section Four:

"INTENTIONAL INFLUENCE" (Proverbs 13:16-15:17)

"The pessimist complains about the wind. The optimist expects it to change. The leader adjusts the sails." ~ Dr. John C. Maxwell

Someone is watching you . . . what you say . . . how you say it . . . how you do it. All of us are influencing someone else. The question is, what is driving you to influence others? Is it out of personal pride or are you being intentional to set a good example for others to follow? Note this example of the power of being able to influence others:

[6] You also became imitators of us and of the Lord, having received the word in much tribulation with the joy of the Holy Spirit, [7] so that you became an example to all the believers in Macedonia and in Achaia. **1 Thessalonians 1:6-7**

The "right" kind of imitation can change the world. And the wrong kind can as well.

What is it that makes a leader a really good leader? A lot of it has to do with how he or she leverages their influence. Are they having a positive influence or are they having a negative influence on other people? This is the critical issue for the leader. There are some leaders who are mesmerized by their "title." They wrongly conclude that the title alone makes them a good leader.

Stanley Huffty makes an excellent point when he says, *"It's not the position that makes the leader; it's the leader that makes the position."*

Influence is a gift; it is a trust. The best leaders are always the leaders who use their influence for the good of others.

Here is the take-a-way for the leader who desires to use his or her influence in the right way. How is it done? What does a Quality Leader have to do to be a good influence on others? Here are a few suggestions:

1. <u>It's not about the title</u>. Remember that job titles come and go but it is the character of the leader that really defines the person. Work on building your character first and the titles will take care of themselves.
2. <u>You do not live in a vacuum</u>. What you do as a leader will impact others for good or for harm. If you have been given the great responsibility of leadership, then you must be keenly aware of the kind of influence you possess. Influence is like currency. Spend it wisely.

3. <u>People are watching you</u>: those you work with and those with whom you live. Are you leading in such a way that you will eventually regret, or will your life be defined as one who learned to leverage influence in the right way? The choice is yours.

Here are some other principles of influence that underscore the importance of setting a good example for others to follow:

Set the example of living a transformed life.

'Don't copy the behavior and customs of this world, but let God transform you into a new person by changing the way you think. Then you will learn to know God's will for you, which is good and pleasing and perfect.' (Romans 12:2)

Live in a way that your actions speak for themselves.

'Work hard so you can present yourself to God and receive His approval. Be a good worker, one who does not need to be ashamed and who correctly explains the word of truth. ' (2 Timothy 2:15)

Integrity matters in everything you believe and practice.

'In the same way, encourage the young men to live wisely. And you yourself must be an example to them by doing good works of every kind. Let everything you do reflect the integrity and seriousness of your teaching. Teach the truth so that your teaching can't be criticized. Then those who oppose us will be ashamed and have nothing bad to say about us.' (Titus 2:6-8)

It's not your life. You belong to the Lord so whatever you do should be done in order to please Him.

'"You are the salt of the earth. But what good is salt if it has lost its flavor? Can you make it salty again? It will be thrown out and trampled underfoot as worthless. "You are the light of the world—like a city on a hilltop that cannot be hidden. No one lights a lamp and then puts it under a basket. Instead, a lamp is placed on a stand, where it gives light to everyone in the house. In the same way, let your good deeds shine out for all to see, so that everyone will praise your heavenly Father.' (Matthew 5:13-16)

God has called us to Intentionally Influence others for good. The thirty-one devotions on the following pages remind us how.

INTENTIONAL INFLUENCE
(Proverbs 13:16-15:17)

DAY ONE: "Before You Leap"

Today May You . . . before you do anything, THINK, PRAY, LISTEN, and then ACT.

Wise people think before they act;

fools don't—and even brag about their foolishness. (Proverbs 13:16 NLT).

Turn your *Declaration Of Quality Wisdom* into this prayer of commitment:

> *Lord Jesus, **Today May I** before I do anything, THINK, PRAY, LISTEN, and then ACT.*

DAY TWO: "Why Being Open To Correction Will Open Doors For You"

Today May You . . . have an open MIND to learn more, an open HEART to change more and an open LIFE to show more of God's grace at work in you.

If you ignore criticism, you will end in poverty and disgrace;

if you accept correction, you will be honored. (Proverbs 13:18 NLT).

Turn your *Declaration Of Quality Wisdom* into this prayer of commitment:

> *Lord Jesus, **Today May I** have an open MIND to learn more, an open HEART to change more and an open LIFE to show more of God's grace at work in me.*

DAY THREE: "Dreams Of Destiny"

Today May You . . . DREAM the kind of DREAMS that only the DREAM MAKER can make happen.

It is pleasant to see dreams come true,

but fools refuse to turn from evil to attain them. (Proverbs 13:19 NLT).

Turn your *Declaration Of Quality Wisdom* into this prayer of commitment:

---

*Lord Jesus, **Today May I** DREAM the kind of DREAMS that only the DREAM MAKER can make happen.*

DAY FOUR: "The Company You Keep Will Keep You"

Today May You . . . surround yourself with the kind of people who will make you a better you.

Walk with the wise and become wise;

associate with fools and get in trouble. (Proverbs 13:20 NLT).

Turn your *Declaration Of Quality Wisdom* into this prayer of commitment:

---

*Lord Jesus, **Today May I** surround myself with the kind of people who will make me a better me.*

DAY FIVE: "Choices Always Have Consequences"

Today May You . . . . run away from trouble and run to the blessings God has promised you.

Trouble chases sinners,

while blessings reward the righteous. (Proverbs 13:21 NLT).

Turn your *Declaration Of Quality Wisdom* into this prayer of commitment:

> *Lord Jesus, **Today May I** run away from trouble and run to the blessings God has promised me.*

DAY SIX: "Right On!"

Today May You . . . make decisions that keep you on the RIGHT path, connect you with the RIGHT people, and help you wind up in the RIGHT place.

Those who follow the right path fear the Lord;
those who take the wrong path despise him. (Proverbs 14:2 NLT).

Turn your *Declaration Of Quality Wisdom* into this prayer of commitment:

> *Lord Jesus, **Today May I** make decisions that keep me on the RIGHT path, connecting me with the RIGHT people, and help me wind up in the RIGHT place.*

DAY SEVEN: "Passion In Your Purpose"

Today May You . . . do enough productive work that will be messy enough to clean up.

Without oxen a stable stays clean,
but you need a strong ox for a large harvest. (Proverbs 14:4 NLT).

Turn your *Declaration Of Quality Wisdom* into this prayer of commitment:

> *Lord Jesus, **Today May I** do enough productive work that will be messy enough to clean up.*

DAY EIGHT: "Just The Facts Please"

Today May You . . . make an intentional decision that everything you THINK, SAY, and DO be based upon what is TRUE.

An honest witness does not lie;

a false witness breathes lies. (Proverbs 14:5 NLT).

Turn your *Declaration Of Quality Wisdom* into this prayer of commitment:

> *Lord Jesus, **Today May I** make an intentional decision that everything I THINK, SAY, and DO be based upon what is TRUE.*

DAY NINE: "Life Plan"

Today May You . . . ask the Lord for His PLAN and then ask Him for the POWER and the COURAGE to live it out.

The prudent understand where they are going,

but fools deceive themselves. (Proverbs 14:8 NLT).

Turn your *Declaration Of Quality Wisdom* into this prayer of commitment:

> *Lord Jesus, **Today May I** ask You for Your PLAN and then ask You for the POWER and the COURAGE to live it out.*

DAY TEN: "A Safe Place For Secrets"

Today May You . . . find a safe place to unpack the secrets of your heart.

Each heart knows its own bitterness, and no one else can fully share its joy. Proverbs 14:10 (NLT).

Turn your *Declaration Of Quality Wisdom* into this prayer of commitment:

> Lord Jesus, *Today May I* find a safe place to unpack the secrets of my heart.

DAY ELEVEN: "The Need To Be Considered A Safe Person For The Hurting"

Today May You . . . be keenly aware, by the discernment of the Spirit, of the people around you who are smiling on the outside but are hurting on the inside.

Laughter can conceal a heavy heart,

but when the laughter ends, the grief remains. (Proverbs 14:13 NLT).

Turn your *Declaration Of Quality Wisdom* into this prayer of commitment:

> Lord Jesus, *Today May I* be keenly aware, by the discernment of the Spirit, of the people around me who are smiling on the outside but are hurting on the inside.

DAY TWELVE: "Being Intentional In Experiencing A Focused And Fruitful Life"

Today May You . . . do whatever it takes to keep your INTEGRITY intact and your love for the Lord INTENSE.

Backsliders get what they deserve;

good people receive their reward. (Proverbs 14:14 NLT).

Turn your *Declaration Of Quality Wisdom* into this prayer of commitment:

> *Lord Jesus, **Today May I** do whatever it takes to keep my INTEGRITY intact and my love for You INTENSE.*

DAY THIRTEEN: "Living In The Land Of Truth"

Today May You . . . be on the lookout for FAITH news and not FAKE news: believe Him, not them.

Only simpletons believe everything they're told!
The prudent carefully consider their steps. (Proverbs 14:15 NLT).

Turn your *Declaration Of Quality Wisdom* into this prayer of commitment:

> *Lord Jesus, **Today May I** be on the lookout for FAITH news and not FAKE news: believe Him, not them.*

DAY FOURTEEN: "The Disciplines Of A Dedicated Disciple Of Jesus"

Today May You . . . THINK before you SPEAK, take a DEEP BREATH before you ACT and PRAY ALWAYS.

The wise are cautious and avoid danger;

fools plunge ahead with reckless confidence.

Short-tempered people do foolish things,

and schemers are hated.

Simpletons are clothed with foolishness,

but the prudent are crowned with knowledge. (Proverbs 14:16-18 NLT).

Turn your *Declaration Of Quality Wisdom* into this prayer of commitment:

> *Lord Jesus, **Today May I** THINK before I SPEAK, take a DEEP BREATH before I ACT and PRAY ALWAYS.*

DAY FIFTEEN: "Do Good Rules"

Today May You . . . treat others the way you want to be treated.

It is a sin to belittle one's neighbor;

blessed are those who help the poor.

If you plan to do evil, you will be lost;

if you plan to do good, you will receive unfailing love and faithfulness. (Proverbs 14:21-22 NLT).

Turn your *Declaration Of Quality Wisdom* into this prayer of commitment:

> *Lord Jesus, **Today May I** treat others the way I want to be treated.*

DAY SIXTEEN: "Money Matters In A Material World"

Today May You . . . make good sense in every financial decision you make, and for God's glory and His purpose, make many dollars for His work.

Work brings profit,

but mere talk leads to poverty!

Wealth is a crown for the wise;

the effort of fools yields only foolishness. (Proverbs 14:23-24 NLT).

Turn your *Declaration Of Quality Wisdom* into this prayer of commitment:

> *Lord Jesus, Today May I make good sense in every financial decision I make, and for God's glory and His purpose, make many dollars for His work.*

DAY SEVENTEEN: "Can I Get A Witness?"

Today May You . . . determine to make every decision you make be based upon the truth, no matter how "inconvenient" it may be for you.

A truthful witness saves lives,

but a false witness is a traitor. (Proverbs 14:25 NLT).

Turn your *Declaration Of Quality Wisdom* into this prayer of commitment:

> *Lord Jesus, Today May I determine to make every decision I make be based upon the truth, no matter how "inconvenient" it may be for me.*

DAY EIGHTEEN: "Anger Management"

Today May You . . . take a deep breath when you want to lash out in anger and instead, reach out in love, and be firm in your response.

People with understanding control their anger;

a hot temper shows great foolishness. (Proverbs 14:29 NLT).

Turn your *Declaration Of Quality Wisdom* into this prayer of commitment:

> *Lord Jesus, **Today May I** take a deep breath when I want to lash out in anger and instead, reach out in love, and be firm in my response.*

DAY NINETEEN: "Secrets To Healthy Living"

Today May You . . . experience a peaceful, easy feeling, and avoid making any decision that will poison your life.

A peaceful heart leads to a healthy body;

jealousy is like cancer in the bones. (Proverbs 14:30 NLT).

Turn your *Declaration Of Quality Wisdom* into this prayer of commitment:

> *Lord Jesus, **Today May I** experience a peaceful, easy feeling, and avoid making any decision that will poison my life.*

DAY TWENTY: "Priceless"

Today May You . . . do an act of kindness for someone who could never repay you.

Those who oppress the poor insult their Maker,

but helping the poor honors him. (Proverbs 14:31 NLT).

Turn your *Declaration Of Quality Wisdom* into this prayer of commitment:

> *Lord Jesus, **Today May I** do an act of kindness for someone who could never repay me.*

DAY TWENTY ONE: "Responsible Citizenship"

Today May You . . . do your part to make your nation great by living a life of godliness.

Godliness makes a nation great,

but sin is a disgrace to any people. (Proverbs 14:34 NLT).

Turn your *Declaration Of Quality Wisdom* into this prayer of commitment:

> *Lord Jesus,* ***Today May I*** *do my part to make my nation great by living a life of godliness.*

DAY TWENTY TWO: "Word Diplomat"

Today May You . . . WATCH what you say, WHO you say it to, and HOW you say it.

A gentle answer deflects anger,

but harsh words make tempers flare.

The tongue of the wise makes knowledge appealing,

but the mouth of a fool belches out foolishness. (Proverbs 15:1-2 NLT).

Turn your *Declaration Of Quality Wisdom* into this prayer of commitment:

> *Lord Jesus,* ***Today May I*** *WATCH what I say, WHO I say it to, and HOW I say it.*

DAY TWENTY THREE: "Word Leverage"

Today May You . . . speak words that produce life and not words that kill people, one cut at a time.

Gentle words are a tree of life;

a deceitful tongue crushes the spirit. (Proverbs 15:4 NLT).

Turn your *Declaration Of Quality Wisdom* into this prayer of commitment:

> *Lord Jesus, **Today May I** speak words that produce life and not words that kill people, one cut at a time.*

DAY TWENTY FOUR: "Saying Yes To The Great And No To The Good"

Today May You . . . always say YES to God's ways and NO to the things that may sound good but are foolish.

The lips of the wise give good advice;

the heart of a fool has none to give. (Proverbs 15:7 NLT).

Turn your *Declaration Of Quality Wisdom* into this prayer of commitment:

> *Lord Jesus, **Today May I** always say YES to God's ways and NO to the things that may sound good but are foolish.*

DAY TWENTY FIVE: "Experiencing A Right Life"

Today May You . . . PURSUE right THOUGHTS and right ACTIONS so that you may live a right LIFE.

The Lord detests the way of the wicked,

but he loves those who pursue godliness. (Proverbs 15:9 NLT).

Turn your *Declaration Of Quality Wisdom* into this prayer of commitment:

> *Lord Jesus, **Today May I** PURSUE right THOUGHTS and right ACTIONS so that I may live a right LIFE.*

DAY TWENTY SIX: "Life Between The Ditches"

Today May You . . . keep your life between the ditches and resist the urge to abandon the right path.

Whoever abandons the right path will be severely disciplined;
whoever hates correction will die. (Proverbs 15:10 NLT).

Turn your *Declaration Of Quality Wisdom* into this prayer of commitment:

> *Lord Jesus, **Today May I** keep my life between the ditches and resist the urge to abandon the right path.*

DAY TWENTY SEVEN: "Emotions Are Real"

Today May You . . . do the things that will make you GLAD and not SAD.

A glad heart makes a happy face;
a broken heart crushes the spirit. (Proverbs 15:13 NLT).

Turn your *Declaration Of Quality Wisdom* into this prayer of commitment:

> *Lord Jesus, **Today May I** do the things that will make me GLAD and not SAD.*

DAY TWENTY EIGHT: "Soul Food"

Today May You . . . feed your mind with HEALTHY thoughts and leave the brainless JUNK FOOD of UNHEALTHY thoughts alone.

A wise person is hungry for knowledge,
while the fool feeds on trash. (Proverbs 15:14 NLT).

Turn your *Declaration Of Quality Wisdom* into this prayer of commitment:

*Lord Jesus, **Today May I** feed my mind with HEALTHY thoughts and leave the brainless JUNK FOOD of UNHEALTHY thoughts alone.*

DAY TWENTY NINE: "The Power Of The Daily Choice"

Today May You . . . make the kind of choices that will produce within you a happy heart and a satisfied soul.

For the despondent, every day brings trouble;
for the happy heart, life is a continual feast. (Proverbs 15:15 NLT).

Turn your *Declaration Of Quality Wisdom* into this prayer of commitment:

*Lord Jesus, **Today May I** make the kind of choices that will produce within me a happy heart and a satisfied soul.*

DAY THIRTY: "The Power Of Living A Satisfied Life"

Today May You . . . be SATISFIED with all He provides and love Him more than to have this gnawing feeling inside that is never SATISFIED.

Better to have little, with fear for the Lord,
than to have great treasure and inner turmoil. (Proverbs 15:16 NLT).

Turn your *Declaration Of Quality Wisdom* into this prayer of commitment:

> Lord Jesus, *Today May I* be SATISFIED with all You provide and love You more than to have this gnawing feeling inside that is never SATISFIED.

DAY THIRTY ONE: "Divine Dining"

Today May You . . . be the REAL DEAL when it comes to having a MEANINGFUL MEAL.

A bowl of vegetables with someone you love

is better than steak with someone you hate. (Proverbs 15:17 NLT).

Turn your *Declaration Of Quality Wisdom* into this prayer of commitment:

> Lord Jesus, *Today May I* be the REAL DEAL when it comes to having a MEANINGFUL MEAL.

Introduction To Section Five:
"DISCIPLINED FOR DESTINY" (Proverbs 15:22-17:17)

"The secret of success in life is for a man to be ready for his time when it comes."
~ Benjamin Disraeli

One of the key attributes of the successful person is their ability to embrace "The Process" and see where it leads. Where many are looking for the easiest off ramp, there is great blessing for those who are willing to exhibit discipline. If they do it well, they are well on their way to be Disciplined For Destiny.

The Apostle Paul had a clear grasp of the process when he was inspired to write these timeless words:

For I am confident of this very thing, that He who began a good work in you will perfect it until the day of Christ Jesus. **Philippians 1:6**

Hurry up and wait. We sense the tension inside our mind. We are eager. We are expectant. And often, we are impatient if our circumstances are not moving along at our set pace. Many impatient leaders grow weary of the process and make a rash decision, and often fail.

One of the great characteristics of a Quality Leader is the ability to trust the process. We live in such a quick fix society where patience and perseverance are dirty words for many leaders. Anyone who has spent any time cooking in the kitchen knows the difference between "fast food" and "crockpot food." You might be able to prepare a quick meal that will fill your stomach but leave your taste buds unsatisfied. In contrast, a meal that has time to simmer and marinate the flavors into one delicious dish is well worth the wait. Great cooking requires time, and time requires a commitment to the process.

This is the way good leadership works. Like preparing a delicious meal, preparation time must be accounted for if we are to be ready for the next growth opportunity that comes our way. We must be committed to do the "little things," the daily disciplines of preparation. It was Benjamin Disraeli who shared, "The secret of success in life is for a man to be ready for his time when it comes." For the Quality Leader, the question is not *if* a defining moment comes his or her way, but *when*. And when the defining moment comes, the leader who commits to do the daily duties of preparation will be prepared to lead.

Here is the take-a-way for the leader who desires to experience steady growth by being patient with the process. How is it done? What does a Quality Leader have to do in order to experience growth, day-by-day and mature as a leader? Here are a few suggestions:

1. You need to create a personal growth plan. Chart out a reasonable list of goals you have for your personal growth. Your goals need to be reasonable and they need to be measurable.
2. Be patient with the process and, just as important, be patient with yourself.
3. Refuse to take growth shortcuts. Do the necessary work on the front end.

When we accept the challenge to be disciplined for destiny, the future we make for ourselves is literally in our hands. The thirty-one devotions on the following pages remind us how.

DISCIPLINED FOR DESTINY
(Proverbs 15:22-17:17)

DAY ONE: "Under Advisement"

Today May You . . . always get better advice than your own.

Plans go wrong for lack of advice;

many advisers bring success. (Proverbs 15:22 NLT).

Turn your *Declaration Of Quality Wisdom* into this prayer of commitment:

> *Lord Jesus, **Today May I** always get better advice than my own.*

DAY TWO: "Right Of Way"

Today May You . . . say the RIGHT THING at the RIGHT TIME in the RIGHT WAY to the RIGHT PERSON.

Everyone enjoys a fitting reply;

it is wonderful to say the right thing at the right time! (Proverbs 15:23 NLT).

Turn your *Declaration Of Quality Wisdom* into this prayer of commitment:

> *Lord Jesus, **Today May I** say the RIGHT THING at the RIGHT TIME in the RIGHT WAY to the RIGHT PERSON.*

DAY THREE: "Proceed With Caution"

Today May You . . . be CAREFUL what you THINK and what you SAY and what you DO.

The heart of the godly thinks carefully before speaking;

the mouth of the wicked overflows with evil words. (Proverbs 15:28 NLT).

Turn your *Declaration Of Quality Wisdom* into this prayer of commitment:

> *Lord Jesus, **Today May I** be CAREFUL what I THINK and what I SAY and what I DO.*

DAY FOUR: "The Benefits Of A Well Placed Smile"

Today May You . . . KEEP a SMILE on your FACE and in your HEART too.

A cheerful look brings joy to the heart;

good news makes for good health. (Proverbs 15:30 NLT).

Turn your *Declaration Of Quality Wisdom* into this prayer of commitment:

> *Lord Jesus, **Today May I** KEEP a SMILE on my FACE and in my HEART too.*

DAY FIVE: "Unending Learning"

Today May You . . . embrace this posture of humility: the more I know the less I know thus the need to keep learning more and more.

If you listen to constructive criticism,

you will be at home among the wise. (Proverbs 15:31 NLT).

Turn your *Declaration Of Quality Wisdom* into this prayer of commitment:

> *Lord Jesus, **Today May I** embrace this posture of humility: the more I know the less I know thus the need to keep learning more and more.*

DAY SIX: "Humility Rules"

Today May You . . . be willing to be HUMBLE when you are WRONG and be willing to be HUMBLE when you are RIGHT.

If you reject discipline, you only harm yourself;
but if you listen to correction, you grow in understanding. (Proverbs 15:32 NLT).

Turn your *Declaration Of Quality Wisdom* into this prayer of commitment:

> *Lord Jesus, **Today May I** be willing to be HUMBLE when I am WRONG and be willing to be HUMBLE when I am RIGHT.*

DAY SEVEN: "How To Get And Use Wisdom"

Today May You . . . seek to be the wisest, most humble person you know.

Fear of the Lord teaches wisdom;
humility precedes honor. (Proverbs 15:33 NLT).

Turn your *Declaration Of Quality Wisdom* into this prayer of commitment:

> *Lord Jesus, **Today May I** seek to be the wisest, most humble person I know.*

DAY EIGHT: "No Limit To Your Dreams"

Today May You . . . be free to dream a dream that only God can fulfill.

We can make our own plans,

but the Lord gives the right answer. (Proverbs 16:1 NLT).

Turn your *Declaration Of Quality Wisdom* into this prayer of commitment:

> *Lord Jesus, **Today May I** be free to dream a dream that only God can fulfill.*

DAY NINE: "Motives Matter"

Today May You . . . keep an open mind as you ask for His mind.

People may be pure in their own eyes,

but the Lord examines their motives. (Proverbs 16:2 NLT).

Turn your *Declaration Of Quality Wisdom* into this prayer of commitment:

> *Lord Jesus, **Today May I** keep an open mind as I ask for Yours.*

DAY TEN: "The Key To Experiencing A Wildly Successful Life"

Today May You . . . give every plan, every action, and every dream you have to the Lord who will bless you with the kind of success only He can give.

Commit your actions to the Lord,

and your plans will succeed. (Proverbs 16:3 NLT).

Turn your *Declaration Of Quality Wisdom* into this prayer of commitment:

> *Lord Jesus, **Today May I** give every plan, every action, and every dream I have to You who will bless me with the kind of success only You can give.*

DAY ELEVEN: "Please Who You Need To Please"

Today May You . . . seek to PLEASE the Lord more than you seek to PLEASE anyone else.

When people's lives please the Lord,

even their enemies are at peace with them. (Proverbs 16:7 NLT).

Turn your *Declaration Of Quality Wisdom* into this prayer of commitment:

> *Lord Jesus, **Today May I** seek to PLEASE You more than I seek to PLEASE anyone else.*

DAY TWELVE: "The Secret To Contentment"

Today May You . . . be content with the ABUNDANCE God provides and not worry about what you DO NOT HAVE.

Better to have little, with godliness,

than to be rich and dishonest. (Proverbs 16:8 NLT).

Turn your *Declaration Of Quality Wisdom* into this prayer of commitment:

> *Lord Jesus, **Today May I** be content with the ABUNDANCE God provides and not worry about what I DO NOT HAVE.*

DAY THIRTEEN: "Plan B"

Today May You . . . be bold enough to dream but humble enough to adjust and go.

We can make our plans,

but the Lord determines our steps. (Proverbs 16:9 NLT).

Turn your *Declaration Of Quality Wisdom* into this prayer of commitment:

> Lord Jesus, ***Today May I*** be bold enough to dream but humble enough to adjust and go.

DAY FOURTEEN: "Integrity Gives You The Right To Influence Others"

Today May You . . . keep INTEGRITY in full view knowing that your HONESTY will give you the right to influence someone's HEART.

The Lord demands accurate scales and balances;

he sets the standards for fairness. (Proverbs 16:11 NLT).

Turn your *Declaration Of Quality Wisdom* into this prayer of commitment:

> Lord Jesus, ***Today May I*** keep INTEGRITY in full view knowing that my HONESTY will give me the right to influence someone's HEART.

DAY FIFTEEN: "True Riches"

Today May You . . . seek to become the RICHEST person you know with the things that matter most.

How much better to get wisdom than gold,

and good judgment than silver! (Proverbs 16:16 NLT).

Turn your *Declaration Of Quality Wisdom* into this prayer of commitment:

> Lord Jesus, *Today May I* seek to become the RICHEST person I know with the things that matter most.

DAY SIXTEEN: "Why People Trip, Stumble, And Fall"

Today May You . . . guard your heart before you break your neck.

Pride goes before destruction,

and haughtiness before a fall. (Proverbs 16:18 NLT).

Turn your *Declaration Of Quality Wisdom* into this prayer of commitment:

> Lord Jesus, *Today May I* guard my heart before I break my neck.

DAY SEVENTEEN: "The Powerful Reason Why Being A Good Listener Matters"

Today May You . . . be wise enough to listen to good instruction and trusting enough to be joyful.

Those who listen to instruction will prosper;

those who trust the Lord will be joyful. (Proverbs 16:20 NLT).

Turn your *Declaration Of Quality Wisdom* into this prayer of commitment:

> Lord Jesus, *Today May I* be wise enough to listen to good instruction and trusting enough to be joyful.

DAY EIGHTEEN: "The Filter Of Wisdom"

Today May You . . . make it your goal to make everything you THINK, SAY, and DO be anchored in wisdom.

From a wise mind comes wise speech;

the words of the wise are persuasive. (Proverbs 16:23 NLT).

Turn your *Declaration Of Quality Wisdom* into this prayer of commitment:

> *Lord Jesus, **Today May I** make it my goal to make everything I THINK, SAY, and DO be anchored in wisdom.*

DAY NINETEEN: "Sweet Words"

Today May You . . . add value to those you love by intentionally using kind words that build them up.

Kind words are like honey—

sweet to the soul and healthy for the body. (Proverbs 16:24 NLT).

Turn your *Declaration Of Quality Wisdom* into this prayer of commitment:

> *Lord Jesus, **Today May I** add value to those I love by intentionally using kind words that build them up.*

DAY TWENTY: "The Motivation Of Work"

Today May You . . . seek to work HARDER and SMARTER so you will be able to be a GIVER to the things that MATTER to the Lord.

It is good for workers to have an appetite;

an empty stomach drives them on. (Proverbs 16:26 NLT).

Turn your *Declaration Of Quality Wisdom* into this prayer of commitment:

> Lord Jesus, ***Today May I*** seek to work HARDER and SMARTER so I will be able to be a GIVER to the things that MATTER to You.

DAY TWENTY ONE: "No Gossip Zone"

Today May You . . . make sure every word you use builds someone up and does not take them down.

A troublemaker plants seeds of strife;

gossip separates the best of friends. (Proverbs 16:28 NLT).

Turn your *Declaration Of Quality Wisdom* into this prayer of commitment:

> Lord Jesus, ***Today May I*** make sure every word I use builds someone up and does not take them down.

DAY TWENTY TWO: "Godly Gray"

Today May You . . . as you get older, get wiser by becoming more godly.

Gray hair is a crown of glory;

it is gained by living a godly life. (Proverbs 16:31 NLT).

Turn your *Declaration Of Quality Wisdom* into this prayer of commitment:

> Lord Jesus, ***Today May I*** as I get older, get wiser by becoming more godly.

DAY TWENTY THREE: "The Power Of Being Patient"

Today May You . . . make it your goal to be more PATIENT than POWERFUL, more SELF-CONTROLLED than OUT OF CONTROL, and more SPIRIT-LED than YOU-LED.

Better to be patient than powerful;

better to have self-control than to conquer a city. (Proverbs 16:32 NLT).

Turn your *Declaration Of Quality Wisdom* into this prayer of commitment:

> Lord Jesus, *Today May I* make it my goal to be more PATIENT than POWERFUL, more SELF-CONTROLLED than OUT OF CONTROL, and more SPIRIT-LED than ME-LED.

DAY TWENTY FOUR: "Holy Coincidences"

Today May You . . . always be prepared to ADJUST and GO when your plan needs to align with His.

We may throw the dice [cast lots],

but the Lord determines how they fall. (Proverbs 16:33 NLT).

Turn your *Declaration Of Quality Wisdom* into this prayer of commitment:

> Lord Jesus, *Today May I* always be prepared to ADJUST and GO when my plan needs to align with Yours.

DAY TWENTY FIVE: "Heart Check"

Today May You . . . keep your integrity in what you think and in what you say and in what you do.

Fire tests the purity of silver and gold,

but the Lord tests the heart. (Proverbs 17:3 NLT).

Turn your *Declaration Of Quality Wisdom* into this prayer of commitment:

> *Lord Jesus, **Today May I** keep my integrity in what I think and in what I say and in what I do.*

DAY TWENTY SIX: "Shutting Out Destructive Voices"

Today May You . . . guard your lips and protect your ears so your heart will be clear and pure.

Wrongdoers eagerly listen to gossip;

liars pay close attention to slander. (Proverbs 17:4 NLT).

Turn your *Declaration Of Quality Wisdom* into this prayer of commitment:

> *Lord Jesus, **Today May I** guard my lips and protect my ears so my heart will be clear and pure.*

DAY TWENTY SEVEN: "Life On The Perch"

Today May You . . . LOOK UP to the Lord before you LOOK DOWN on those who are not as fortunate as you.

Those who mock the poor insult their Maker;

those who rejoice at the misfortune of others will be punished. (Proverbs 17:5 NLT).

Turn your *Declaration Of Quality Wisdom* into this prayer of commitment:

> *Lord Jesus, Today May I LOOK UP to the Lord before I LOOK DOWN on those who are not as fortunate as me.*

DAY TWENTY EIGHT: "When Tolerance Is Spelled L-O-V-E"

Today May You . . . FORGIVE when you find a FAULT, LOVE when you would rather LASH out, and GIVE GRACE because you need it too.

Love prospers when a fault is forgiven,

but dwelling on it separates close friends. (Proverbs 17:9 NLT).

Turn your *Declaration Of Quality Wisdom* into this prayer of commitment:

> *Lord Jesus, Today May I FORGIVE when I find a FAULT, LOVE when I would rather LASH out, and GIVE GRACE because I need it too.*

DAY TWENTY NINE: "Connect With Me And Then Correct Me"

Today May You . . . be willing to receive CORRECTION when a CORRECTION is needed.

A single rebuke does more for a person of understanding

than a hundred lashes on the back of a fool. (Proverbs 17:10 NLT).

Turn your *Declaration Of Quality Wisdom* into this prayer of commitment:

> *Lord Jesus, Today May I be willing to receive CORRECTION when a CORRECTION is needed.*

DAY THIRTY: "The Best Way To Stop An Argument Is Not To Start One"

Today May You . . . control your tongue so your life may be flooded with peace.

Starting a quarrel is like opening a floodgate,

so stop before a dispute breaks out. (Proverbs 17:14 NLT).

Turn your *Declaration Of Quality Wisdom* into this prayer of commitment:

> *Lord Jesus, **Today May I** control my tongue so my life may be flooded with peace.*

DAY THIRTY ONE: "The Best Kind Of Friend"

Today May You . . . be the kind of friend you need to be for you.

A friend is always loyal,

and a brother is born to help in time of need. (Proverbs 17:17 NLT).

Turn your *Declaration Of Quality Wisdom* into this prayer of commitment:

> *Lord Jesus, **Today May I** be the kind of friend I need to be for me.*

Introduction To Section Six:
"STRATEGIC SELF-AWARENESS" (Proverbs 17:18-20:13)

I always wanted to be somebody, but I should have been more specific.

~ Lily Tomlin

Be still (cease striving) and know that I am God. (Psalm 46:10)
Before the Throne of mercy and grace, listen to who God says you are.
Listen for His voice on your calling.

Who Am I?

This is the deep and very philosophical question that was posed to my freshman college Introduction to Philosophy class. The braver students spoke right up and began to wax eloquent and espouse their undergraduate wisdom. Some spoke of what they knew, only because that is what they had always known, was most obvious to them, and had been *taught* to them for a long, long time. "I am an American . . . I am a freshman . . . I am a Christian."

The professor of record immediately sensed the fresh(man) blood in the water and went for the kill. His target that day was two students whose worldviews were poles apart. One of the students eventually finished the course and wound up believing that he was nothing more than a human vegetable. In other words, just brain and soul mush. The other student was a Christian who was on the bent side of an unswerving fundamentalism who had all of the "right" answers but failed to win the argument. During the course of one lecture, the professor (who happened to also be an ordained Baptist minister and who also taught a class many tagged "Misunderstanding and Applying the Bible") pushed all of this kid's buttons and got the response he wanted: a burst of volcanic anger and hopeless frustration.

This raises a good question: why it is so difficult to answer, on the surface at least, a simply worded question? Who am I? Allow me to ask it again, this time, more drawn out: who . . . am . . . I . . . ? What is my identity? Do I know who I am and am I so confident in knowing who I am that I am empowered to accomplish great things in my life?

Before I can know what to do, I need to know who I am. Before I can live out an incredible legacy, I must know my unique vocation or calling. My STORY, My PURPOSE, and My MOTIVES all come from the seedbed of who I AM. Before I can plan an effective STRATEGY and INFLUENCE the right people, and EMPOWER them to do their very best, I have to know who I am. I need to get in tune with my "vocational call." What is a vocational call? A vocational call is who God says I am. In order to embrace that call, it means I need to connect with the person God has called and made me to be. Understanding one's vocational call gives greater clarity of one's identity.

This is the truth:

- How do you discover your PURPOSE? Go back to your Identity.
- How do you make sense of your STORY? Go back to your Identity.
- How do you experience a QUALITY LIFE? You know. Go back to your Identity.

In case you might be wondering, I did pass the Philosophy class. Apparently, I was able to answer "the question" in a way that met the demands of the class syllabus. My essay was a bit longer than the student who had the guts to answer the question of "Who Am I?" with this pithy answer, "I Am." His answer reminds me of the way Jesus answered the question, "Who are you?" I AM who I AM." It takes a pretty confident person to know who they are, where they have come from and where they are going. I submit to you that Jesus was supremely confident in His identity; He was free to be Himself and impact His world. This was not without a challenge. Even for Jesus, there were some around Him who sought to mold His identity into someone He was not. There are forces around us, and within us, which seek to accomplish two things: get us to *do* before we *become*, and mold us into *someone* we are not. For example:

Have you ever gotten the cart before the horse? Or in other words, have you violated the principle of "being before doing?" I have. I'm pretty sure you have too. Have you ever felt the pressure from others to be someone you are not? I have and I know you have too.

Do you long for the freedom to be yourself? We all do.

The Primary Need To Be.

Knowing one's identity is one of the core foundations of being. Some have said, correctly, that *being* precedes *doing*. Many get it completely backwards and seek to do before they become. This kind of thinking comes out of a works-based, performance-oriented world-view. There are many who have perfected this way of living. Sadly, their weary soul never catches up with the torrid pace of a hurried life. No one is really immune to this attempt for others to form *who you are* in *their* opinion. Remember, even Jesus had others suggest He was someone He was not.

18 One day Jesus left the crowds to pray alone. Only his disciples were with him, and he asked them, "Who do people say I am?"
19 "Well," they replied, "some say John the Baptist, some say Elijah, and others say you are one of the other ancient prophets risen from the dead."
20 Then he asked them, "But who do you say I am?"
Peter replied, "You are the Messiah sent from God!" Luke 9:18-20

Having Clarity About Our Identity Empowers Us.
Before the Passover celebration, Jesus knew that his hour had come to leave this world and return to his Father. He had loved his disciples during his ministry on earth, and now he loved them to the very end. 2 It was time for supper, and the devil had already prompted Judas, son of Simon Iscariot, to betray Jesus. 3 Jesus knew that the Father had given him authority over everything and that he had come from God and would return to God. 4 So he got up from the table, took off his robe, wrapped a towel around his waist, 5 and poured water into a basin. Then he began to wash the disciples' feet, drying them with the towel he had around him. John 13:1-5

There are three spiritual insights we can gather from verse 3:
"Jesus knew that the Father had given him authority over everything and that he had come from God and would return to God."

- Jesus knew His purpose and source— the Father had given him authority over everything
- Jesus knew His history—from where He came
- Jesus knew His destiny—where He was going

Here is a great application of the power of knowing who you are (and Whose you are too!):
A healthy view of your identity (who you are) empowers you to go beyond yourself and serve others.

4 "So he got up from the table, took off his robe, wrapped a towel around his waist, 5 and poured water into a basin. Then he began to wash the disciples' feet, drying them with the towel he had around him."

Knowing who you are is the first step towards living a fulfilled life. When a Quality Leader has a healthy self-image, he or she . . .

- Is secure in who they are,
- Has not left their soul behind,
- Is empowered to serve others.

So, one of the greatest gifts you can ever give yourself is your very own self-awareness. Your ability to embrace and celebrate who you are is a game changer. Think of your own self-awareness as you strategically read over and pray through these next 31 devotions.

STRATEGIC SELF-AWARENESS
(Proverbs 17:18-20:13)

DAY ONE: "Crazy Money"

Today May You . . . not allow your HEART to get ahead of your HEAD or you might lose more than your MIND.

It's poor judgment to guarantee another person's debt
or put up security for a friend. (Proverbs 17:18 NLT).

Turn your *Declaration Of Quality Wisdom* into this prayer of commitment:

> *Lord Jesus, **Today May I** not allow my HEART to get ahead of my HEAD or I might lose more than my MIND.*

DAY TWO: "Rx For The Heart"

Today May You . . . be the good medicine to those who hearts are breaking.

A cheerful heart is good medicine,
but a broken spirit saps a person's strength. (Proverbs 17:22 NLT).

Turn your *Declaration Of Quality Wisdom* into this prayer of commitment:

> *Lord Jesus, **Today May I** be the good medicine to those who hearts are breaking.*

DAY THREE: "When Less Is More"

Today May You . . . use the RIGHT words at the RIGHT time in the RIGHT way.

A truly wise person uses few words;

a person with understanding is even-tempered. (Proverbs 17:27 NLT).

Turn your *Declaration Of Quality Wisdom* into this prayer of commitment:

> *Lord Jesus, **Today May I** use the RIGHT words at the RIGHT time in the RIGHT way.*

DAY FOUR: "Wisdom Source"

Today May You . . . be a plentiful resource of wisdom that wisdom hunters can come and draw from you.

Wise words are like deep waters;

wisdom flows from the wise like a bubbling brook. (Proverbs 18:4 NLT).

Turn your *Declaration Of Quality Wisdom* into this prayer of commitment:

> *Lord Jesus, **Today May I** be a plentiful resource of wisdom that wisdom hunters can come and draw from me.*

DAY FIVE: "Hide-a-Way"

Today May You . . . run to the Lord when hell throws everything at you and by His grace may you depend upon His name when you feel unsafe.

The name of the Lord is a strong fortress;

the godly run to him and are safe. (Proverbs 18:10 NLT).

Turn your *Declaration Of Quality Wisdom* into this prayer of commitment:

> *Lord Jesus, Today May I run to You when hell throws everything at me and by Your grace may I depend upon Your name when I feel unsafe.*

DAY SIX: "Humility With Honor"

Today May You . . . never become proud of your humility.

Haughtiness goes before destruction;
humility precedes honor. (Proverbs 18:12 NLT).

Turn your *Declaration Of Quality Wisdom* into this prayer of commitment:

> *Lord Jesus, Today May I never become proud of my humility.*

DAY SEVEN: "Open Mind To Success"

Today May You . . . make it your goal to learn more than you did yesterday and to use what you learn to add value to more people.

Intelligent people are always ready to learn.
Their ears are open for knowledge. (Proverbs 18:15 NLT).

Turn your *Declaration Of Quality Wisdom* into this prayer of commitment:

> *Lord Jesus, Today May I make it my goal to learn more than I did yesterday and to use what I learn to add value to more people.*

DAY EIGHT: "Power Gifts"

Today May You . . . BE THE GIFT that ADDS VALUE to important people.

Giving a gift can open doors;

it gives access to important people! (Proverbs 18:16 NLT).

Turn your *Declaration Of Quality Wisdom* into this prayer of commitment:

> Lord Jesus, *Today May I* BE THE GIFT that ADDS VALUE to important people.

DAY NINE: "The Winner Takes It All"

Today May You . . . protect the relationships that are important to you by winning their love, not by winning the argument.

An offended friend is harder to win back than a fortified city.

Arguments separate friends like a gate locked with bars. (Proverbs 18:19 NLT).

Turn your *Declaration Of Quality Wisdom* into this prayer of commitment:

> Lord Jesus, *Today May I* protect the relationships that are important to me by winning their love, not by winning the argument.

DAY TEN: "Wise Words That Satisfy"

Today May You . . . feed the people who hunger for the kinds of words that produce VALIDATION for those who need to experience SATISFACTION.

Wise words satisfy like a good meal;

the right words bring satisfaction. (Proverbs 18:20 NLT).

Turn your *Declaration Of Quality Wisdom* into this prayer of commitment:

---

*Lord Jesus, **Today May I** feed the people who hunger for the kinds of words that produce VALIDATION for those who need to experience SATISFACTION.*

DAY ELEVEN: "The Power Of The Tongue"

Today May You . . . SPEAK words of PRAISE, not words of POISON.

The tongue can bring death or life;

those who love to talk will reap the consequences. (Proverbs 18:21 NLT).

Turn your *Declaration Of Quality Wisdom* into this prayer of commitment:

---

*Lord Jesus, **Today May I** SPEAK words of PRAISE, not words of POISON.*

DAY TWELVE: "What Real Friends Do"

Today May You . . . be the kind of trusted friend your intimate circle of friends needs from you.

There are "friends" who destroy each other,

but a real friend sticks closer than a brother. (Proverbs 18:24 NLT).

Turn your *Declaration Of Quality Wisdom* into this prayer of commitment:

> *Lord Jesus, **Today May I** be the kind of trusted friend my intimate circle of friends needs from me.*

DAY THIRTEEN: "got Honesty?"

Today May You . . . be HONEST with others, HONEST with yourself, and HONEST to God.

Better to be poor and honest

than to be dishonest and a fool. (Proverbs 19:1 NLT).

Turn your *Declaration Of Quality Wisdom* into this prayer of commitment:

> *Lord Jesus, **Today May I** be HONEST with others, HONEST with myself, and HONEST to God.*

DAY FOURTEEN: "The Do It Life"

Today May You . . . know what you are DOING before you DO it and take your time DOING what you know to DO so you may DO it well and enjoy it too.

Enthusiasm without knowledge is no good;

haste makes mistakes. (Proverbs 19:2 NLT).

Turn your *Declaration Of Quality Wisdom* into this prayer of commitment:

> *Lord Jesus, **Today May I** know what I am DOING before I DO it and take my time DOING what I know to DO so I may DO it well and enjoy it too.*

DAY FIFTEEN: "Be Smart. Live Right"

Today May You . . . BE SMART and trust Him, don't OUTSMART yourself and then blame the Lord when it does not work out like you thought it would.

People ruin their lives by their own foolishness

and then are angry at the Lord. (Proverbs 19:3 NLT).

Turn your *Declaration Of Quality Wisdom* into this prayer of commitment:

> *Lord Jesus, **Today May I** BE SMART and trust You, don't OUTSMART myself and then blame You when it does not work out like I thought it would.*

DAY SIXTEEN: "Love To Grow You"

Today May You . . . love yourself enough to grow yourself enough to be a blessing to others.

To acquire wisdom is to love yourself;

people who cherish understanding will prosper. (Proverbs 19:8 NLT).

Turn your *Declaration Of Quality Wisdom* into this prayer of commitment:

> *Lord Jesus, **Today May I** love myself enough to grow myself enough to be a blessing to others.*

DAY SEVENTEEN: "Mind Wars"

Today May You . . . win the battle between your EARS by what comes out of your HEART and through your MOUTH.

Sensible people control their temper;

they earn respect by overlooking wrongs. (Proverbs 19:11 NLT).

Turn your *Declaration Of Quality Wisdom* into this prayer of commitment:

> *Lord Jesus, **Today May I** win the battle between my EARS by what comes out of my HEART and through my MOUTH.*

DAY EIGHTEEN: "Living A Big Life"

Today May You . . . have a BIG heart to meet the BIG needs of those who may be less fortunate than you.

If you help the poor, you are lending to the Lord—

and he will repay you! (Proverbs 19:17 NLT).

Turn your *Declaration Of Quality Wisdom* into this prayer of commitment:

> *Lord Jesus, **Today May I** have a BIG heart to meet the BIG needs of those who may be less fortunate than me.*

DAY NINETEEN: "The Wise Person Always Learns"

Today May You . . . be willing to LEARN so you will be able to be WISE the REST of your LIFE.

Get all the advice and instruction you can,

so you will be wise the rest of your life. (Proverbs 19:20 NLT).

Turn your *Declaration Of Quality Wisdom* into this prayer of commitment:

> Lord Jesus, *Today May I* be willing to LEARN so I will be able to be WISE the REST of my LIFE.

DAY TWENTY: "Plan It. Live It. Adjust It"

Today May You . . . PLAN like you know where you are going, but be open to the idea that your PLAN might change.

You can make many plans,
but the Lord's purpose will prevail. (Proverbs 19:21 NLT).

Turn your *Declaration Of Quality Wisdom* into this prayer of commitment:

> Lord Jesus, *Today May I* PLAN like I know where I am going but be open to the idea that my PLAN might change.

DAY TWENTY ONE: "The Attractive Life"

Today May You . . . live an attractive life by being LOYAL and HONEST.

Loyalty makes a person attractive.
It is better to be poor than dishonest. (Proverbs 19:22 NLT).

Turn your *Declaration Of Quality Wisdom* into this prayer of commitment:

> Lord Jesus, *Today May I* live an attractive life by being LOYAL and HONEST.

DAY TWENTY TWO: "Awesome!"

Today May You . . . have an AWESOME respect for your AWESOME God who watches after you in an AWESOME way.

Fear of the Lord leads to life,

bringing security and protection from harm. (Proverbs 19:23 NLT).

Turn your *Declaration Of Quality Wisdom* into this prayer of commitment:

> *Lord Jesus, **Today May I** have an AWESOME respect for my AWESOME God who watches after me in an AWESOME way.*

DAY TWENTY THREE: "A Legacy Of Generational Honor"

Today May You . . . be a person of HONOR and never allow yourself to be a shameful EMBARRASSMENT and become a person of public DISGRACE (Ephesians 6:2-3).

Children who mistreat their father or chase away their mother

are an embarrassment and a public disgrace. (Proverbs 19:26 NLT).

Turn your *Declaration Of Quality Wisdom* into this prayer of commitment:

> *Lord Jesus, **Today May I** be a person of HONOR and never allow myelf to be a shameful EMBARRASSMENT and become a person of public DISGRACE (Ephesians 6:2-3).*

DAY TWENTY FOUR: "An Open Mind To Learn More"

Today May You . . . live like the more you learn the less you know thus the need to keep on learning more.

If you stop listening to instruction, my child,

you will turn your back on knowledge. (Proverbs 19:27 NLT).

Turn your *Declaration Of Quality Wisdom* into this prayer of commitment:

> *Lord Jesus, Today May I live like the more I learn the less I know, thus the need to keep on learning more.*

DAY TWENTY FIVE: "Focused Living"

Today May You . . . take the HIGH road and walk over those who are UNDER the road.

Avoiding a fight is a mark of honor;

only fools insist on quarreling. (Proverbs 20:3 NLT).

Turn your *Declaration Of Quality Wisdom* into this prayer of commitment:

> *Lord Jesus, Today May I take the HIGH road and walk over those who are UNDER the road.*

DAY TWENTY SIX: "Motivation Matters"

Today May You . . . be motivated to do the work TODAY that will provide for your needs TOMORROW.

Those too lazy to plow in the right season

will have no food at the harvest. (Proverbs 20:4 NLT).

Turn your *Declaration Of Quality Wisdom* into this prayer of commitment:

*Lord Jesus, **Today May I** be motivated to do the work TODAY that will provide for my needs TOMORROW.*

DAY TWENTY SEVEN: "Good To Have A Good Friend For Good"

Today May You . . . be a GOOD FRIEND by being a GOOD LISTENER so you will be able to give GOOD ADVICE that will help your friend have a GOOD DAY.

Though good advice lies deep within the heart,
a person with understanding will draw it out. (Proverbs 20:5 NLT).

Turn your *Declaration Of Quality Wisdom* into this prayer of commitment:

*Lord Jesus, **Today May I** be a GOOD FRIEND by being a GOOD LISTENER so I will be able to give GOOD ADVICE that will help my friend have a GOOD DAY.*

DAY TWENTY EIGHT: "Friendship Qualities That Matter"

Today May You . . . be the most LOYAL and RELIABLE friend you know.

Many will say they are loyal friends,
but who can find one who is truly reliable? (Proverbs 20:6 NLT).

Turn your *Declaration Of Quality Wisdom* into this prayer of commitment:

*Lord Jesus, **Today May I** be the most LOYAL and RELIABLE friend I know.*

DAY TWENTY NINE: "The Predictable Life"

Today May You . . . treat everyone you meet with impeccable fairness.

False weights and unequal measures —

the Lord detests double standards of every kind. (Proverbs 20:10 NLT).

Turn your *Declaration Of Quality Wisdom* into this prayer of commitment:

> *Lord Jesus, **Today May I** treat everyone I meet with impeccable fairness.*

DAY THIRTY: "The Importance Of Being A Good Listener"

Today May You . . . LISTEN to His voice to know what to do, and may you SEE where He leads you to go and DO what He wants.

Ears to hear and eyes to see—

both are gifts from the Lord. (Proverbs 20:12 NLT).

Turn your *Declaration Of Quality Wisdom* into this prayer of commitment:

> *Lord Jesus, **Today May I** LISTEN to Your voice to know what to do, and may I SEE where You lead me to go and DO what You want.*

DAY THIRTY ONE: "Rest In Peace To Rest in Life"

Today May You . . . get enough of the right kind of REST so you will be able to enjoy the REST of your life.

If you love sleep, you will end in poverty.

Keep your eyes open, and there will be plenty to eat! (Proverbs 20:13 NLT).

Turn your *Declaration Of Quality Wisdom* into this prayer of commitment:

*Lord Jesus, **Today May I** get enough of the right kind of REST so I will be able to enjoy the REST of my life.*

Introduction To Section Seven:
"PURSUING THE PROMISES" (Proverbs 20:15-23:11)

If you don't know where you are going any road will take you there
Lewis Carroll (Alice in Wonderland)

Promises are great! Especially when the ones you need to come true can mean the difference between life and death. The Promises of God are not some iffy pie in the sky way of thinking. His, all of them, are true. When all you've got to hang on to when your life is in sinking sand, go with the promises! David knew, by experience, the value of trusting God for His promises. He found his story in the pit.

"Promotion From The Pit: Praising God When It Hurts"

¹I waited patiently for the LORD; And He inclined to me and heard my cry. ²He brought me up out of the pit of destruction, out of the miry clay, And He set my feet upon a rock making my footsteps firm. ³He put a new song in my mouth, a song of praise to our God; Many will see and fear And will trust in the LORD. ⁴How blessed is the man who has made the LORD his trust, And has not turned to the proud, nor to those who lapse into falsehood. ⁵Many, O LORD my God, are the wonders which You have done, And Your thoughts toward us; There is none to compare with You. If I would declare and speak of them, They would be too numerous to count. **(Psalm 40:1-5 NASB)**

INTRODUCTION:

Where is God when it hurts? That is a familiar, yet very personal, question that rises from the depths of our soul; into our minds; and sometimes those words escape and even leave our mouth.

Where is God when it hurts? It's a good question that we can begin to answer in these passages of Scriptures. One thing that we can be very sure of is that God cares for us and in His care, He will provide all of us a comfort that lasts as we offer our praise to Him.

1. **A Comfort That Comes At The Right Time—40:1**

¹I waited patiently for the LORD; And He inclined to me and heard my cry.

Depression is a dark companion to the human experience. We do not like it; we seek to do everything we know to avoid it; and yet it comes with a vengeance with no respect to person. It plays no favorites; and it never plays fair. Depression is like a pit of destruction. It swallows us and the people we love. And if we allow it, the very shadow of depression will depress us and pull us down into the pit too.

And yet, as believers in the Risen Lord Jesus, we can have a unique perspective that the unbeliever cannot grasp: WE WIN!

In my case, I began a new business venture that had success written all over it. In my mind I had every advantage in my favor: I was widely known in my community, I was associated with an internationally recognized brand, and I was full of confidence. Then, all of the wheels fell off of the momentum train. Everything I tried to do in order to make it successful failed. And the more I tried to make any reasonable idea stick, everything slid off of the wall of desperation. After three months of repeated failures, I became discouraged and then eventually became depressed and fell into the proverbial pit of destruction and miry clay.

I had to make a choice, a purposed decision, during my depression: to either give up, become a victim, or to take a chance on the character of God. This is what David did. Note the testimony of David, the Psalmist of Psalm 40: *He waited patiently for the Lord.*

He trusted in the character of God; that God is good, and that God loves him (this is called worship). Even while finding himself in the most difficult of circumstances, the Psalmist waited patiently for the Lord . . . to deliver him.

- He believed in his heart that God cared for him; and then one day, it happened!

- God inclined His ear to the Psalmist and heard the cry of His child.

- God knows where we are today. God hears the cry of our heart. God will transport us from the pit.

The comfort that lasts will come in the right time—and God is never late, ever.

2. A Comfort That Comes In The Right Way—40:2-3

²He brought me up out of the pit of destruction, out of the miry clay, And He set my feet upon a rock making my footsteps firm. ³He put a new song in my mouth, a song of praise to our God; Many will see and fear And will trust in the LORD.

Absolutely nothing I did got me out of my pit. Like quicksand, the more I struggled in my own strength, the weight of my depression pulled me down even further. I needed more than human strength. I needed His.

- The comfort we need is not earned by having enough human strength to muster it up.

- The comfort we need is not gained by denying the reality of our circumstances.

- The comfort we need is GRACE-DRIVEN. That simply means that God is on a mission to engage us and help us do something we can never do on our own.

Listen to this example of being GRACE-DRIVEN:

- It is God who brings us up out of the pit of destruction, out of the miry clay.

- It is God who sets our feet upon a rock making our footsteps firm.

- It is God who puts a new song in our mouth, a song of praise to our God.

- It is God who will use our difficult circumstances to help others who are watching us and who place their trust in the Lord.

Grace says that God never wastes anything in our life—even the most difficult of things.

And we know that God causes all things to work together for good to those who love God, to those who are called according to *His* purpose. **Romans 8:28 (NASB95)**

The comfort that lasts will come in the right way—by the GRACE of God.

3. A Comfort That Comes From The Right Source—40:4

⁴How blessed is the man who has made the LORD his trust, And has not turned to the proud, nor to those who lapse into falsehood.

The Psalmist testifies about his own life. He claims that we are blessed when we make the Lord our trust. For the believer, it comes down to trust. Do we trust Him only when our circumstances are easy and most desirable or do we trust Him even when life is most difficult? Will I praise and worship Him only when things are going my way?

In other words, how real, how authentic is our faith? Is our faith experience best described as a "Churchianity" (meaningless religious traditions) or a biblical "Christianity"? Do we have a personal relationship with Jesus Christ, or do we just know about Him? How we come to grips with these questions will make all the difference in this world . . . and in the next.

What does it mean to trust the Lord? It means we accept His free gift of eternal life that came by His death and sacrifice on the Cross. We believe that "Jesus paid it all." We believe that His grace is sufficient always. We believe that we can do exactly what the writer of Proverbs said:

⁵Trust in the LORD with all your heart And do not lean on your own understanding.   ⁶In all your ways acknowledge Him, And He will make your paths straight. **Proverbs 3:5-6 (NASB95)**

The comfort that lasts comes from the right source—our trust in the Lord.

4. A Comfort That Comes At The Right Time, In The Right Way, and From The Right Source is a Comfort That Will Last—40:5

⁵Many, O LORD my God, are the wonders which You have done, And Your thoughts toward us; There is none to compare with You. If I would declare and speak of them, They would be too numerous to count.

It has been granted to the believer the challenge to try and count the blessings that God has bestowed upon us. Quickly, I count my ten fingers and ten toes and have hardly begun to make a list of His blessings. We can never grasp how much God loves us. I have personally discovered, and perhaps you have as well, the more time I invest in counting my blessings the less time and energy is spent concentrating on the negative things that seek to capture my attention. Need a gentle reminder of all the "wonders" you can be thankful?

- You can read this page
- You got up this morning and took your first glance at an unspoiled day
- You have a God-given purpose for your life
- You are a child of the King
- You have a story that has redemptive perspective where nothing is wasted
- You are passionately loved by God with no strings attached

The Psalmist was enamored with his God. He was in awe of not only what God has done, but was just as impressed by all of the thoughts that God was thinking about him.

Can you even fathom this: God, the Maker of Heaven and Earth; the Creator and Sustainer of the Universe thinks about me and you.

Focus your attention and try to picture the colorful images that King David is painting in your mind with these precious words from Psalm 139.

¹O LORD, You have searched me and known *me.* ²You know when I sit down and when I rise up; You understand my thought from afar. ³You scrutinize my path and my lying down, And are intimately acquainted with all my ways. ⁴Even before there is a word on my tongue, Behold, O LORD, You know it all. ⁵You have enclosed me behind and before, And laid Your hand upon me. ⁶*Such* knowledge is too wonderful for me; It is *too* high, I cannot attain to it. ⁷Where can I go from Your Spirit? Or where can I flee from Your presence? ⁸If I ascend to heaven, You are there; If I make my bed in Sheol, behold, You are there. ⁹If I take the wings of the dawn, If I dwell in the remotest part of the sea, ¹⁰Even there Your hand will lead me, And Your right hand will lay hold of me. ¹¹If I say, "Surely the darkness will overwhelm me, And the light around me will be night," ¹²Even the darkness is not dark to You, And the night is as bright as the day. Darkness and light are alike *to You.* ¹³For You formed my inward parts; You wove me in my mother's womb. ¹⁴I will give thanks to You, for I am fearfully and wonderfully made; Wonderful are Your works, And my soul knows it very well. ¹⁵My frame was not hidden from You, When I was made in secret, *And* skillfully wrought in the depths of the earth; ¹⁶Your eyes have seen my unformed substance; And in Your book were all written The days that were ordained *for me,* When as yet there was not one of them. ¹⁷How precious also are Your thoughts to me, O God! How vast is the sum of them! ¹⁸If I should count them, they would outnumber the sand. When I awake, I am still with You. **Psalms 139:1-18 (NASB95)**

This is God's wonderful promise to His children today:

- He has given us a Comfort That Lasts

- God knows us. God loves us. And God has a place for us when He calls us home to live with Him forever.

¹The LORD is my shepherd, I shall not want. ²He makes me lie down in green pastures; He leads me beside quiet waters. ³He restores my soul; He guides me in the paths of righteousness For His name's sake. ⁴Even though I walk through the valley of the shadow of death, I fear no evil, for You are with me; Your rod and Your staff, they comfort me. ⁵You prepare a table before me in the presence of my enemies; You have anointed my head with oil; My cup overflows. ⁶Surely goodness and lovingkindness will follow me all the days of my life, And I will dwell in the house of the LORD forever. **Psalms 23:1-6 (NASB95)**

This next section from the Proverbs will give you some focus as you carefully read and pray through the 31 readings that will help you Pursue The Promises.

Daily Declarations For Positive People

PURSUING THE PROMISES
(Proverbs 20:15-23:11)

DAY ONE: "Treasure Trove"

Today May You . . . make it your treasure to embrace words that add value to you and to everyone who hears you speak.

Wise words are more valuable

than much gold and many rubies. (Proverbs 20:15 NLT).

Turn your *Declaration Of Quality Wisdom* into this prayer of commitment:

> *Lord Jesus, **Today May I** make it my treasure to embrace words that add value to me and to everyone who hears me speak.*

DAY TWO: "Strategic Plans To Win"

Today May You . . . be selective and only fight the battles you can win.

Plans succeed through good counsel;

don't go to war without wise advice. (Proverbs 20:18 NLT).

Turn your *Declaration Of Quality Wisdom* into this prayer of commitment:

> *Lord Jesus, **Today May I** be selective and only fight the battles I can win.*

DAY THREE: "Guarding Yourself From The Garbage"

Today May You . . . GUARD what your EARS hear so that toxic WORDS will not leave your MOUTH.

A gossip goes around telling secrets,

so don't hang around with chatterers. (Proverbs 20:19 NLT).

Turn your *Declaration Of Quality Wisdom* into this prayer of commitment:

> *Lord Jesus, **Today May I** GUARD what my EARS hear so that toxic WORDS will not leave my MOUTH.*

DAY FOUR: "No Vindictive Zone"

Today May You . . . allow the Lord to keep you on an EVEN keel and stay RIGHT so you will not fall into the vindictive trap of trying to get EVEN and wind up WRONG.

Don't say, "I will get even for this wrong."
Wait for the Lord to handle the matter. (Proverbs 20:22 NLT).

Turn your *Declaration Of Quality Wisdom* into this prayer of commitment:

> *Lord Jesus, **Today May I** allow You to keep me on an EVEN keel and stay RIGHT so I will not fall into the vindictive trap of trying to get EVEN and wind up WRONG.*

DAY FIVE: "Faith It Out"

Today May You . . . FAITH it out *now* before you try to FIGURE it out *then*.

The Lord directs our steps,

so why try to understand everything along the way? (Proverbs 20:24 NLT).

Turn your *Declaration Of Quality Wisdom* into this prayer of commitment:

> Lord Jesus, *Today May I* FAITH it out *now* before I try to FIGURE it out *then*.

DAY SIX: "Praying Before You Promise"

Today May You . . . THINK before you make a promise that only Jesus can help you KEEP.

Don't trap yourself by making a rash promise to God

and only later counting the cost. (Proverbs 20:25 NLT).

Turn your *Declaration Of Quality Wisdom* into this prayer of commitment:

> Lord Jesus, *Today May I* THINK before I make a promise that only You can help me KEEP.

DAY SEVEN: "The Transparent Life"

Today May You . . . live a transparent life before the Lord and may His AGENDA become yours.

The Lord's light penetrates the human spirit,

exposing every hidden motive. (Proverbs 20:27 NLT).

Turn your *Declaration Of Quality Wisdom* into this prayer of commitment:

> Lord Jesus, *Today May I* live a transparent life before You and may Your AGENDA become mine.

DAY EIGHT: "When Unfailing Love Influences Everything You Do"

Today May You . . . lead with unfailing LOVE in every decision you make, with every person you touch and be absolutely secure in His love for you.

Unfailing love and faithfulness protect the king;

his throne is made secure through love. (Proverbs 20:28 NLT).

Turn your *Declaration Of Quality Wisdom* into this prayer of commitment:

> *Lord Jesus, **Today May I** lead with unfailing LOVE in every decision I make, with every person I touch and be absolutely secure in Your love for me.*

DAY NINE: "Heart Check"

Today May You . . . check your HEART before you trust your EYES.

People may be right in their own eyes,

but the Lord examines their heart. (Proverbs 21:2 NLT).

Turn your *Declaration Of Quality Wisdom* into this prayer of commitment:

> *Lord Jesus, **Today May I** check my HEART before I trust my EYES.*

DAY TEN: "Obedience Matters"

Today May You . . . be more intentional in giving Him your willing OBEDIENCE than offering Him a hollow SACRIFICE.

The Lord is more pleased when we do what is right and just

than when we offer him sacrifices. (Proverbs 21:3 NLT).

Turn your *Declaration Of Quality Wisdom* into this prayer of commitment:

> *Lord Jesus, **Today May I** be more intentional in giving You my willing OBEDIENCE than offering You a hollow SACRIFICE.*

DAY ELEVEN: "Working The Plan To Succeed"

Today May You . . . WORK a good plan and then WORK hard to see the plan succeed.

Good planning and hard work lead to prosperity,

but hasty shortcuts lead to poverty. (Proverbs 21:5 NLT).

Turn your *Declaration Of Quality Wisdom* into this prayer of commitment:

> *Lord Jesus, **Today May I** WORK a good plan and then WORK hard to see the plan succeed.*

DAY TWELVE: "Wealth, Honestly Speaking"

Today May You . . . make a commitment to earn an HONEST dollar by telling and living the TRUTH before others and before God.

Wealth created by a lying tongue

is a vanishing mist and a deadly trap. (Proverbs 21:6 NLT).

Turn your *Declaration Of Quality Wisdom* into this prayer of commitment:

> *Lord Jesus, **Today May I** make a commitment to earn an HONEST dollar by telling and living the TRUTH before others and before God.*

DAY THIRTEEN: "Ears To Hear"

Today May You . . . LISTEN to the needs around you and LEARN what you can do to LEVERAGE your LEADERSHIP and be a blessing to the LEAST of these.

Those who shut their ears to the cries of the poor

will be ignored in their own time of need. (Proverbs 21:13 NLT).

Turn your *Declaration Of Quality Wisdom* into this prayer of commitment:

> *Lord Jesus, **Today May I** LISTEN to the needs around me and LEARN what I can do to LEVERAGE my LEADERSHIP and be a blessing to the LEAST of these.*

DAY FOURTEEN: "The Right Kind Of Life"

Today May You . . . set your sight on LIVING RIGHT and pursuing the kind of LOVE that never FAILS and then fully experiencing LIFE, RIGHTEOUSNESS, and HONOR.

Whoever pursues righteousness and unfailing love

will find life, righteousness, and honor. (Proverbs 21:21 NLT).

Turn your *Declaration Of Quality Wisdom* into this prayer of commitment:

> Lord Jesus, *Today May I* set my sight on LIVING RIGHT and pursuing the kind of LOVE that never FAILS and then fully experiencing LIFE, RIGHTEOUSNESS, and HONOR.

DAY FIFTEEN: "Mouth Guard"

Today May You . . . HUSH your mouth and KEEP your witness.

Watch your tongue and keep your mouth shut,

and you will stay out of trouble. (Proverbs 21:23 NLT).

Turn your *Declaration Of Quality Wisdom* into this prayer of commitment:

> Lord Jesus, *Today May I* HUSH my mouth and KEEP my witness.

DAY SIXTEEN: "Thankful To Be Thankful"

Today May You . . . be THANKFUL that you have the ability to help others be THANKFUL as well.

Some people are always greedy for more,

but the godly love to give! (Proverbs 21:26 NLT).

Turn your *Declaration Of Quality Wisdom* into this prayer of commitment:

> Lord Jesus, *Today May I* be THANKFUL that I have the ability to help others be THANKFUL as well.

DAY SEVENTEEN: "Seek And You Will Find"

Today May You . . . SEEK His wisdom, not yours; and His plan, not yours, because His WAYS are much higher than yours.

No human wisdom or understanding or plan
can stand against the Lord. (Proverbs 21:30 NLT).

Turn your *Declaration Of Quality Wisdom* into this prayer of commitment:

> *Lord Jesus, **Today May I** SEEK Your wisdom, not mine; and Your plan, not mine, because Your WAYS are much higher than mine.*

DAY EIGHTEEN: "How Work And Prayer Go Together"

Today May You . . . WORK like it all depends upon you and PRAY like it all depends upon Him.

The horse is prepared for the day of battle,
but the victory belongs to the Lord. (Proverbs 21:31 NLT).

Turn your *Declaration Of Quality Wisdom* into this prayer of commitment:

> *Lord Jesus, **Today May I** WORK like it all depends upon me and PRAY like it all depends upon You.*

DAY NINETEEN: "Character Vs. Comfort"

Today May You . . . live like CHARACTER matters more than your material COMFORT.

Choose a good reputation over great riches;
being held in high esteem is better than silver or gold. (Proverbs 22:1 NLT).

Turn your *Declaration Of Quality Wisdom* into this prayer of commitment:

Lord Jesus, Today May I live like CHARACTER matters more than my material COMFORT.

DAY TWENTY: "Planning For The Worst And Hoping For The Best"

Today May You . . . plan for the WORST and hope for the BEST.

A prudent person foresees danger and takes precautions.

The simpleton goes blindly on and suffers the consequences. (Proverbs 22:3 NLT).

Turn your *Declaration Of Quality Wisdom* into this prayer of commitment:

Lord Jesus, Today May I plan for the WORST and hope for the BEST.

DAY TWENTY ONE: "The Prioritized Life"

Today May You . . . set yourself up for long term SUCCESS by HOW you live and WHO you live for.

True humility and fear of the Lord

lead to riches, honor, and long life. (Proverbs 22:4 NLT).

Turn your *Declaration Of Quality Wisdom* into this prayer of commitment:

Lord Jesus, Today May I set myself up for long term SUCCESS by HOW I live and WHO I live for.

DAY TWENTY TWO: "The Best Debt"

Today May You . . . make sure the only thing you OWE anyone is LOVE.

Just as the rich rule the poor,

so the borrower is servant to the lender. (Proverbs 22:7 NLT).

Turn your *Declaration Of Quality Wisdom* into this prayer of commitment:

*Lord Jesus, **Today May I** make sure the only thing I OWE anyone is LOVE.*

DAY TWENTY THREE: "The Power Of The Blessing"

Today May You . . . BLESS those who need a BLESSING from you.

Blessed are those who are generous,

because they feed the poor. (Proverbs 22:9 NLT).

Turn your *Declaration Of Quality Wisdom* into this prayer of commitment:

*Lord Jesus, **Today May I** BLESS those who need a BLESSING from me.*

DAY TWENTY FOUR: "Bless Your Heart So You Can Bless Others"

Today May You . . . keep the right words in your HEART so you can bless the HEART of another.

Listen to the words of the wise;

apply your heart to my instruction.

For it is good to keep these sayings in your heart

and always ready on your lips. (Proverbs 22:17-18 NLT).

Turn your *Declaration Of Quality Wisdom* into this prayer of commitment:

> Lord Jesus, *Today May I* keep the right words in my HEART so I can bless the HEART of another.

DAY TWENTY FIVE: "Open Heart, Open Mind, Growing Life"

Today May You . . . keep an OPEN heart to have a LEARNING heart so you will have a TRUSTING heart in the Lord.

I am teaching you today—yes, you—

so you will trust in the Lord. (Proverbs 22:19 NLT).

Turn your *Declaration Of Quality Wisdom* into this prayer of commitment:

> Lord Jesus, *Today May I* keep an OPEN heart to have a LEARNING heart so I will have a TRUSTING heart in You.

DAY TWENTY SIX: "The Right Company You Keep Will Keep You Safe"

Today May You . . . GUARD your heart so you will not LOSE your soul.

Don't befriend angry people

or associate with hot-tempered people,

or you will learn to be like them

and endanger your soul. (Proverbs 22:24-25 NLT).

Turn your *Declaration Of Quality Wisdom* into this prayer of commitment:

*Lord Jesus, **Today May I** GUARD my heart so I will not LOSE my soul.*

DAY TWENTY SEVEN: "Losing Your Cents Will Cost You Many Dollars"

Today May You . . . not allow your heart to mess with your mind.

Don't agree to guarantee another person's debt

or put up security for someone else.

If you can't pay it,

even your bed will be snatched from under you. (Proverbs 22:26-27 NLT).

Turn your *Declaration Of Quality Wisdom* into this prayer of commitment:

*Lord Jesus, **Today May I** not allow my heart to mess with my mind.*

DAY TWENTY EIGHT: "Good Business Matters"

Today May You . . . make every business decision with a commitment to live out the teachings of Jesus with your own PERSONAL INTEGRITY and WORK ETHIC.

Don't cheat your neighbor by moving the ancient boundary markers

set up by previous generations.

Do you see any truly competent workers?

They will serve kings

rather than working for ordinary people. (Proverbs 22:28-29 NLT).

Turn your *Declaration Of Quality Wisdom* into this prayer of commitment:

> *Lord Jesus, Today May I make every business decision with a commitment to live out the teachings of Jesus with my own PERSONAL INTEGRITY and WORK ETHIC.*

DAY TWENTY NINE: "Jehovah Jireh, My Provider"

Today May You . . . TRUST GOD FOR WHAT YOU NEED and then allow Him, in His way, to PROVIDE ALL OF YOUR NEEDS.

Don't wear yourself out trying to get rich. Be wise enough to know when to quit.
In the blink of an eye wealth disappears, for it will sprout wings and fly away like an eagle. (Proverbs 23:4-5 NLT).

Turn your *Declaration Of Quality Wisdom* into this prayer of commitment:

> *Lord Jesus, Today May I TRUST You FOR WHAT I NEED and then allow You, in Your way, to PROVIDE ALL OF MY NEEDS.*

DAY THIRTY: "Learning To Be A Good Steward Of Time and Of People"

Today May You . . . save your breath for the RIGHT people, at the RIGHT time, and for the RIGHT reason.

Don't waste your breath on fools,
for they will despise the wisest advice. (Proverbs 23:9 NLT).

Turn your *Declaration Of Quality Wisdom* into this prayer of commitment:

*Lord Jesus, **Today May I** save my breath for the RIGHT people, at the RIGHT time, and for the RIGHT reason.*

DAY THIRTY ONE: "The Honest Legacy"

Today May You . . . be on the Lord's side and treat people with honesty and respect, especially the ones who are on the weaker side of the power relationship and cannot defend themselves.

Don't cheat your neighbor by moving the ancient boundary markers; don't take the land of defenseless orphans.
For their Redeemer is strong; he himself will bring their charges against you. (Proverbs 23:10-11 NLT).

Turn your *Declaration Of Quality Wisdom* into this prayer of commitment:

*Lord Jesus, **Today May I** be on the Lord's side and treat people with honesty and respect, especially the ones who are on the weeker side of the power relationship and cannot defend themselves.*

Introduction To Section Eight:
"COMMITTED TO THE CALL" (Proverbs 23:17-28:2)

*"Nothing is easier than saying words.
Nothing is harder than living them day after day."*
— Arthur Gordon

Words are cheap, unless they are backed up by the currency of action. Many great ideas and best intentions have been set aside because of a lack of commitment. The book of Proverbs always puts us in the fork of the road. Will we simply be believers who have filled our hearts with Biblical trivia, or will we put what we learn into action? When we become committed to the call, our passion sustains us, and our focus keeps us on message. Want to impact the world?

THE NINE STRATEGIC STEPS FOR IMPACTING THE WORLD THROUGH YOUR LIFE AND MINISTRY

Deep down, every believer who loves Jesus wants to make a significant difference in the world. You are only given one life to live and give, and the opportunities for greatness are few and far between if you do not yield yourself to God. If you want to be used by God and leave a legacy that will impact the world through your life and ministry, then there are at least nine essential things that you must do in order to impact the world.

In the presence of God and of Christ Jesus, who will judge the living and the dead, and in view of his appearing and his kingdom, I give you this charge: Preach the Word; be prepared in season and out of season; correct, rebuke and encourage--with great patience and careful instruction. For the time will come when men will not put up with sound doctrine. Instead, to suit their own desires, they will gather around them a great number of teachers to say what their itching ears want to hear. They will turn their ears away from the truth and turn aside to myths. But you, keep your head in all situations, endure hardship, do the work of an evangelist, discharge all the duties of your ministry. **2 Tim. 4:1-5** (NIV)

A.   You Must Preach The Word
<u>Preach the Word</u>; be prepared in season and out of season; correct, rebuke and encourage--with great patience and careful instruction. **2 Tim. 4:2** (NIV)

***PERSONAL APPLICATION:

There are a few assumptions here. One is that you must be proactive and preach. You must stand as God's ambassador and speak for Him. Two, you must keep your preaching focused upon one and only one thing: the Word of God. What is the "Word of God"? It is the Scriptures, the Bible, every one of the sixty-six books of the Bible, God's perfect word to us. But why are we to preach? Because it is through the preaching of God's Word that people come to know Jesus Christ.

> *For the message of the cross is foolishness to those who are perishing, but to us who are being saved it is the power of God.* **1 Cor. 1:18 (NIV)**
> *For since in the wisdom of God the world through its wisdom did not know him, God was pleased through the foolishness of what was preached to save those who believe.* **1 Cor. 1:21 (NIV)**

B.   You Must Be Ready At Any Moment To Share The Gospel

Preach the Word; <u>be prepared in season and out of season</u>; correct, rebuke and encourage--with great patience and careful instruction. **2 Tim. 4:2** (NIV)

***PERSONAL APPLICATION:

There should never be a time when we cannot share the life-changing Gospel. Hard times and easy times come and go; different seasons will always be with us. No matter what our circumstance, we are to be ready, 24/7, to preach the Good News.

The Amplified New Testament says:

> *"Keep your sense of urgency (stand by, be at hand and ready, whether the opportunity seems to be favorable or unfavorable, whether it is convenient or inconvenient, whether it be welcome or unwelcome, you as preacher of the Word are to show people in what way their lives are wrong)."*

> *Now about our brother Apollos: I strongly urged him to go to you with the brothers. He was quite unwilling to go now, but he will go when he has the opportunity.* **1 Cor. 16:12 (NIV)**
> *But mark this: There will be terrible times in the last days.* **2 Tim. 3:1 (NIV)**

C.   You Must Reprove Or Correct Those Who Are Under The Conviction Of Sin And Lead Them To Confess And Repent Of The Sin.

Preach the Word; be prepared in season and out of season; <u>correct</u>, rebuke and encourage--with great patience and careful instruction. **2 Tim. 4:2** (NIV)

***PERSONAL APPLICATION:

We are doing no one any favors when we wink at sin and fail to confront it. It is true: we are to hate the sin, but love the sinner. And the love that we are to share is a "tough love", a love that tells it like it is.

> *Have nothing to do with the fruitless deeds of darkness, but rather expose them.* **Ephes. 5:11 (NIV)**

D.   You Must Rebuke Those Who Are Playing With Fire And Will Be Burned Unless They Are Warned.

Preach the Word; be prepared in season and out of season; correct, <u>rebuke</u> and encourage--with great patience and careful instruction. **2 Tim. 4:2** (NIV)

***PERSONAL APPLICATION:

There are two kinds of Christians—those who are "mile-markers" and those who are a "fork in the road." The "mile-marker" Christian is indifferent when a person is living a sinful life before him or her. Instead of bringing a warning, this Christian is content to put his head in the sand and hope it all goes away. On the other hand, the Christian who is a "fork in the road" is willing to take the flack of making a stand and confront a person who is living in a destructive sinful lifestyle.

> ¹⁵"If your brother sins against you, go and show him his fault, just between the two of you. If he listens to you, you have won your brother over. ¹⁶But if he will not listen, take one or two others along, so that 'every matter may be established by the testimony of two or three witnesses.' ¹⁷If he refuses to listen to them, tell it to the church; and if he refuses to listen even to the church, treat him as you would a pagan or a tax collector. **Matthew 18:15-17 (NIV)**
>
> Those who sin are to be rebuked publicly, so that the others may take warning. **1 Tim. 5:20 (NIV)**
>
> He must hold firmly to the trustworthy message as it has been taught, so that he can encourage others by sound doctrine and refute those who oppose it. **Titus 1:9 (NIV)**
>
> These, then, are the things you should teach. Encourage and rebuke with all authority. Do not let anyone despise you. **Titus 2:15 (NIV)**
>
> Warn a divisive person once, and then warn him a second time. After that, have nothing to do with him. **Titus 3:10 (NIV)**

E.   You Must Exhort Those Who Have Fallen Into A Deep Hole And Cannot Get Out By Themselves. [How? With Great Patience And Instruction]

Preach the Word; be prepared in season and out of season; correct, rebuke and <u>encourage--with great patience and careful instruction</u>. **2 Tim. 4:2** (NIV)

***PERSONAL APPLICATION:

It is never easy to play the "heavy" and share the hard truth to a person who is floundering in sin. Many of us have become frustrated and impatient with those who have disappointed us after making poor choices. But God's Word is clear. If we really want to have a legacy that impacts the world, then we need to embrace the instructions from Scripture.

> Love is patient, love is kind. It does not envy, it does not boast, it is not proud. **1 Cor. 13:4 (NIV)**

But encourage one another daily, as long as it is called Today, so that none of you may be hardened by sin's deceitfulness. **Hebrews 3:13 (NIV)**

Be shepherds of God's flock that is under your care, serving as overseers--not because you must, but because you are willing, as God wants you to be; not greedy for money, but eager to serve; **1 Peter 5:2 (NIV)**

F. You Must Be Sober, Keep Your Head, In All Things

But you, <u>keep your head in all situations</u>, endure hardship, do the work of an evangelist, discharge all the duties of your ministry. **2 Tim. 4:5** (NIV)

***PERSONAL APPLICATION:

It is only natural for us to be caught up in the emotion of the moment when people around us are making decisions that are destructive. If we are not careful, we can also become calloused to the dangers around us and fall into the same pit of sin. God has called us to live a sober life, a disciplined life, and a life that stays above the fray and keeps a level head.

"Watch and pray so that you will not fall into temptation. The spirit is willing, but the body is weak." **Matthew 26:41 (NIV)**

So, if you think you are standing firm, be careful that you don't fall! **1 Cor. 10:12 (NIV)**

Be on your guard; stand firm in the faith; be men of courage; be strong. **1 Cor. 16:13 (NIV)**

Be self-controlled and alert. Your enemy the devil prowls around like a roaring lion looking for someone to devour. **1 Peter 5:8 (NIV)**

G. You Are To Endure Hardship

But you, keep your head in all situations, <u>endure hardship</u>, do the work of an evangelist, discharge all the duties of your ministry. **2 Tim. 4:5** (NIV)

***PERSONAL APPLICATION:

God never said that it would be easy for His people to have a ministry that impacts the world. It takes an amazing amount of grace and faith and a lot of discipline on our part. Life presents to us a myriad of opportunities to face obstacles, endure them, all the while trusting Christ to help us persevere to the end.

All men will hate you because of me, but he who stands firm to the end will be saved. **Matthew 10:22 (NIV)**

Therefore, my dear brothers, stand firm. Let nothing move you. Always give yourselves fully to the work of the Lord, because you know that your labor in the Lord is not in vain. **1 Cor. 15:58 (NIV)**

For it has been granted to you on behalf of Christ not only to believe on him, but also to suffer for him, **Philip. 1:29 (NIV)**

Therefore, since we are surrounded by such a great cloud of witnesses, let us throw off everything that hinders and the sin that so easily entangles, and let us run with perseverance the race marked out for us. **Hebrews 12:1 (NIV)**

Blessed is the man who perseveres under trial, because when he has stood the test, he will receive the crown of life that God has promised to those who love him. **James 1:12 (NIV)**

H.   You Are To Do The Work Of An Evangelist

But you, keep your head in all situations, endure hardship, <u>do the work of an evangelist</u>, discharge all the duties of your ministry. **2 Tim. 4:5** (NIV)

***PERSONAL APPLICATION:

God has not called all of us to become a professional traveling evangelist. Not everyone has the gift that God granted to Billy Graham. But God has called all of us to do the work of an evangelist. And what is that work? It is a willingness to do anything needed in order to bring a person to saving faith in Jesus Christ.

But you will receive power when the Holy Spirit comes on you; and you will be my witnesses in Jerusalem, and in all Judea and Samaria, and to the ends of the earth." **Acts 1:8 (NIV)**

For we cannot help speaking about what we have seen and heard." **Acts 4:20 (NIV)**

It is written: "I believed; therefore I have spoken." With that same spirit of faith we also believe and therefore speak, **2 Cor. 4:13 (NIV)**

But in your hearts set apart Christ as Lord. Always be prepared to give an answer to everyone who asks you to give the reason for the hope that you have. But do this with gentleness and respect, **1 Peter 3:15 (NIV)**

I.   You Are To Fulfill Your Ministry

But you, keep your head in all situations, endure hardship, do the work of an evangelist, <u>discharge [or fulfill] all the duties of your ministry</u>. **2 Tim. 4:5** (NIV)

***PERSONAL APPLICATION:

The idea is that our ministry is to be filled to "the brim." Time is too precious to waste by doing ministry that is half-done. The need is too great to give God only a portion of your service to Him. We must take the attitude that our lives are dedicated to service unto Him. We must fulfill our ministry if we are going to leave a legacy that impacts the world.

"My food," said Jesus, "is to do the will of him who sent me and to finish his work. **John 4:34 (NIV)**

I have brought you glory on earth by completing the work you gave me to do. **John 17:4 (NIV)**

The third time he said to him, "Simon son of John, do you love me?" Peter was hurt because Jesus asked him the third time, "Do you love me?" He said, "Lord, you know all things; you know that I love you." Jesus said, "Feed my sheep. **John 21:17 (NIV)**

However, I consider my life worth nothing to me, if only I may finish the race and complete the task the Lord Jesus has given me--the task of testifying to the gospel of God's grace. **Acts 20:24 (NIV)**

Keep watch over yourselves and all the flock of which the Holy Spirit has made you overseers. Be shepherds of the church of God, which he bought with his own blood. **Acts 20:28 (NIV)**

I thank Christ Jesus our Lord, who has given me strength, that he considered me faithful, appointing me to his service. **1 Tim. 1:12 (NIV)**

6For I am already being poured out like a drink offering, and the time has come for my departure. 7I have fought the good fight, I have finished the race, I have kept the faith. 8Now there is in store for me the crown of righteousness, which the Lord, the righteous Judge, will award to me on that day--and not only to me, but also to all who have longed for his appearing. **2 Tim. 4:6-8 (NIV)**

I will place shepherds over them who will tend them, and they will no longer be afraid or terrified, nor will any be missing," declares the LORD. **Jeremiah 23:4 (NIV)**

When you set your heart to be Committed to the Call, your life will never be the same again. Carefully read and then pray through the next 31 devotionals and see for yourself what commitment to the call will do for you.

COMMITTED TO THE CALL
(Proverbs 23:17-28:2)

DAY ONE: "Hope Floats Your Dreams"

Today May You . . . gladly ACCEPT all that the Lord has provided for you and keep your HOPE alive.

Don't envy sinners, but always continue to fear the Lord.

You will be rewarded for this; your hope will not be disappointed. (Proverbs 23:17-18 NLT).

Turn your *Declaration Of Quality Wisdom* into this prayer of commitment:

> *Lord Jesus, **Today May I** gladly ACCEPT all that You have provided for me and keep my HOPE alive.*

DAY TWO: "Heart Give-A-Way"

Today May You . . . give Him your HEART so that your EYES can follow His ways and ENJOY your life.

O my son, give me your heart.

May your eyes take delight in following my ways. (Proverbs 23:26 NLT).

Turn your *Declaration Of Quality Wisdom* into this prayer of commitment:

> *Lord Jesus, **Today May I** give You my HEART so that my EYES can follow Your ways and ENJOY my life.*

DAY THREE: "The Discerning Heart"

Today May You . . . give your heart to only those who will PROTECT it and not POISON it.

Don't envy evil people

or desire their company.

For their hearts plot violence,

and their words always stir up trouble. (Proverbs 24:1-2 NLT).

Turn your *Declaration Of Quality Wisdom* into this prayer of commitment:

*Lord Jesus, **Today May I** give my heart to only those who will PROTECT it and not POISON it.*

DAY FOUR: "The Power Of Common Sense Wisdom"

Today May You . . . make a focused effort to gain practical wisdom in your life and then have the common sense to know what to do with it.

A house is built by wisdom and becomes strong through good sense. Through knowledge its rooms are filled with all sorts of precious riches and valuables. The wise are mightier than the strong, and those with knowledge grow stronger and stronger. (Proverbs 24:3-5 NLT).

Turn your *Declaration Of Quality Wisdom* into this prayer of commitment:

*Lord Jesus, **Today May I** make a focused effort to gain practical wisdom in my life and then have the common sense to know what to do with it.*

DAY FIVE: "Stress Test"

Today May You . . . put in the necessary WORK that will empower you to STAND when the pressure is on.

If you fail under pressure,
your strength is too small. (Proverbs 24:10 NLT).

Turn your *Declaration Of Quality Wisdom* into this prayer of commitment:

> *Lord Jesus, **Today May I** put in the necessary WORK that will empower me to STAND when the pressure is on.*

DAY SIX: "Taste And See For Yourself

Today May You . . . acquire a taste for wisdom that will SATISFY every desire for SUCCESS.

My child, eat honey, for it is good, and the honeycomb is sweet to the taste. In the same way, wisdom is sweet to your soul. If you find it, you will have a bright future, and your hopes will not be cut short. (Proverbs 24:13-14 NLT).

Turn your *Declaration Of Quality Wisdom* into this prayer of commitment:

> *Lord Jesus, **Today May I** acquire a taste for wisdom that will SATISFY every desire for SUCCESS.*

DAY SEVEN: "Why Grace And Compassion Matter"

Today May You . . . REJOICE when GRACE has comforted you and may you have COMPASSION on those who need His GRACE too.

The godly may trip seven times, but they will get up again.
But one disaster is enough to overthrow the wicked. Don't rejoice when your enemies fall; don't be happy when they stumble. For the Lord will be displeased with you and will turn his anger away from them. (Proverbs 24:16-18 NLT).

Turn your *Declaration Of Quality Wisdom* into this prayer of commitment:

> *Lord Jesus, **Today May I** REJOICE when GRACE has comforted me and may I have COMPASSION on those who need His GRACE too.*

DAY EIGHT: "Right Living Leads To A Right Life"

Today May You . . . do the RIGHT things in the RIGHT way to get the RIGHT results at the RIGHT time.

Do your planning and prepare your fields
before building your house. (Proverbs 24:27 NLT).

Turn your *Declaration Of Quality Wisdom* into this prayer of commitment:

> *Lord Jesus, **Today May I** do the RIGHT things in the RIGHT way to get the RIGHT results at the RIGHT time.*

DAY NINE: "The Best Way To Pay Someone Back"

Today May You . . . make sure the only "Payback Currency" comes out of the love account.

Don't testify against your neighbors without cause; don't lie about them. And don't say, "Now I can pay them back for what they've done to me! I'll get even with them!" (Proverbs 24:28-29 NLT).

Turn your *Declaration Of Quality Wisdom* into this prayer of commitment:

> *Lord Jesus, **Today May I** make sure the only "Payback Currency" comes out of the love account.*

DAY TEN: "A Solid Theology Of Work"

Today May You . . . work HARDER and SMARTER.

I walked by the field of a lazy person, the vineyard of one with no common sense. I saw that it was overgrown with nettles. It was covered with weeds and its walls were broken down. Then, as I looked and thought about it, I learned this lesson: A little extra sleep, a little more slumber, a little folding of the hands to rest—then poverty will pounce on you like a bandit; scarcity will attack you like an armed robber. (Proverbs 24:30-34 NLT).

Turn your *Declaration Of Quality Wisdom* into this prayer of commitment:

> *Lord Jesus, **Today May I** work HARDER and SMARTER.*

DAY ELEVEN: "Promotion Comes From The Lord"

Today May You . . . allow the Lord to PROMOTE you before you PROMOTE yourself.

Don't demand an audience with the king

or push for a place among the great. It's better to wait for an invitation to the head table than to be sent away in public disgrace. (Proverbs 25:6-7 NLT).

Turn your *Declaration Of Quality Wisdom* into this prayer of commitment:

> *Lord Jesus, **Today May I** allow You to PROMOTE me before I PROMOTE myself.*

DAY TWELVE: "Becoming The Very Best Version Of You"

Today May You . . . be willing to take some good advice that will make you an even better version of you.

Timely advice is lovely, like golden apples in a silver basket. To one who listens, valid criticism is like a gold earring or other gold jewelry. (Proverbs 25:11-12 NLT).

Turn your *Declaration Of Quality Wisdom* into this prayer of commitment:

> *Lord Jesus, **Today May I** be willing to take some good advice that will make me an even better version of myself.*

DAY THIRTEEN: "The Refreshing Messenger"

Today May You . . . be a refreshing blessing to those who are a blessing to you.

Trustworthy messengers refresh like snow in summer.

They revive the spirit of their employer. (Proverbs 25:13 NLT).

Turn your *Declaration Of Quality Wisdom* into this prayer of commitment:

> *Lord Jesus, **Today May I** be a refreshing blessing to those who are a blessing to me.*

DAY FOURTEEN: "Why You Need To Keep Promises You Make"

Today May You . . . seek to UNDER promise and OVER deliver on the way you serve others.

A person who promises a gift but doesn't give it

is like clouds and wind that bring no rain. (Proverbs 25:14 NLT).

Turn your *Declaration Of Quality Wisdom* into this prayer of commitment:

> *Lord Jesus, **Today May I** seek to UNDER promise and OVER deliver on the way I serve others.*

DAY FIFTEEN: "Why You Need To Take The High Road"

Today May You . . . take the HIGH ROAD no matter how LOW your adversary may GO.

If your enemies are hungry, give them food to eat. If they are thirsty, give them water to drink. You will heap burning coals of shame on their heads, and the Lord will reward you. (Proverbs 25:21-22 NLT).

Turn your *Declaration Of Quality Wisdom* into this prayer of commitment:

> *Lord Jesus, **Today May I** take the HIGH ROAD no matter how LOW my adversary may GO.*

DAY SIXTEEN: "The Power Of A Timely Word"

Today May You . . . PRAY about WHO needs a GOOD and ENCOURAGING WORD from YOU and SHARE IT.

Good news from far away

is like cold water to the thirsty. (Proverbs 25:25 NLT).

Turn your *Declaration Of Quality Wisdom* into this prayer of commitment:

> *Lord Jesus, **Today May I** PRAY about WHO needs a GOOD and ENCOURAGING WORD from ME and SHARE IT.*

DAY SEVENTEEN: "The Blessing Of Counting To Ten"

Today May You . . . take a deep breath and, before you do or say anything that you would later regret, count to ten.

A person without self-control

is like a city with broken-down walls. (Proverbs 25:28 NLT).

Turn your *Declaration Of Quality Wisdom* into this prayer of commitment:

> *Lord Jesus, **Today May I** take a deep breath and, before I do or say anything that I would later regret, count to ten.*

DAY EIGHTEEN: "The Best Way To Defeat A Person Who Is Difficult"

Today May You . . . know WHEN to ignore a difficult person and WHEN to put a difficult person in their place.

Don't answer the foolish arguments of fools, or you will become as foolish as they are. Be sure to answer the foolish arguments of fools, or they will become wise in their own estimation. (Proverbs 26:4-5 NLT).

Turn your *Declaration Of Quality Wisdom* into this prayer of commitment:

> *Lord Jesus, **Today May I** know WHEN to ignore a difficult person and WHEN to put a difficult person in their place.*

DAY NINETEEN: "Home Field Advantage"

Today May You . . . make sure you put the right people on your team.

An employer who hires a fool or a bystander

is like an archer who shoots at random. (Proverbs 26:10 NLT).

Turn your *Declaration Of Quality Wisdom* into this prayer of commitment:

> *Lord Jesus, **Today May I** make sure I put the right people on my team.*

DAY TWENTY: "Boundaries Matter"

Today May You . . . know when it's the right time to stay in your own hula hoop and stay out of others.

Interfering in someone else's argument

is as foolish as yanking a dog's ears. (Proverbs 26:17 NLT).

Turn your *Declaration Of Quality Wisdom* into this prayer of commitment:

> *Lord Jesus, **Today May I** know when it's the right time to stay in my own hula hoop and stay out of others.*

DAY TWENTY ONE: "Spiritual Firefighter"

Today May You . . . resist the urge to join a gossip party and instead look for ways to speak well of those who are being slandered.

Fire goes out without wood,

and quarrels disappear when gossip stops. (Proverbs 26:20 NLT).

Turn your *Declaration Of Quality Wisdom* into this prayer of commitment:

> *Lord Jesus, **Today May I** resist the urge to join a gossip party and instead look for ways to speak well of those who are being slandered.*

DAY TWENTY TWO: "The Benefits Of Living By The Golden Rule"

Today May You . . . set your heart to live by the GOLDEN rule and not be ruled by a poisonous plot.

If you set a trap for others, you will get caught in it yourself. If you roll a boulder down on others, it will crush you instead.

A lying tongue hates its victims, and flattering words cause ruin. (Proverbs 26:27-28 NLT).

Turn your *Declaration Of Quality Wisdom* into this prayer of commitment:

> *Lord Jesus, **Today May I** set my heart to live by the GOLDEN rule and not be ruled by a poisonous plot.*

DAY TWENTY THREE: "Present And Accounted For"

Today May You . . . live in the PRESENT and trust God to give you what you need for the FUTURE.

Don't brag about tomorrow,

since you don't know what the day will bring. (Proverbs 27:1 NLT).

Turn your *Declaration Of Quality Wisdom* into this prayer of commitment:

> *Lord Jesus, **Today May I** live in the PRESENT and trust God to give me what I need for the FUTURE.*

DAY TWENTY FOUR: "Learning How To Accept Praise"

Today May You . . . be okay with someone else telling you how great you really are.

Let someone else praise you, not your own mouth—

a stranger, not your own lips. (Proverbs 27:2 NLT).

Turn your *Declaration Of Quality Wisdom* into this prayer of commitment:

> *Lord Jesus, **Today May I** be okay with someone else telling me how great I really am.*

DAY TWENTY FIVE: "The Fine Art Of Accepting Constructive Criticism"

Today May You . . . be WILLING to hear a CONSTRUCTIVE CRITIQUE from those who are WILLING to tell you the TRUTH about yourself.

An open rebuke is better than hidden love! Wounds from a sincere friend are better than many kisses from an enemy. (Proverbs 27:5-6 NLT).

Turn your *Declaration Of Quality Wisdom* into this prayer of commitment:

> Lord Jesus, *Today May I* be WILLING to hear a CONSTRUCTIVE CRITIQUE from those who are WILLING to tell me the TRUTH about myself.

DAY TWENTY SIX: "Loving The Sweet Life"

Today May You . . . LISTEN and LEARN from those who LOVE you so that you may live a SWEET LIFE.

The heartfelt counsel of a friend
is as sweet as perfume and incense. (Proverbs 27:9 NLT).

Turn your *Declaration Of Quality Wisdom* into this prayer of commitment:

> Lord Jesus, *Today May I* LISTEN and LEARN from those who LOVE me so that I may live a SWEET LIFE.

DAY TWENTY SEVEN: "Fanclub"

Today May You . . . cultivate the kinds of friendships that when everything hits the fan your friends will be your biggest fans.

Never abandon a friend—either yours or your father's. When disaster strikes, you won't have to ask your brother for assistance. It's better to go to a neighbor than to a brother who lives far away. (Proverbs 27:10 NLT).

Turn your *Declaration Of Quality Wisdom* into this prayer of commitment:

> *Lord Jesus, **Today May I** cultivate the kinds of friendships that when everything hits the fan my friends will be my biggest fans.*

DAY TWENTY EIGHT: "The Courageous Life"

Today May You . . . be COURAGEOUSLY CAUTIOUS as you live your life.

A prudent person foresees danger and takes precautions.
The simpleton goes blindly on and suffers the consequences. (Proverbs 27:12 NLT).

Turn your *Declaration Of Quality Wisdom* into this prayer of commitment:

> *Lord Jesus, **Today May I** be COURAGEOUSLY CAUTIOUS as I live my life.*

DAY TWENTY NINE: "The Sharp Life"

Today May You . . . be on the lookout for sharp friends who will make you sharper and don't allow dull acquaintances to suck the life out of you and make you lose your edge.

As iron sharpens iron,
so a friend sharpens a friend. (Proverbs 27:17 NLT).

Turn your *Declaration Of Quality Wisdom* into this prayer of commitment:

> *Lord Jesus, **Today May I** be on the lookout for sharp friends who will make me sharper and don't allow dull acquaintances to suck the life out of me and make me lose my edge.*

DAY THIRTY: "Caregiver"

Today May You . . . make your very BEST EFFORT to take special CARE of the people God places in your CARE.

"Know the state of your flocks, and put your heart into caring for your herds," (Proverbs 27:23 NLT).

Turn your *Declaration Of Quality Wisdom* into this prayer of commitment:

> *Lord Jesus, **Today May I** make my very BEST EFFORT to take special CARE of the people You place in my CARE.*

DAY THIRTY ONE: "This Is My Country"

Today May You . . . pray for the kind of LEADERSHIP in your city, state, and country who would choose to be wise and knowledgeable and that the people would enjoy stability.

"When there is moral rot within a nation, its government topples easily. But wise and knowledgeable leaders bring stability." (Proverbs 28:2 NLT).

Turn your *Declaration Of Quality Wisdom* into this prayer of commitment:

> *Lord Jesus, **Today May I** pray for the kind of LEADERSHIP in my city, state, and country who would choose to be wise and knowledgeable and that the people would enjoy stability.*

Introduction To Section Nine:
"LOVING TO LEAD" (Proverbs 28:3-31:31)

"Leadership ability is always the lid on personal and organizational effectiveness. If a person's leadership is strong, the organization's lid is high. But if it's not, then the organization is limited" ~ John C. Maxwell

"A man's gift makes room for him and brings him before great men."
~ Solomon, Proverbs 18:16 (NASB) ~

It has been said that when a person, especially a leader, stops growing, he or she is dying. If this sounds too dramatic for your taste, consider the consequences if I am correct. Leadership, good and bad, always impacts not only the leader but other people as well. If we are growing as leaders, then most likely, those under us will be growing as well. However, if we are stagnant and have not been pressed to grow, chances are those whom we serve will be stagnant as well. There are few sadder things to behold than to gaze at an organization that was once great but has fallen off its perch into ruin.

In Jim Collin's foundational study on organizational health, "Good to Great," he had a list of companies that had gone from "good to great." One of those "great" companies was the now bankrupt Circuit City. What is the bottom-line lesson for any leader? If we lose our focus and quit growing, we will eventually join the other Circuit Cities into the scrapheap of failed leadership. John Maxwell says it so well when he states, *"Leadership ability is always the lid on personal and organizational effectiveness. If a person's leadership is strong, the organization's lid is high. But if it's not, then the organization is limited."* Let's put it another way: are *you* hindering anyone in his or her own development as a leader because of *your* lack of ability?

So here is the take-a-way for the leader who desires to grow and keep on growing. How is it done? What does a Quality Leader have to do in order to increase his or her leadership ability and stay sharp and grow? Here are a few suggestions:

1. Read, read, read every good book you can get on personal and organizational leadership. Don't read the books from the guys who are writing about an abstract theory they have never experienced. Read from the leaders who have experienced growth!
2. Surround yourself with people who are a whole lot smarter than you are. No one, especially you, has all of the answers. Get a team around you who can compensate for your weak areas.
3. Stay humble and teachable. The best leaders know this to be true: "The more I learn, the less I know." Never stop learning!

One of the most challenging qualities of a good leader is to master the mind: to keep things positive. While all of the distracting white noise surrounds him or her, and the false messages that swirl in the mind look to trespass and seek to "rent space," the quality leader disciplines the mind: they always discipline their mind to think on positive virtues. Here is how it's done.

And now, dear brothers and sisters, one final thing. Fix your thoughts on what is true, and honorable, and right, and pure, and lovely, and admirable. Think about things that are excellent and worthy of praise. (Philippians 4:8 NLT).

Introduction:

An "ok" or "average" life is easy to pull off: just do nothing except allow your mind to trend downward and believe the worst-case scenario, always. No one in their right mind would want to have this kind of life as their legacy, but many people, many believers, settle for it. Why? Well, for two reasons. One is just ignorance. They have never been instructed on how to create habits of positive thinking. And when positive habits of thinking are put into place, success usually follows closely behind. The other reason some remain in the trap of "stinking thinking" is most common: many people are just lazy thinkers. They have no creativity, no vision for success, no willingness to do the hard work of constructive thinking.

It is essential we get ahold of this life principle that applies to every culture: we become what we think. Our thinking influences our self-value and our ability to fulfill our purpose. Our confidence, how we think and what we think influences what we do. If you want to become the very best version of you, learning how to think positively is key.

What the Bible says (Observation):

In this one verse, the Apostle Paul gives us the template to right thinking. And he does it in two ways: How we are to do it, "Fix your thoughts," what we are to do, and what we are to fix our minds on . . .

- ◊ What is true, as in authentic, real, genuine
- ◊ What is honorable, or honest, noble, highly respected
- ◊ What is right, as in righteous behavior lived out before God and other people
- ◊ What is pure, as in undefiled, morally free from impurities
- ◊ What is lovely, what is gracious, as in seeing images of kindness, always seeing the positive in someone else, to build them up
- ◊ What is admirable, as in things that are worthy enough to allow space in your mind

What the Bible means (Interpretation):

- ◊ What is true, as in authentic, real, genuine

It is not coincidental that Paul begins this list of key words with TRUE. Without the foundation of truth, every other virtue on this list is lacking in relevance. No truth? Then honor becomes subjective. No truth? Then what is right is left in the eye of the beholder. No foundation of truth? Purity is corrupt. No truth? There is nothing lovely about that at all. Finally, no truth? Admirable? No way!

Truth is the currency that finances how you build your life into the very best version of you. No matter how challenging it may be to fix your thoughts on what is true, you must commit to it. We live in a day and time where the truth is being attacked on all fronts: in the media, politics, education, and even from certain parts of the Church. Many who claim to be Christ followers openly dispute many of the truths of Scripture and would rather water them down in the politically correct doctrines of humanism. If you want to live a set free life, then think on what is true.

[31] Jesus said to the people who believed in him, "You are truly my disciples if you remain faithful to my teachings. [32] And you will know the truth, and the truth will set you free." John 8:31-32

- ◊ What is honorable, or honest, noble, highly respected

Honorable thoughts are uplifting thoughts. Some of the most notable leaders in history are the men and women who dedicated their lives to a big idea that would transform the world.

- ❖ It was Martin Luther King who fixed his thoughts on "I have a dream" that changed a nation.
- ❖ It was Mother Theresa who fixed her thoughts on having the right perspective when she said "Not all of us can do great things. But we can do small things with great love." and challenged our hearts.
- ❖ It was Jesus who fixed his thoughts on the power of us being able to love each other just as He has loved us with a love that will transform the world.

[9] "I have loved you even as the Father has loved me. Remain in my love. [10] When you obey my commandments, you remain in my love, just as I obey my Father's commandments and remain in his love. [11] I have told you these things so that you will be filled with my joy. Yes, your joy will overflow! [12] This is my commandment: Love each other in the same way I have loved you. [13] There is no greater love than to lay down one's life for one's friends. [14] You are my friends if you do what I command. [15] I no longer call you slaves, because a master doesn't confide in his slaves. Now you are my friends, since I have told you everything the Father told me. [16] You didn't choose me. I chose you. I appointed you to go and produce lasting fruit, so that the Father will give you whatever you ask for, using my name. [17] This is my command: Love each other. (John 15:9-16)

◊ What is right, as in righteous behavior lived out before God and other people

When you make the conscious decision to fix your mind on what is right, you are declaring to "see the kind of life" you seek to live. What you think will determine how you live your life.

It has been said that people do not care how much you know but want to know how much you care. That is true. If you want to become the very best version of you, then you need to live the right kind of life.

The steps of a *good* man are ordered by the Lord,
And He delights in his way. (Psalm 37:23 NKJV)

Blessed *is* the man
Who walks not in the counsel of the [l]ungodly,
Nor stands in the path of sinners,
Nor sits in the seat of the scornful;
[2] But his delight *is* in the law of the Lord,
And in His law he [l]meditates day and night.

³ He shall be like a tree
Planted by the rivers of water,
That brings forth its fruit in its season,
Whose leaf also shall not wither;
And whatever he does shall prosper. (Psalm 1:1-3 NKJV)

◊ What is pure, as in undefiled, morally free from impurities

When I was living in the dorms during my seminary days Steve, my RA (resident assistant), challenged me and the other guys on the floor with this profound challenge: *"The best thing you can offer anyone is your own personal holiness."* Wow! It moved me then and it moves me now as I write. In a world where rampant compromise is being made in the name of "personal freedom," personal purity is set aside for what is expedient and desired. Is it really possible in today's world to live by a set of Biblical values and adhere to a moral lifestyle? Yes, of course it is. But it's only possible by the grace of God and a decision to set your mind to think on what is pure. If you can practice this self-discipline of purity then you are well on your way to becoming the best version of you.

Since you have purified your souls in obeying the truth through the Spirit in sincere love of the brethren, love one another fervently with a pure heart, (1 Peter 1:22 NKJV)

Blessed *are* the pure in heart, For they shall see God. (Matthew 5:8 NKJV)

◊ What is lovely, what is gracious, as in seeing images of kindness, always seeing the positive in someone else, to build them up

A lovely mindset is one that always looks for the good in a person and in a circumstance. When someone tells you to "have a lovely day," what are they saying? They are wishing for you to have a day of joy, a day where things are going your way, a day where you see the glass as always half full and never half empty. In an ugly world, the person who has a lovely mindset will become the very best version of themselves and help others see life through the lens of a lovely perspective too.

² Dear brothers and sisters, when troubles of any kind come your way, consider it an opportunity for great joy. ³ For you know that when your faith is tested, your endurance has a chance to grow. ⁴ So let it grow, for when your endurance is fully developed, you will be perfect and complete, needing nothing. (James 1:2-4 NLT).

And we know that God causes everything to work together for the good of those who love God and are called according to his purpose for them. (Romans 8:28 NLT).

◊   What is admirable, as in things that are worthy enough to allow space in your mind

What are you willing to rent space in your head? Or let's look at the question in another way: are there any trespassers in your mind that are sucking the life out of you? Worry? Anger? Bitterness? Unforgiveness? Greed? Loss of focus? The need to win an argument about a topic that won't matter a hundred years from now? Things that are not eternal in nature?

Thinking positive thoughts, when you think about it, is really just a stewardship issue. How you spend your time and energy thinking will define how you will become the very best version of you.

And just in case we missed the point, Paul sums it up again when he says, "Think about things that are excellent and worthy of praise."

So, there you go. The key to great leadership is to have a mind that is set upon things that are excellent and worthy of praise. As you turn the page and begin to work through the final 31 devotions, ask the Lord to give you focus and clarity that will empower you to live out what you are learning before others. They are waiting for you my friend, as one who is Loving To Lead.

LOVING TO LEAD
(Proverbs 28:3-31:31)

DAY ONE: "Being Careful How You Use Your Power"

Today May You . . . never take advantage of anyone who is having a difficult time.

'A poor person who oppresses the poor is like a pounding rain that destroys the crops.' (Proverbs 28:3 NLT).

Turn your *Declaration Of Quality Wisdom* into this prayer of commitment:

> *Lord Jesus, **Today May I** never take advantage of anyone who is having a difficult time.*

DAY TWO: "Living As A Good Citizen"

Today May You . . . be a person who is known as a good citizen in your community.

'Evil people don't understand justice, but those who follow the Lord understand completely.' (Proverbs 28:5 NLT)

Turn your *Declaration Of Quality Wisdom* into this prayer of commitment:

> *Lord Jesus, **Today May I** be a person who is known as a good citizen in my community.*

DAY THREE: "Prayers That Please"

Today May You . . . have the kind of prayer life that pleases the Lord.

'God detests the prayers of a person who ignores the law.' (Proverbs 28:9 NLT).

Turn your *Declaration Of Quality Wisdom* into this prayer of commitment:

> *Lord Jesus, **Today May I** have the kind of prayer life that pleases You.*

DAY FOUR: "A Life Of Essential Values"

Today May You . . . be sure your Christian VALUES are the most VALUABLE possessions you live out before God and others.

Better to be poor and honest

than to be dishonest and rich. (Proverbs 28:6 NLT).

Turn your *Declaration Of Quality Wisdom* into this prayer of commitment:

> *Lord Jesus, **Today May I** be sure my Christian VALUES are the most VALUABLE possessions I live out before God and others.*

DAY FIVE: "Glad To Be Glad"

Today May You . . . make your finest effort to help everyone you know be glad.

When the godly succeed, everyone is glad.

When the wicked take charge, people go into hiding. (Proverbs 28:12 NLT).

Turn your *Declaration Of Quality Wisdom* into this prayer of commitment:

Lord Jesus, Today May I make my finest effort to help everyone I know be glad.

DAY SIX: "The Need To Keep Short Accounts With God"

Today May You . . . keep short accounts with God and stay clean before Him and before others.

People who conceal their sins will not prosper,

but if they confess and turn from them, they will receive mercy. (Proverbs 28:13 NLT).

Turn your *Declaration Of Quality Wisdom* into this prayer of commitment:

Lord Jesus, Today May I keep short accounts with You and stay clean before You and before others.

DAY SEVEN: "Hunger Works"

Today May You . . . work like your meals depend upon it.

A hard worker has plenty of food,

but a person who chases fantasies ends up in poverty. (Proverbs 28:19 NLT).

Turn your *Declaration Of Quality Wisdom* into this prayer of commitment:

Lord Jesus, Today May I work like my meals depend upon it.

DAY EIGHT: "Win Like A Turtle"

Today May You . . . remember that in any significant race of life that the TURTLE always wins, always.; so, stay STEADY, stay TRUSTWORTHY, stay out of TROUBLE.

The trustworthy person will get a rich reward,

but a person who wants quick riches will get into trouble. (Proverbs 28:20 NLT).

Turn your *Declaration Of Quality Wisdom* into this prayer of commitment:

> *Lord Jesus, **Today May I** remember that in any significant race of life that the TURTLE always wins, always.; so, help me to stay STEADY, stay TRUSTWORTHY, stay out of TROUBLE.*

DAY NINE: "Being On The Right Team"

Today May You . . . surround yourself with the kind of people who love you enough to tell you the truth.

In the end, people appreciate honest criticism

far more than flattery. (Proverbs 28:23 NLT).

Turn your *Declaration Of Quality Wisdom* into this prayer of commitment:

> *Lord Jesus, **Today May I** surround myself with the kind of people who love me enough to tell me the truth.*

DAY TEN: "Why Having An Attitude Of Gratitude Leads To Prosperity"

Today May You . . . have an ATTITUDE of GRATITUDE for every blessing the Lord sends your way.

Greed causes fighting;

trusting the Lord leads to prosperity. (Proverbs 28:25 NLT).

Turn your *Declaration Of Quality Wisdom* into this prayer of commitment:

> Lord Jesus, **Today May I** have an ATTITUDE of GRATITUDE for every blessing You send my way.

DAY ELEVEN: "The Benefits Of Having A Tender Heart For The Poor"

Today May You . . . have a keen awareness of the material needs of others who are not as fortunate as you and have a tender heart for them.

Whoever gives to the poor will lack nothing,

but those who close their eyes to poverty will be cursed. (Proverbs 28:27 NLT).

Turn your *Declaration Of Quality Wisdom* into this prayer of commitment:

> Lord Jesus, **Today May I** have a keen awareness of the material needs of others who are not as fortunate as I am and have a tender heart for them.

DAY TWELVE: "Why Encouragement Is Superior To Flattery"

Today May You . . . be INTENTIONAL in your ENCOURAGEMENT towards your friends and build them up; resist the urge to FLATTER them and fatten up their pride and ego.

To flatter friends

is to lay a trap for their feet. (Proverbs 29:5 NLT).

Turn your *Declaration Of Quality Wisdom* into this prayer of commitment:

> *Lord Jesus, **Today May I** be INTENTIONAL in my ENCOURAGEMENT towards my friends and build them up; and resist the urge to FLATTER them and fatten up their pride and ego.*

DAY THIRTEEN: "A Big Heart Is A Caring Heart"

Today May You . . . have a BIG heart for the people who need your COMPASSION and your CARE.

The godly care about the rights of the poor;

the wicked don't care at all. (Proverbs 29:7 NLT).

Turn your *Declaration Of Quality Wisdom* into this prayer of commitment:

> *Lord Jesus, **Today May I** have a BIG heart for the people who need my COMPASSION and my CARE.*

DAY FOURTEEN: "The Right Way To Handle Your Anger"

Today May You . . . be SPIRIT FILLED when you want to give someone a PIECE of your mind; give them His PEACE instead.

Fools vent their anger,

but the wise quietly hold it back. (Proverbs 29:11 NLT).

Turn your *Declaration Of Quality Wisdom* into this prayer of commitment:

> *Lord Jesus, **Today May I** be SPIRIT FILLED when I want to give someone a PIECE of my mind; give them Your PEACE instead.*

DAY FIFTEEN: "The Focused Life"

Today May You . . . keep your life between the DITCHES and stay on the JOYFUL PATH.

When people do not accept divine guidance, they run wild.

But whoever obeys the law is joyful. (Proverbs 29:18 NLT).

Turn your *Declaration Of Quality Wisdom* into this prayer of commitment:

> Lord Jesus, *Today May I* keep my life between the DITCHES and stay on the JOYFUL PATH.

DAY SIXTEEN: "The Benefit Of Thinking Before You Speak"

Today May You . . . THINK before you SPEAK.

There is more hope for a fool

than for someone who speaks without thinking. (Proverbs 29:20 NLT).

Turn your *Declaration Of Quality Wisdom* into this prayer of commitment:

> Lord Jesus, *Today May I* THINK before I SPEAK.

DAY SEVENTEEN: "Practice What Can Be Preached"

Today May You . . . practice the things that make you a HUMBLE hero and not a HUMILIATED heel.

Pride ends in humiliation,

while humility brings honor. (Proverbs 29:23 NLT).

Turn your *Declaration Of Quality Wisdom* into this prayer of commitment:

*Lord Jesus, **Today May I** practice the things that make me a HUMBLE hero and not a HUMILIATED heel.*

DAY EIGHTEEN: "No Fear Zone"

Today May You . . . be more concerned about what the Lord says about you than what people say about you and to you.

Fearing people is a dangerous trap,

but trusting the Lord means safety. (Proverbs 29:25 NLT).

Turn your *Declaration Of Quality Wisdom* into this prayer of commitment:

*Lord Jesus, **Today May I** be more concerned about what You say about me than what people say about me and to me.*

DAY NINETEEN: "The Blessing Of Giving Your Big Problems To A Bigger God"

Today May You . . . give your big problems to a BIGGER God.

Who but God goes up to heaven and comes back down?

Who holds the wind in his fists?

Who wraps up the oceans in his cloak?

Who has created the whole wide world?

What is his name—and his son's name?

Tell me if you know! (Proverbs 30:4 NLT).

Turn your *Declaration Of Quality Wisdom* into this prayer of commitment:

> *Lord Jesus, Today May I give my big problems to a BIGGER God.*

DAY TWENTY: "The Word-Driven Life"

Today May You . . . KNOW the Word, LIVE BY the Word, and POINT others to the Word.

Every word of God proves true.

He is a shield to all who come to him for protection. (Proverbs 30:5 NLT).

Turn your *Declaration Of Quality Wisdom* into this prayer of commitment:

> *Lord Jesus, Today May I KNOW the Word, LIVE BY the Word, and POINT others to the Word.*

DAY TWENTY ONE: "Your Word Is Your Bond"

Today May You . . . be a person of your word and be satisfied with whatever provisions God may send your way.

O God, I beg two favors from you;

let me have them before I die.

First, help me never to tell a lie.

Second, give me neither poverty nor riches!

Give me just enough to satisfy my needs.

For if I grow rich, I may deny you and say, "Who is the Lord?"

And if I am too poor, I may steal and thus insult God's holy name. (Proverbs 30:7-9 NLT).

Turn your *Declaration Of Quality Wisdom* into this prayer of commitment:

> *Lord Jesus, **Today May I** be a person of my word and be satisfied with whatever provisions You may send my way.*

DAY TWENTY TWO: "The Secret To Having A Great Workplace"

Today May You . . . seek to build up your teammates when others would seek to tear them down.

Never slander a worker to the employer,

or the person will curse you, and you will pay for it. (Proverbs 30:10 NLT).

Turn your *Declaration Of Quality Wisdom* into this prayer of commitment:

> *Lord Jesus, **Today May I** seek to build up my teammates when others would seek to tear them down.*

DAY TWENTY THREE: "Expecting An Amazing Life"

Today May You . . . not MUDDLE in the MUNDANE; but instead live your life always AMAZED by an AMAZING God who delights in showing off His glory to you.

There are three things that amaze me—

no, four things that I don't understand:

how an eagle glides through the sky,

how a snake slithers on a rock,

how a ship navigates the ocean,

how a man loves a woman. (Proverbs 30:18-19 NLT).

Turn your *Declaration Of Quality Wisdom* into this prayer of commitment:

> *Lord Jesus, **Today May I** not MUDDLE in the MUNDANE but instead live my life always AMAZED by an AMAZING God who delights in showing off His glory to me.*

DAY TWENTY FOUR: "How You Manage Your Anger Is A Choice"

Today May You . . . choose to give up a chance to stir up anger and instead stir up love, peace, and grace instead.

As the beating of cream yields butter

and striking the nose causes bleeding,

so stirring up anger causes quarrels. (Proverbs 30:33 NLT).

Turn your *Declaration Of Quality Wisdom* into this prayer of commitment:

> *Lord Jesus, **Today May I** choose to give up a chance to stir up anger and instead stir up love, peace, and grace instead.*

DAY TWENTY FIVE: "The Power And Responsibility Of Being An Advocate"

Today May You . . . use your INFLUENCE to INTERCEDE for those who are INNOCENT.

Speak up for those who cannot speak for themselves;

ensure justice for those being crushed.

Yes, speak up for the poor and helpless,

and see that they get justice. (Proverbs 31:8-9 NLT).

Turn your *Declaration Of Quality Wisdom* into this prayer of commitment:

> *Lord Jesus, Today May I use my INFLUENCE to INTERCEDE for those who are INNOCENT.*

DAY TWENTY SIX: "Character Counts"

Today May You . . . pursue with your whole heart the kind of relationships where the depth of their character matters so much more than the shallowness of their self-centeredness.

Who can find a virtuous and capable wife?

She is more precious than rubies.

Her husband can trust her,

and she will greatly enrich his life.

She brings him good, not harm,

all the days of her life. (Proverbs 31:10-12 NLT).

Turn your *Declaration Of Quality Wisdom* into this prayer of commitment:

> *Lord Jesus, Today May I pursue with my whole heart the kind of relationships where the depth of their character matters so much more than the shallowness of their self-centeredness.*

DAY TWENTY SEVEN: "The 'All In' Life"

Today May You . . . work hard like it all depended upon you and pray like it all depended upon Him.

She goes to inspect a field and buys it;

with her earnings she plants a vineyard.

She is energetic and strong,

a hard worker.

She makes sure her dealings are profitable;

her lamp burns late into the night. (Proverbs 31:16-18 NLT).

Turn your *Declaration Of Quality Wisdom* into this prayer of commitment:

> *Lord Jesus, **Today May I** work hard like it all depended upon me and pray like it all depended upon You.*

DAY TWENTY EIGHT: "A Big Hearted Life"

Today May You . . . have a BIG HEART that will care for the BIG NEEDS of people who need BIG LOVE from YOU.

She extends a helping hand to the poor

and opens her arms to the needy. (Proverbs 31:20 NLT).

Turn your *Declaration Of Quality Wisdom* into this prayer of commitment:

> *Lord Jesus, **Today May I** have a BIG HEART that will care for the BIG NEEDS of people who need BIG LOVE from ME.*

DAY TWENTY NINE: "The Right Wardrobe Sets You Apart"

Today May You . . . put on the right kind of WARDROBE that will inspire confidence in everyone around you.

She is clothed with strength and dignity,

and she laughs without fear of the future. (Proverbs 31:25 NLT).

Turn your *Declaration Of Quality Wisdom* into this prayer of commitment:

> Lord Jesus, **Today May I** put on the right kind of WARDROBE that will inspire confidence in everyone around me.

DAY THIRTY: "Transformational Words"

Today May You . . . give someone a piece of your HEART before you give them a piece of your MIND.

When she speaks, her words are wise,

and she gives instructions with kindness. (Proverbs 31:26 NLT).

Turn your *Declaration Of Quality Wisdom* into this prayer of commitment:

> Lord Jesus, **Today May I** give someone a piece of my HEART before I give them a piece of my MIND.

DAY THIRTY ONE: "The Secret To Beauty"

Today May You . . . have an inner beauty that is simply stunning to all who know you and shows your love for the Lord.

Charm is deceptive, and beauty does not last;

but a woman who fears the Lord will be greatly praised. (Proverbs 31:30 NLT).

Turn your *Declaration Of Quality Wisdom* into this prayer of commitment:

> Lord Jesus, **Today May I** have an inner beauty that is simply stunning to all who know me and shows my love for You.

My Quality Life Mission Statement Manifesto based upon Proverbs 3:5-6

*W*hereas, I will trust in the Lord with all of my heart in regard to my PERSONAL life, my PROFESSIONAL life, and my SPIRITUAL life and

*W*hereas, I will not depend upon my own understanding in regard to my PERSONAL life, my PROFESSIONAL life, and my SPIRITUAL life and

*W*hereas, I will seek His will in regard to my PERSONAL life, my PROFESSIONAL life, and my SPIRITUAL life and

*W*hereas, I will trust Him to put me on the perfect path in regard to my PERSONAL life, my PROFESSIONAL life, and my SPIRITUAL life, so

I will live a Quality Life and create a legacy that will glorify the Lord, be an inspiration for those who desire to experience a Quality Life too, and I will be able, when my time on earth is done, to finish well.

"But you should keep a clear mind in every situation. Don't be afraid of suffering for the Lord. Work at telling others the Good News, and fully carry out the ministry God has given you. As for me, my life has already been poured out as an offering to God. The time of my death is near. I have fought the good fight, I have finished the race, and I have remained faithful. And now the prize awaits me—the crown of righteousness, which the Lord, the righteous Judge, will give me on the day of his return. And the prize is not just for me but for all who eagerly look forward to his appearing."
2 Timothy 4:5-8 NLT

Soli Deo

RESOURCES FOR THE QUALITY LEADER

**My Quality Life Plan:
7 Essential Phases (Choices) That Will Change My World**

- Who I Am — *Identity*
- Where I've Been — *History*
- What I Want To Do — *Purpose*
- Why I Want To Do It — *Motive*
- How I Need To Do It — *Strategy*
- Who I Want To Impact — *Influence*
- What I Want Them To Do — *Empowerment*

My Spiritual Life Plan

©Copyright 2014 Dr. Denny Bates / www.dennybates.com

Quality Wisdom For A Modern Age

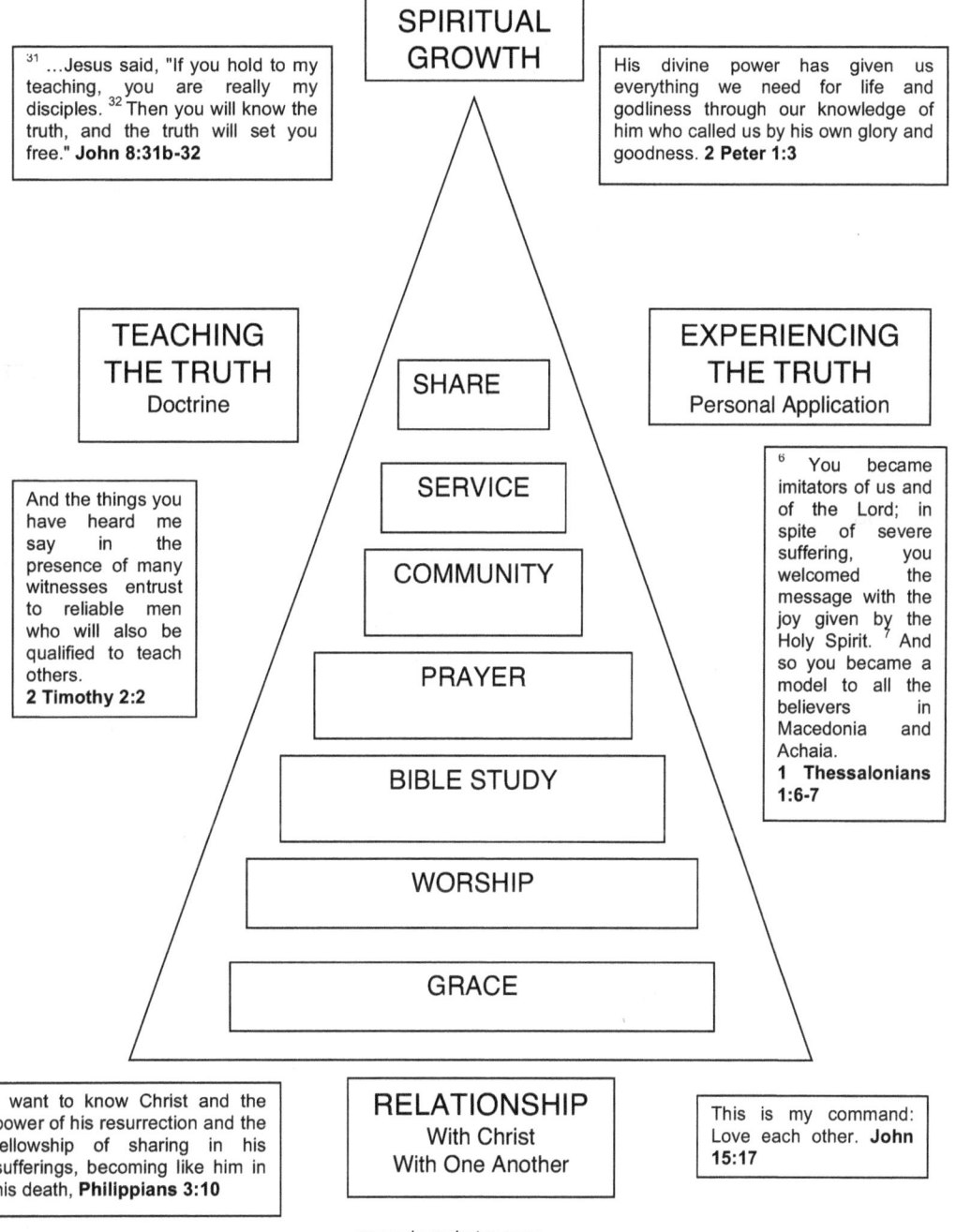

HOW YOU CAN HAVE
A RELATIONSHIP WITH JESUS

- ✓ **GOD LOVES YOU AND HAS A WONDERFUL PLAN FOR YOUR LIFE**

For I know the plans I have for you," declares the LORD, "plans to prosper you and not to harm you, plans to give you hope and a future. **Jeremiah 29:11 (NIV)**

- ✓ AS A RESULT OF MAN GOING HIS OWN WAY AND REJECTING GOD, A CHASM, A GREAT DIVIDE, HAS COME SEPARATING A JUST AND HOLY GOD FROM SINFUL MAN

for all have sinned and fall short of the glory of God, **Romans 3:23 (NIV)**

For the wages of sin is death, but the gift of God is eternal life in Christ Jesus our Lord. **Romans 6:23 (NIV)**

- ✓ GOD SENT HIS SON, HIS PERFECT SON TO BECOME OUR SACRIFICE. HE WHO IS SINLESS TOOK UPON HIMSELF OUR SINS, OFFERING TO RESTORE OUR BROKEN RELATIONSHIP WITH GOD, BRIDGING THE GAP BETWEEN GOD AND MAN

We all, like sheep, have gone astray, each of us has turned to his own way; and the LORD has laid on him the iniquity of us all. **Isaiah 53:6 (NIV)**

The next day John saw Jesus coming toward him and said, "Look, the Lamb of God, who takes away the sin of the world!" **John 1:29 (NIV)**

- ✓ GOD HAS GIVEN EACH MAN A CHOICE EITHER TO ACCEPT THE FREE GIFT OF SALVATION AND LIVE FOREVER OR TO REJECT HIS GRACIOUS GIFT AND SPEND ETERNITY FOREVER SEPARATED FROM GOD

For God so loved the world that he gave his one and only Son, that whoever believes in him shall not perish but have eternal life. **John 3:16 (NIV)**

[12]Yet to all who received him, to those who believed in his name, he gave the right to become children of God-- [13]children born not of natural descent, nor of human decision or a husband's will, but born of God. **John 1:12-13 (NIV)**

SUBJECT INDEX

An Introduction to the Subject Index for

Quality Wisdom For A Modern Age:

Years ago, I had a friend share with me that a good book can become a great book if it has a useful subject index. I agree with him. What is provided for you in the coming pages is a comprehensive subject index that covers how to experience quality wisdom for a modern age. This devotional book is much more than a book of helpful information. It is treasure trove of inspirational thoughts and never-ending starting points for a dynamic personal and small group Bible study.

How to use this valuable resource:

You can use it as a Bible Study on a topic that you want to become more familiar with in your search for spiritual growth. For example, you may wish to study the topic of ***Abundance***.

Abundant—Abundance
    A. fruit of His blessing. Pg. 9
    Choosing an A. mindset for life. Pg. 48
    Duty.
        Be content with the A. God provides and not worry about what you DO NOT HAVE. Pg. 81
        Do whatever it takes to keep your eyes on the prize of experiencing the A. life. Pg. 26
        Live your life with an A. mindset. Pg. 48
    Fact.
        Give freely and become more wealthy. Pg. 48
    Secret to experiencing an A. life. Pg. 9

See how it works? In this illustration, you have been shown eight Bible study points based upon the topic of Abundance. There are literally hundreds of more subjects in this comprehensive study resource that will provide you many years of enriching times of study, reflection, and personal growth.

A

Abandon—Abandons
    Warning.
        Whoever A. the right path will be severely disciplined. Pg. 72

Abundant—Abundance
    A. fruit of His blessing. Pg. 9
    Choosing an A. mindset for life. Pg. 48

Duty.

> Be content with the A. God provides and not worry about what you DO NOT HAVE. Pg. 81
> Do whatever it takes to keep your eyes on the prize of experiencing the A. life. Pg. 26
> Live your life with an A. mindset. Pg. 48

Fact.

> Give freely and become more wealthy. Pg. 48

Secret to experiencing an A. life. Pg. 9

Access

Fact.

> Giving a gift can open doors; it gives A. to important people! Pg. 97

Accounts

Duty.

> Keep short A. with God and stay clean before Him and before others. Pg. 156

Accurate—Accuracy

Fact.

> The Lord demands A. scales and balances; he sets the standards for fairness. Pg. 82

Act

Before you leap. Pg. 61

Duty.

> Before you do anything, THINK, PRAY, LISTEN, and then A. Pg. 61

Fact.

> Wise people think before they A. Pg. 61

Action—Actions

Fact.

> Commit your A. to the Lord, and your plans will succeed. Pg. 80
> We can make our plans, but the Lord determines our steps. Pg. 82

Kind of.

> Crooked. Pg. 6

Adjust

Duty.

> Always be prepared to A. and GO when your plan needs to align with His. Pg. 86
> PLAN like you know where you are going but be open to the idea that your PLAN might change. Pg. 102

Fact.

> Be bold enough to dream but humble enough to A. and go. Pg. 82
> Must learn to A. and go. Pg. 34
> We can make our plans, but the Lord determines our steps. Pg. 82

Admirable

Duty.

Fix your mind on what is A., as in things that are worthy enough to allow space in your mind. Pg. 153

Advice—Advisers—Advising—Advisor
   Duty.
      Always get better A. than your own. Pg. 77
      Be a GOOD FRIEND by being a GOOD LISTENER so you will be able to give GOOD A. that will help your friend have a GOOD DAY. Pg. 105
      Be willing to take some good advice that will make you an even better version of you. Pg. 139
      Get all the A. and instruction you can, so you will be wise the rest of your life. Pg. 101
      Be willing to SPEAK the truth and ENCOURAGE your friends to make the kind of choice that will add great VALUE to them. Pg. 55
      Get A. that is much better than yours. Pg. 52
      Have a heart of humility that will be open to A. and SUCCEED. Pg. 58
   Fact.
      Many A. bring success. Pg. 77
      Plans succeed through good counsel; don't go to war without wise A. Pg. 114
      The godly give good A. to their friends. Pg. 55
      The lips of the wise give good A. Pg. 71
      The mouth of the godly person gives wise A. Pg. 36
      There is safety in having many A. Pg. 45
      Though good A. lies deep within the heart, a person with understanding will draw it out. Pg. 105
      Those who take A. are wise. Pg. 57
      Timely A. is lovely, like golden apples in a silver basket. To one who listens, valid criticism is like a gold earring or other gold jewelry. Pg. 139
   Kind of.
      Wholesome. Pg. 27
      Always follow God's A. Pg. 26
   The blessing of passing on good A. Pg. 55
   Warning.
      A. of the wicked is treacherous. Pg. 51
      Don't go to war without wise advice. Pg. 114
      Don't waste your breath on fools, for they will despise the wisest A. Pg. 126
      People who despise A. are asking for trouble. Pg. 58
      Plans go wrong for lack of A. Pg. 77
      Protect yourself from taking your own A. and not His. Pg. 9
      The heart of a fool has no wise A. to give. Pg. 71
      The wicked lead their friends astray. Pg. 55

Advocate
   Duty.
      Speak up for the poor and helpless, and see that they get justice. Pg. 164
      Speak up for those who cannot speak for themselves; ensure justice for those being crushed. Pg. 164

Use your INFLUENCE to INTERCEDE for those who are INNOCENT. Pg. 164
The power and responsibility of begin an A. Pg. 164

Agenda
Duty.
Live a transparent life before the Lord and may His A. become yours. Pg. 116

Allen, James
Quote of.
As the physically weak man can make himself strong by careful and patient training, so the man of weak thoughts can make them strong by exercising himself in right thinking. Pg. xi

Amaze—Amazed—Amazing
Duty.
Do not MUDDLE in the MUNDANE but instead live your life always A. by an A. God who delights in showing off His glory to you. Pg. 163
Expecting an A. life. Pg. 163
Fact.
Three things that A. me—no, four things that I don't understand:
How an eagle glides through the sky. Pg. 163
How a snake slithers on a rock. Pg. 163
How a ship navigates the ocean. Pg. 163
How a man loves a woman. Pg. 163

Ambition
Warning.
The A. of treacherous people traps them. Pg. 38

Ambush
Warning.
Words of the wicked are like a murderous A. Pg. 51

Anger—Angry
A. Management. Pg. 68
Duty.
Be SPIRIT FILLED when you want to give someone a PIECE of your mind, give them His PEACE instead. Pg. 159
Choose to give up a chance to stir up A. and instead stir up love, peace, and grace instead. Pg. 164
Control your tongue so your life may be flooded with peace. Pg. 89
Fact.
A gentle answer deflects A. Pg. 70
Fools vent their A., but the wise quietly hold it back. Pg. 159
How you manage your A. is a choice. Pg. 164
People ruin their lives by their own foolishness and then are A. at the Lord. Pg. 100
People with understanding control their A. Pg. 68

Sensible people control their temper; they earn respect by overlooking wrongs. Pg. 101

Take a deep breath when you want to lash out in A. and instead reach out in love and be firm in your response. Pg. 68

The right way to handle your A. Pg. 159

Warning.

As the beating of cream yields butter and striking the nose causes bleeding, so stirring up A. causes quarrels. Pg. 164

But one disaster is enough to overthrow the wicked. Don't rejoice when your enemies fall; don't be happy when they stumble. For the Lord will be displeased with you and will turn his A. away from them. Pg. 137

Don't befriend A. people or associate with hot-tempered people, or you will learn to be like them and endanger your soul. Pg. 124

Harsh words make tempers flare. Pg. 70

Answer

Fact.

We can make our own plans, but the Lord gives the right A. Pg. 80

Ants

Qualities of.

Gather food for the winter. Pg. 24

Labor hard all summer. Pg. 24

Appetite

Fact.

It is good for workers to have an A.; an empty stomach drives them on. Pg. 85

Approve—Approves—Approval

Fact.

The Lord A. of those who are godly. Pg. 50

Archer

Fact.

An employer who hires a fool or a bystander is like an A. who shoots at random. Pg. 142

Argue—Argument—Arguments

Duty.

Control your tongue so your life may be flooded with peace. Pg. 89

Know when it's the right time to stay in your own hula hoop and stay out of the others. Pg. 142

Know WHEN to ignore a difficult person and WHEN to put a difficult person in their place. Pg. 142

Protect the relationships that are important to you by winning their love, not by winning the A. Pg. 97

Take the HIGH road and walk over those who are UNDER the road. Pg. 104

Fact.

A. separate friends like a gate locked with bars. Pg. 97
Avoiding a fight is a mark of honor; only fools insist on quarreling. Pg. 104
The best way to stop an A. is not to start one. Pg. 89
The best way to defeat a person who is difficult. Pg. 142
Warning.
Don't answer the foolish arguments of fools, or you will become as foolish as they are. Pg. 142
Interfering in someone else's A. is as foolish as yanking a dog's ears. Pg. 142

Ashamed
How to not be A. Pg. 60

Attitude
Duty.
Have an A. of GRATITUDE for every blessing the Lord sends your way. Pg. 158
Why having an attitude of gratitude leads to prosperity. Pg. 158

Attractive
Fact.
Loyalty makes a person A. It is better to be poor than dishonest. Pg. 102

Authentic—Authenticity
Duty.
Be the REAL DEAL when it comes to having a MEANINGFUL MEAL. Pg. 74
Live a transparent life before the Lord and may His AGENDA become yours. Pg. 116
Fact.
A bowl of vegetables with someone you love is better than steak with someone you hate. Pg. 74
The transparent life. Pg. 116

Awe—Awesome
Duty.
Have an A. respect for your A. God who watches after you in an A. way. Pg. 103
Respect. Pg. 2

B

Backslider—Backsliders
Warning.
B. get what they deserve. Pg. 65

Balances
Fact.
The Lord demands accurate scales and B.; he sets the standards for fairness. Pg. 82

Barnabas
- Fact.
  - B. mentioned 29 x in the NT. Pg. 40
  - Nick name was B. Pg. 40
- Meaning of.
  - Son of Encouragement. Pg. 40
- Qualities of.
  - A man of character. Pg. 41
  - Courage. Pg. 41
  - Exhortation that was needed (Sponsorship). Pg. 41
  - Saw potential in Paul. Pg. 41
  - Was a mentor in action. Pg. 40
  - Was beloved or dear. Pg. 40
  - Was a generous man. Pg. 40
  - Was a good man. Pg. 41
  - Was a networker. Pg. 41
  - Was a shepherd. Pg. 41
  - Was an encourager. Pg. 41
  - Was evangelistic. Pg. 41
  - Was called by God. Pg. 40
  - Was full of the Holy Spirit and faith. Pg. 41
  - Was teaching and preaching. Pg. 40
  - Was willing to be sent out. Pg. 41
- Real Name.
  - Joseph. Pg. 40

Battle—Battles
- Duty.
  - Be selective and only fight the B. you can win. Pg. 114
- Fact.
  - The horse is prepared for the day of B., but the victory belongs to the Lord. Pg. 121
- How to win the B. and the war. Pg. 57

Beauty—Beautiful
- Duty.
  - Have an inner B. that is simply stunning to all who know you and of your love for the Lord. Pg. 167
- Fact.
  - Charm is deceptive, and B. does not last; but a woman who fears the Lord will be greatly praised. Pg. 167
- The secret to B. Pg. 167

Be—Being
- Fact.
  - B. proceeds doing. Pg. 91
- The primary need to B. Pg. 91

Believe—Believer
- Charge.
  - Live the life. you B. Pg. 50
  - THINK good thoughts, do good DEEDS, and make a good CONTRIBUTION to your community. Pg. 50
- Duty.
  - Be on the lookout for FAITH news and not FAKE news: B. Him, not them. Pg. 66
- Kind of.
  - Word-centered B. Pg. 15
- Warning.
  - Only simpletons B. everything they're told! Pg. 66

Benefit—Benefits
- Of putting God's Word in your heart. Pg. 7
- Wise words bring many B. Pg. 51

Bitter—Bitterness
- Fact.
  - Each heart knows its own B., and no one else can fully share its joy. Pg. 65

Bless—Blessed—Blessing—Blessings
- Duty.
  - Be a refreshing B. to those who are a B. to you. Pg. 140
  - B. those who need a B. from you. Pg. 123
  - B. your heart so you can B. others. Pg. 123
  - Have a BIG heart to meet the BIG needs of those who may be less fortunate than you. Pg. 101
  - Have an ATTITUDE of GRATITUDE for every B. the Lord sends your way. Pg. 158
  - Keep the right words in your HEART so you can B. the HEART of another. Pg. 123
  - Listen to the words of the wise; apply your heart to my instruction. For it is good to keep these sayings in your heart and always ready on your lips. Pg. 123
  - Love yourself enough to grow yourself enough to be a B. to others. Pg. 100
- Fact.
  - B. are those who are generous, because they feed the poor. Pg. 123
  - The godly are showered with B. Pg. 31
  - Too blessed to be stressed. Pg. 35
  - Trustworthy messengers refresh like snow in summer. They revive the spirit of their employer. Pg. 140
- Of the Lord.
  - Makes a person rich. Pg. 35
- The power of the B. Pg. 123

Body
- Fact.
  - A peaceful heart leads to a healthy B. Pg. 69

Bone—Bones
Fact.
>Jealousy is like cancer in the B. Pg. 69

Bonhoeffer, Dietrich
Quote of.
>*God does not give us everything we want, but He does fulfill His promises, leading us along the best and straightest paths to Himself.* Pg. x

Borrow—Borrower
Fact.
>Just as the rich rule the poor, so the B. is servant to the lender. Pg. 123

Boundary
Warning.
>Don't cheat your neighbor by moving the ancient B. markers set up by previous generations. Pg. 125

Brother
Duty.
>Never abandon a friend—either yours or your father's. When disaster strikes, you won't have to ask your B. for assistance. It's better to go to a neighbor than to a B. who lives far away. Pg. 146

Fact.
>A friend is always loyal, and a B. is born to help in time of need. Pg. 89

Warning.
>There are "friends" who destroy each other, but a real friend sticks closer than a B. Pg. 98

Bubbling Brook
Fact.
>Wisdom flows from the wise like a B. B. Pg. 95

Build Up
Duty.
>Add value to those you love by intentionally using kind words that build them up. Pg. 84
>
>Make sure every word you use builds someone up and not take them down. Pg. 85

Business
Do not make it your goal to be a "Christian" businessman or businesswoman. Pg. 30

Duty.
>Make every B. decision with a commitment to live out the teachings of Jesus with your own PERSONAL INTEGRITY and WORK ETHIC. Pg. 125
>
>Make sure your moral compass is true in every B. and personal relationship transaction you make. Pg. 37

Good B. matters. Pg. 125

Qualities of a successful businessman and businesswoman.

Blessed by God. Pg. 30
Lives for God. Pg. 30
Loves like God. Pg. 30
Trusts God. Pg. 30

C
Call—Calling
Committed to the C. Pg. 128

Cancer
Fact.
Jealousy is like C. in the bones. Pg. 69

Care—Careful
Duty.
Make it your very BEST EFFORT to take special C. of the people God Places under your C. Pg. 147

For others.
Be keenly aware, by the discernment of the Spirit, of the people around you who are smiling on the outside but are hurting on the inside. Pg. 65

Reason why you are to take very good C. of your heart.
It determines the course of your life. Pg. 16

Warning.
Be C. what you THINK and what you SAY and what you DO. Pg. 78
Guard your heart above all else. Pg. 16

Caregiver
Caregiver. Pg. 147
Duty.
"Know the state of your flocks, and put your heart into caring for your herds," Pg. 147
Make it your very BEST EFFORT to take special CARE of the people God Places under your CARE. Pg. 147

Carroll, Lewis
Quote of.
If you don't know where you are going any road will take you there. Pg. 108

Caution
Warning.
Be CAREFUL what you THINK and what you SAY and what you DO. Pg. 78
Proceed with C. Pg. 78

Challenge—Challenging
Fact.
Grace says that God never wastes anything in our life—even the most difficult of things. Pg. 110

Character
- C. Vs. comfort. Pg. 121
- Duty.
  - Live like C. matters more than your material COMFORT. Pg. 121
  - Pursue with your whole heart the kind of relationships where the depth of their C. matters so much more than the shallowness of their self-centeredness. Pg. 165
  - Set in your heart to be THE REAL DEAL in your C. with those who are depending upon you to be HONEST and TRUE. Pg. 47
- Fact.
  - C. counts Pg. 165
  - Choose a good reputation over great riches; being held in high esteem is better than silver or gold. Pg. 121

Charm
- Fact.
  - C.is deceptive, and beauty does not last; but a woman who fears the Lord will be greatly praised. Pg. 167

Chatterers
- Warning.
  - A gossip goes around telling secrets, so don't hang around with C. Pg. 115

Cheat
- Warning.
  - Don't C. your neighbor by moving the ancient boundary markers set up by previous generations. Pg. 125

Cheer—Cheerful
- Fact.
  - A C. look brings joy to the heart. Pg. 78

Children
- Warning.
  - C. who mistreat their father or chase away their mother are an embarrassment and a public disgrace. Pg. 103

Choice—Choices
- Duty.
  - Make the kind of choices that will produce within you a happy heart and a satisfied soul. Pg. 73
- Fact.
  - C. will always have consequences. Pg. 62
  - We may throw the dice [cast lots], but the Lord determines how they fall. Pg. 86
- The power of the daily C. Pg. 73
- Wise C. will watch over you. Pg. 6

Circumstance—Circumstances
> Fact.
>> We may throw the dice [cast lots], but the Lord determines how they fall. Pg. 86

City
> Fact.
>> The whole city celebrates when the godly succeed. Pg. 39
>> The whole city shouts for joy when the wicked die. Pg. 39
>> Upright citizens are good for a city and make it prosper. Pg. 39
>
> Duty.
>> Pray for the kind of LEADERSHIP in your C., state, and country who would choose to be wise and knowledgeable and that the people would enjoy stability. Pg. 147
>
> Warning.
>> The talk of the wicked tears a C. apart. Pg. 39

Citizen—Citizenship
> By the book. Pg. 39
>
> Duty.
>> Be a person who is known as a good C. in your community. Pg. 154
>> Do your part to make your nation great by living a life of godliness. Pg. 70
>
> Fact.
>> The whole city celebrates when the godly succeed. Pg. 39
>
> Living as a good C. Pg. 154
> Responsible C. Pg. 70

City
> Fact.
>> A person without self-control is like a C. with broken-down walls. Pg. 141
>> Better to have self-control than to conquer a C. Pg. 86

Clarity
> Fact.
>> Having C. about our identity empowers us. Pg.92

Cling

> Duty.
>> C. to every bit of wisdom you can collect . . . and use it. Pg. 27

Clothes—Clothed
> Duty.
>> Put on the right kind of WARDROBE where you inspire confidence in everyone around you. Pg. 166
>
> Fact.
>> The virtuous woman is C. with strength and dignity. Pg. 166
>> The right kind of wardrobe sets you apart. Pg. 166

Coincidence—Coincidences
>Fact.
>>We may throw the dice [cast lots], but the Lord determines how they fall. Pg. 86
>Duty.
>>Always be prepared to ADJUST and GO when your plan needs to align with His. Pg. 86
>Kind of.
>>Holy. Pg. 86

Collins, Jim
>What causes a company to go from good to great. Pg. 148

Command—Commands
>Blessing of obedience.
>>Obey His C. and live. Pg. 26
>>Those who respect a C. will succeed. Pg. 58
>Duty.
>>Always treasure the Lord's C. Pg. 26
>>To store His C. in your heart. Pg. 7
>To be treasured. Pg. 4

Comfort
>Character Vs. C. Pg. 121
>Duty.
>>Live like CHARACTER matters more than your material C. Pg. 121

Commit—Committed
>Fact.
>>C. your actions to the Lord, and your plans will succeed. Pg. 80

Common Sense
>Benefit.
>>Can go to bed without fear. Pg. 12
>>Need not to be afraid of destruction that comes upon the wicked. Pg. 12
>>Need not to be afraid of sudden disaster. Pg. 12
>>The Lord will keep your foot from being caught in a trap. Pg. 12
>>The Lord is your security. Pg. 12
>>Will be able to lie down and sleep soundly. Pg. 12
>>Will keep you safe on your way. Pg. 12
>>Will keep your feet from stumbling. Pg. 12
>>Will refresh your soul. Pg. 12
>Challenge.
>>Hang on to C.S. and discernment. Pg. 12
>Duty.
>>Make a focused effort to gain practical wisdom in your life and then have the C.S. to know what to do with it. Pg. 135
>Fact.

A house is built by wisdom and becomes strong through good S. Pg. 135
Kind of life. Pg. 5
God grants a treasure of C.S. to the honest. Pg. 5
Great value of embracing C.S. and discernment. Pg. 12
The power of C.S. wisdom. Pg. 135

Communicate—Communication
  Duty.
    Control your tongue so your life may be flooded with peace. Pg. 89
  Fact.
    It is wonderful to say the right thing at the right time! Pg. 77

Community
  Duty.
    Add value to your C. by living a godly life and by living as an upright citizen. Pg. 39
    Be a person who is known as a good citizen in your community. Pg. 154
    Hang with the kind of people who will make you a better you. Pg. 62
  Fact.
    Evil people don't understand justice, but those who follow the Lord understand completely. Pg. 154
    The company you keep will keep you. Pg. 62
    The whole city celebrates when the godly succeed. Pg. 39
    The whole city shouts for joy when the wicked die. Pg. 39

Company
  Duty.
    Hang with the kind of people who will make you a better you. Pg. 62
  Fact.
    The C. you keep will keep you. Pg. 62
    The right C. you keep will keep you safe. Pg. 124

Compass
  Duty.
    Make sure your moral C. is true in every business and personal relationship transaction you make. Pg. 37
  Kind of.
    Moral C. Pg. 37

Compassion
  Duty.
    Be keenly aware, by the discernment of the Spirit, of the people around you who are smiling on the outside but are hurting on the inside. Pg. 65
    LOOK UP to the Lord before you LOOK DOWN on those who are not as fortunate as you. Pg. 87
    REJOICE when GRACE has comforted you and may you have C. on those who need His GRACE too. Pg. 137
  The need to be considered a safe person for the hurting. Pg. 65
  Why grace and C. matter. Pg. 137

Competent—Competence
Duty.
Assure those who trust you that they can be CONFIDENT in your C. to keep a CONFIDENCE. Pg. 45

Condemn—Condemns—Condemned
Warning.
The Lord C. those who plan wickedness. Pg. 50

Confess—Confession
Duty.
You must reprove or correct those who are under the conviction of sin and lead them to C. and repent of the sin. Pg. 129
Fact.
People who conceal their sins will not prosper, but if they C. and turn from them, they will receive mercy. Pg. 156

Confidence
Duty.
Assure those who trust you that they can be CONFIDENT in your COMPETENCE to keep a C. Pg. 45
Fact.
Those who are trustworthy can keep a C. Pg. 45

Value of keeping a secret. Pg. 45
Warning.
A gossip goes around telling secrets. Pg. 45

Conflict
Duty.
Control your tongue so your life may be flooded with peace. Pg. 89

Take the HIGH road and walk over those who are UNDER the road. Pg. 104
Fact.
Avoiding a fight is a mark of honor; only fools insist on quarreling. Pg. 104
Warning.
Pride leads to C. Pg. 57

Content—Contentment
Be C. Pg. 2
Duty.
Be C. with the ABUNDANCE God provides and not worry about what you DO NOT HAVE. Pg. 81
Fact.
Better to have little, with fear for the Lord, than to have great treasure. and inner turmoil. Pg. 73

Better to have little, with godliness, than to be rich and dishonest. Pg. 81

The secret to C. Pg. 81

Control
Duty.
C. your tongue so your life may be flooded with peace. Pg. 89
Fact.
Better to have self-control than to conquer a city. Pg. 86

Correct—Corrects—Correction
Charge.
Be open to the Lord's loving C. Pg. 10
Love humility so that you may embrace discipline and C. and LEARN. Pg. 50
Connect with me and then correct me. Pg. 88
Duty.
Be willing to receive C. when a C. is needed. Pg. 88
C. the wise. Pg. 29
You must reprove or C. those who are under the conviction of sin and lead them to confess and repent of the sin. Pg. 129
Fact.
A single rebuke does more for a person of understanding than a hundred lashes on the back of a fool. Pg. 88
If you accept C., you will be honored. Pg. 61
If you listen to constructive criticism, you will be at home among the wise. Pg. 78
If you listen to C., you grow in understanding. Pg. 79
The Lord C. those He loves. Pg. 10
To learn, you must love discipline. Pg. 50
Response to.
Don't be upset when He C. you. Pg. 10
Warning.
Do not reject the Lord's discipline. Pg. 10
If you ignore criticism, you will end in poverty and disgrace. Pg. 61
It is stupid to hate C. Pg. 50
Those who ignore C. will go astray. Pg. 34
Whoever hates C. will die. Pg. 72
Why being open to C. will open doors for you. Pg. 61

Corrupt—Corruption
Warning.
"When there is moral rot within a nation, its government topples easily. Pg. 147

Cost
Warning.
Don't trap yourself by making a rash promise to God and only later counting the C. Pg. 116

Corrupt
Warning.
Stay away from C. speech. Pg. 16

Country
    Duty.
        Pray for the kind of LEADERSHIP in your city, state, and country who would choose to be wise and knowledgeable and that the people would enjoy stability. Pg. 147
    This is my C. Pg. 147

Courage—Courageous
    Challenge.
        Have the kind of INNER courage to SAY what is RIGHT and SAY what is WRONG. Pg. 32
    Duty.
        Be COURAGEOUSLY CAUTIOUS as you live your life. Pg. 146
    Fact.
        It's hard to let go of control and power. It takes courage to pass on the baton to others you have trained. Pg. 22
        In your core. Pg. 32
    The C. Life. Pg. 146

Counsel
    Fact.
        Plans succeed through good C.; don't go to war without wise advice. Pg. 114
        The heartfelt C. of a friend is as sweet as perfume and incense. Pg. 145

Credibility
    Duty.
        Make decisions that will add value to others and C. to your legacy. Pg. 32

Criticize—Criticism
    Duty.
        Be WILLING to hear a CONSTRUCTIVE CRITIQUE from those who are WILLING to tell you the TRUTH about you. Pg. 145
    Fact.
        If you listen to constructive C, you will be at home among the wise. Pg. 78
        In the end, people appreciate honest C. far more than flattery. Pg. 157
    The fine art of accepting constructive C. Pg. 145
    Warning.
        If you ignore C., you will end in poverty and disgrace. Pg. 61

Crown
    Fact.
        Gray hair is a C. of glory; it is gained by living a godly life. Pg. 85
    Wealth is a C. for the wise. Pg. 67
    Wisdom will present you with a beautiful C. Pg. 14

Cruel—Cruelty
    Warning.

Your C. will destroy you. Pg. 46

Currency
Warning.
Make sure the only "Payback C." comes out of the love account. Pg. 138

Curse—Cursed
Warning.
Whoever gives to the poor will lack nothing, but those who close their eyes to poverty will be C. Pg. 158

D

Day
Kind of.
Joyful. Pg. 28

Death
Fact.
The way of the godly leads to life; that path does not lead to D. Pg. 55
Warning.
The tongue can bring D. or life. Pg. 98

Debt
Duty.
Make sure the only thing you OWE anyone is LOVE. Pg. 123
Fact.
It's poor judgment to guarantee another person's D. or put up security for a friend. Pg. 94
It's safer not to guarantee another person's D. Pg. 46
The best D. Pg. 123
Warning.
Do not allow your heart to mess with your mind. Pg. 125
Don't agree to guarantee another person's D. or put up security for someone else. If you can't pay it, even your bed will be snatched from under you. Pg. 125
Guaranteeing another's D. Pg. 23
There's danger in putting up security for a stranger's D. Pg. 46

Deceive—Deceives—Deceitful
Warning.
A D. tongue crushes the spirit. Pg.70
The tongue that D. will be cut off. Pg. 36

Decide—Decision—Decisions
Benefits from thinking wise thoughts.
Will help you make wise D. Pg. 28
Challenge:

ALWAYS make the right D. when you come to the Fork in The Road between living a life for Jesus or a life for you. Pg. 13

Make D. that keep you on the RIGHT path, connecting with the RIGHT people, and winding up in the RIGHT place. Pg. 63

Duty.

Experience a peaceful, easy feeling, and avoid making any D. that will poison your life. Pg. 69

Lead with unfailing LOVE in every D. you make, with every person you touch and be absolutely secure in His love for you. Pg. 117

Fact.

Make an intentional D. that everything you THINK, SAY, and DO be based upon what is TRUE. Pg. 64

We can make our plans, but the Lord determines our steps. Pg. 82

Kind of.

Wise decisions. Pg. 30

Warning.

Many impatient leaders grow weary of the process and make a rash D, and often fail. Pg. 75

Deed—Deeds

Duty.

Let your good D. shine out for all to see. Pg. 60

Kind of.

Destructive. Pg. 6

Defend

Reason why you are to D. your heart.

It determines the course of your life. Pg. 16

Warning.

Guard your heart above all else. Pg. 16

Delight—Delights

Fact.

The Lord D. in those with integrity. Pg. 47

Depend

When leaders D. upon you. Pg. 45

Depression

Fact.

D. is a dark companion to the human experience. Pg. 108

Is like a pit of destruction. Pg. 108

Warning.

If we allow it, the very shadow of D. will depress us and pull us down into the pit too. Pg. 108

Despair
    Duty.
        Keep yourself from stumbling into the pit of D. Pg. 25

Despondent
    Fact.
        For the D., every day brings trouble. Pg. 73

Destiny
    Disciplined for D. Pg. 75
    Dreams of D. Pg. 62

Destruction
    Fact.
        Pride goes before D., and haughtiness before a fall. Pg. 83
        Haughtiness goes before D. Pg. 96

Dice
    Fact.
        We may throw the D. [cast lots], but the Lord determines how they fall. Pg. 86

Die
    Warning.
        Whoever hates correction will D. Pg. 72

Disaster
    Duty.
        Never abandon a friend—either yours or your father's. When D. strikes, you won't have to ask your brother for assistance. It's better to go to a neighbor than to a brother who lives far away. Pg. 146
    Warning.
        Babbling of a fool invites D. Pg. 33

Discern—Discernment
    Benefit.
        Can go to bed without fear. Pg. 12
        Need not to be afraid of destruction that comes upon the wicked. Pg. 12
        Need not to be afraid of sudden disaster. Pg. 12
        The Lord will keep your foot from being caught in a trap. Pg. 12
        The Lord is your security. Pg. 12
        Will be able to lie down and sleep soundly. Pg. 12
        Will keep you safe on your way. Pg. 12
        Will keep your feet from stumbling. Pg. 12
        Will refresh your soul. Pg. 12
    Duty.

Be keenly aware, by the D. of the Spirit, of the people around you who are smiling on the outside but are hurting on the inside. Pg. 65

Challenge.
>Hang on to common sense and D. Pg. 12

Great value of embracing common sense and D. Pg. 12

Disciple—Discipleship
The disciplines of a dedicated D. of Jesus. Pg. 66

Discipline—Disciplined—Disciplines
Charge.
> Be open to the Lord's loving correction. Pg. 10
>
> Love humility so that you may embrace D. and correction and LEARN. Pg. 50

D. for destiny. Pg. 75

Duty.
> Be SPIRIT FILLED when you want to give someone a PIECE of your mind, give them His PEACE instead. Pg. 159
>
> We must be committed to do the "little things," the daily D. of preparation. Pg. 75
>
> Win the battle between your EARS by what comes out of your HEART and through your MOUTH. Pg. 100

Fact.
> Corrective D. from one's parents is a way to life. Pg. 25
>
> Fools vent their anger, but the wise quietly hold it back. Pg. 159
>
> People who accept D. are on the pathway to life. Pg. 34
>
> The Lord corrects those He loves. Pg. 10
>
> To learn, you must love D. Pg. 50

Response to.
> Don't be upset when He corrects you. Pg. 10

The Ds. of a dedicated disciple of Jesus. Pg. 66

Warning.
> Do not reject the Lord's D. Pg. 10
>
> If you reject D., you only harm yourself. Pg. 79
>
> It is stupid to hate correction. Pg. 50
>
> Whoever abandons the right path will be severely D. Pg. 72

Discord
Warning. A person who sows D. in a family. The Lord hates, detests them. Pg. 24

Disgrace
Duty.
> Be a person of HONOR and never allow yourself to be a shameful E. and become a person of public DISGRACE. Pg. 103

Warning.
> Children who mistreat their father or chase away their mother are an embarrassment and a public disgrace. Pg. 103
>
> Don't lose your honor because of sexual sins. Pg. 18

If you ignore criticism, you will end in poverty and D. Pg. 61
Pride leads to D. Pg. 37
Sin is a D. to any people. Pg. 70

Dishonest—Dishonesty
Fact.
Better to have little, with godliness, than to be rich and D. Pg. 81
Loyalty makes a person attractive. It is better to be poor than D. Pg. 102
Better to be poor and honest than to be D. and a fool. Pg. 99
Warning.
D. destroys treacherous people. Pg. 38

Dispute
Duty.
Starting a quarrel is like opening a floodgate, so stop before a D. breaks out. Pg. 89
Fact.
The best way to stop an argument is not to start one. Pg. 89

Disraeli, Benjamin
Fact.
The secret of success in life is for a man to be ready for his time when it comes. Pg. 75
Quote of. Pg. 75

Ditch—Ditches
Duty.
Keep it between the D. and resist the urge to abandon the right path. Pg. 72

Divine
D. dining. Pg. 74

Do—Doing
Duty.
Know what you are D. before you D. it and take your time DO. what you know to D. so you may D. it well and enjoy it too. Pg. 99

Door—Doors
Fact.
Giving a gift can open D.; it gives access to important people! Pg. 97

Why being open to correction will open D. for you. Pg. 61

Dyer, Wayne
Quote of.
Transformation literally means going beyond your form. Pg. xi

Dream—Dreams—Dreamer—Dreaming
    A D. fulfilled is a tree of life. Pg. 57
    D. the kind of Ds. that only the D. MAKER can answer. Pg. 62
    Discovering the hope that fuels your D. Pg. 57
    Duty.
        Be bold enough to D. but humble enough to adjust and go. Pg. 82
        Be free to D. a D. that only God can answer. Pg. 80
        Commit your actions to the Lord, and your plans will succeed. Pg. 80
        Give every plan, every action, and every D. you have to the Lord who will bless you with the kind of success only He can give. Pg. 80
        Keep your hope alive and DARE to D. for dreams that only God can answer. Pg. 57
    Fact.
        It is pleasant to see D. come true. Pg. 62
        No limit to your D. Pg. 80
        We can make our own plans, but the Lord gives the right answer. Pg. 80
    Hope floats your D. Pg. 133
    Of destiny. Pg. 62
    Warning.
        Fools refuse to turn from evil to attain D. Pg. 62

E

Eagle
    Fact.
        Three things that amaze me—no, four things that I don't understand:
            How an E. glides through the sky. Pg. 163
    Warning.
        Don't wear yourself out trying to get rich. Be wise enough to know when to quit. In the blink of an eye wealth disappears, for it will sprout wings and fly away like an E. Pg. 126

Ear—Ears
    Duty.
        GUARD what your E. hear so that toxic WORDS will not leave your MOUTH. Pg. 114
        Guard your lips and protect your E. so your heart will be clear and pure. Pg. 87
        Win the battle between your E. by what comes out of your HEART and through your MOUTH. Pg. 100
    E. to hear. Pg. 119
    Fact.
        E. to hear and eyes to see—both are gifts from the Lord. Pg. 106

Eat
    Warning.
        If you love sleep, you will end in poverty. Keep your eyes open, and there will be plenty to E.! Pg. 107

Embarrass—Embarrassment
    Duty.
        Be a person of HONOR and never allow yourself to be a shameful E. and become a person of public DISGRACE. Pg. 103
    Warning.
        Children who mistreat their father or chase away their mother are an E. and a public disgrace. Pg. 103

Emerson, Ralph Waldo
    Quote of. Pg. 40
The only person you are destined to become is the person you decide to be.

Emotion—Emotions
    Duty.
        Do the things that will make you GLAD and not SAD. Pg. 72
    E. are real. Pg. 72

Employer
    Duty.
        Make sure you put the right people on your team. Pg. 142
    Fact.
        An E. who hires a fool or a bystander is like an archer who shoots at random. Pg. 142
    Warning.
        Never slander a worker to the E., or the person will curse you, and you will pay for it. Pg. 163

Enable—Enabler
    Charge.
        Seek to be an encourager and not an E. Pg. 23

Encourage—Encouragers—Encouragement—Encouraging
    Charge.
        Empowered to E. Pg. 40
        Seek to be an E. and not an enabler. Pg. 23
    Duty.
        Add value to those you love by intentionally using kind words that build them up. Pg. 84
        Be INTENTIONAL in your E. of your friends and build them up and resist the urge to FLATTER them and fatten up their pride and ego. Pg. 158
        Be willing to SPEAK the truth and E. your friends to make the kind of choice that will add great VALUE to them. Pg. 55
        E. one another day after day. Pg. 42
        E. the exhausted and strengthen the feeble. Pg. 42
        E. the fainthearted. Pg. 43
        Make sure every word you use builds someone up and not take them down. Pg. 85
        PRAY about WHO needs a GOOD and E. WORD from YOU and SHARE IT. Pg. 141

Save your energy of worrying about things you can't control and spend that energy
building up someone who needs some E. Pg. 54
Treat everyone you meet with impeccable fairness. Pg. 106
We are to bear the burdens of the weak. Pg. 41
We are to build up and encourage our neighbor. Pg. 41
We are to build others up with love. Pg. 41
We are to encourage one another and build each other up. Pg. 41, 43
We are to encourage with our words. Pg. 42
You must exhort those who have fallen into a deep hole and cannot get out by
themselves. [how? With great patience and instruction.] Pg. 130

Fact.
An edified disciple is a soul-winning disciple. Pg. 42
An E. word cheers a person up. Pg. 54
Are essential. Pg. 23
Good news from far away is like cold water to the thirsty. Pg. 141
Is not only a spiritual gift the Lord gives to the Body of Christ, but it is also an intentional
act of kindness that ANYONE who loves the Lord can do. Pg. 42
The words of the godly E. many. Pg. 34
The quality disciple is a direct product of an edified relationship. Pg. 42
Those who refresh others will themselves be refreshed. Pg. 48
We all need it. Pg. 40

How we are to E.
List. Pg. 41

Kind of.
Strong e. Pg. 43

List of Scriptures on E. Pg. 42

Son of.
Barnabas. Pg. 40

Strategic Plan of E. Pg. 42
Tools of E. Pg. 43
Why E. is superior to flattery. Pg. 158

Endure

Duty.
You are to E. hardship. Pg. 131

Enemy—Enemies

Duty.
If your E. are hungry, give them food to eat. If they are thirsty, give them water to drink.
You will heap burning coals of shame on their heads, and the Lord will reward you.
Pg. 140

Fact.
An open rebuke is better than hidden love! Wounds from a sincere friend are better than
many kisses from an E. Pg. 145
When people's lives please the Lord, even their E. are at peace with them. Pg. 81

Warning.

But one disaster is enough to overthrow the wicked. Don't rejoice when your E. fall; don't be happy when they stumble. For the Lord will be displeased with you and will turn his anger away from them. Pg. 137

Energy
- Duty.
  - Save your E. of worrying about things you can't control and spend that E. building up someone who needs some encouragement. Pg. 54

Enhance—Enhanced
- Fact.
  - The earnings of the godly E. their lives. Pg. 33

Entangle—Entangled—Entanglement
- Warning.
  - Be on your guard and not become E. with the kind of people who want to pull you down. Pg. 6

Enthusiasm
- Fact.
  - E. without knowledge is no good. Pg. 99

Evangelism
- Duty.
  - You are to do the work of an evangelist. Pg. 132

Evil
- Benefits of wisdom.
  - Will save you from E. people. Pg. 6
- Charge.
  - Turn away from E. Pg. 9
- Duty.
  - Keep your feet from following E. Pg. 17
- Fact.
  - E. people don't understand justice, but those who follow the Lord understand completely. Pg. 154
  - E. people get rich for the moment. Pg. 47
- Warning.
  - Don't envy E. people or desire their company. For their hearts plot violence, and their words always stir up trouble. Pg. 135
  - E. people squander their money on sin. Pg. 33
  - If you plan to do E., you will be lost. Pg. 67
  - The mouth of the wicked overflows with E. words. Pg. 78
- Words. Pg. 78

Eye—Eyes
- Duty.
  - Do whatever it takes to keep your E. on the prize of experiencing the abundant life. Pg. 26
  - Check your HEART before you trust your E. Pg. 117
  - Fix your E. on what lies before you. Pg. 17
  - Give Him your HEART so that your E. can follow His ways and ENJOY your life. Pg. 134
  - Give Him your heart. May your E. take delight in following His ways. Pg. 134
- Fact.
  - Ears to hear and E. to see—both are gifts from the Lord. Pg. 106
  - People may be pure in their own E., but the Lord examines their motives. Pg. 80
  - People may be right in their own E., but the Lord examines their heart. Pg. 117
- Haughty.
  - The Lord hates, detests them. Pg. 24
- Warning.
  - If you love sleep, you will end in poverty. Keep your E. open, and there will be plenty to eat! Pg. 107
  - Whoever gives to the poor will lack nothing, but those who close their E. to poverty will be cursed. Pg. 158

Example
- Duty.
  - Be an E. by doing good works of every kind. Pg. 60
  - Set the E. of living a transformed life. Pg. 60

Expectation—Expectations
- Warning.
  - The E. of the wicked come to nothing. Pg. 36

F

Face
- Duty.
  - KEEP a SMILE on your F. and in your HEART too. Pg. 78
- Fact.
  - A glad heart makes a happy F. Pg. 72

Fair—Fairness
- Fact.
  - The Lord demands accurate scales and balances; he sets the standards for F. Pg. 82
- Duty.
  - Treat everyone you meet with impeccable F. Pg. 106
- Warning.
  - False weights and unequal measures — the Lord detests double standards of every kind. Pg. 106

Faith
- Duty.
  - F. it out *now* before you try to FIGURE it out *then*. Pg. 115
- Fact.
  - The Lord directs our steps, so why try to understand everything along the way? Pg. 115

Fall
- Fact.
  - Pride goes before destruction, and haughtiness before a F. Pg. 83

False
- Fact.
  - A F. witness is a traitor. Pg. 68
- Warning.
  - A F. witness breathes lies. Pg. 64

Family
- Warning.
  - A person who sows discord in a F. The Lord hates, detests them. Pg. 24
  - Children who mistreat their father or chase away their mother are an embarrassment and a public disgrace. Pg. 103

Father
- Blessing of having godly parents.
  - Their command is a lamp. Pg. 25
  - Their corrective discipline is the way to life. Pg. 25
  - Their instruction is a light. Pg. 25
  - When you sleep, they will protect you. Pg. 25
  - When you wake up, they will advise you. Pg. 25
  - When you walk, their counsel will lead you. Pg. 25
- Duty.
  - Keep their words always in your heart. Pg. 25
  - Obey your father's commands. Pg. 25
  - Tie their words around your neck. Pg. 25
- Warning.
  - Children who mistreat their F. or chase away their mother are an embarrassment and a public disgrace. Pg. 103

Fault
- Fact.
  - Love prospers when a F. is forgiven. Pg. 88
- Warning.
  - Dwelling on a F. separates close friends. Pg. 88

Favor—Favored
- Duty.

Live your life in the F. of God. Pg. 35
How one can find F. with both God and people. Pg. 8
Whoever finds wisdom receives F. from the Lord. Pg. 28

Fear—Fearing
Duty.
Be more concerned about what the Lord says about you than what people say about you and to you. Pg. 161
Fact.
Better to have little, with F. for the Lord, than to have great treasure and inner turmoil. Pg. 73
True humility and F. of the Lord lead to riches, honor, and long life. Pg. 122
F. of the Lord leads to life, bringing security and protection from harm. Pg. 103
F. people is a dangerous trap, but trusting the Lord means safety. Pg. 161
No F. zone. Pg. 161
Of the Lord. Pg. 2, 4, 9, 30, 73, 79, 103, 122
Teaches wisdom. Pg. 79

Feast
Fact.
For the happy heart, life is a continual feast. Pg. 73

Feed—Feeds
Warning.
The fool F. on trash. Pg. 72

Feet
Duty.
Keep your F. from following evil. Pg. 17
Mark out a straight path for your F. Pg. 17
F. that race to do wrong. The Lord hates, detests them. Pg. 24

Field—Fields
Duty.
Do your planning and prepare your F. before building your house. Pg. 137

Fight
Charge.
Don't pick a F. without reason. Pg. 13
The best way to stop an argument is not to start one. Pg. 89
Fact.
Avoiding a F. is a mark of honor; only fools insist on quarreling. Pg. 104

Fire
Fact.
F. goes out without wood, and quarrels disappear when gossip stops. Pg. 143

F. tests the purity of silver and gold, but the Lord tests the heart. Pg. 87

Spiritual firefighter. Pg. 143

Flatter—Flattery—Flattering
Duty.
Be INTENTIONAL in your ENCOURAGEMENT of your friends and build them up and resist the urge to F. them and fatten up their pride and ego. Pg. 158
Fact.
In the end, people appreciate honest criticism far more than F. Pg. 157
Warning.
A lying tongue hates its victims, and F. words cause ruin. Pg. 143
To F. friends is to lay a trap for their feet. Pg. 158
Why encouragement is superior to F. Pg. 158

Flourish
Fact.
The godly F. like leaves in spring. Pg. 49

Focus—Focused
Duty.
Don't get sidetracked. Pg. 17
Fix your eyes on what lies before you. Pg. 17
F. your passion to keep your purity. Pg. 18
Keep your feet from following evil. Pg. 17
Keep your life between the DITCHES and stay on the JOYFUL PATH. Pg. 160
Look straight ahead. Pg. 17
Mark out a straight path for your feet. Pg. 17
Stay on the safe path. Pg. 17
To be laser F. upon His Words. Pg. 15

Food
Fact.
A hard worker has plenty of F., but a person who chases fantasies ends up in poverty. Pg. 156
Those too lazy to plow in the right season will have no F. at the harvest. Pg. 104
Duty.
Work like your meals depended upon it. Pg. 156

Fool—Fools—Foolish
Duty.
Always say YES to God's ways and NO to the things that may sound good but are F. Pg. 71
Be sure to answer the F. arguments of fools, or they will become wise in their own estimation. Pg. 142
Fact.
A F. is quick-tempered. Pg. 52
An employer who hires a F. or a bystander is like an archer who shoots at random. Pg. 142

A single rebuke does more for a person of understanding than a hundred lashes on the back of a F. Pg. 88
Are put to shame. Pg. 14
Avoiding a fight is a mark of honor; only F. insist on quarreling. Pg. 104
Better to be poor and honest than to be dishonest and a F. Pg. 99
F. broadcast their foolishness. Pg. 53
Fs. deceive themselves. Pg. 64
F. don't think before they act—and even brag about their foolishness. Pg. 61
F. think their own way is right. Pg. 52
F. vent their anger, but the wise quietly hold it back. Pg. 159
Short-tempered people do foolish things. Pg. 66
The heart of a F. is worthless. Pg. 34
There is more hope for a F. than for someone who speaks without thinking. Pg. 160

Babbling F fall flat on their faces. Pg. 31

Warning.
    Associate with F. and get in trouble. Pg. 62
    Babbling of a F invites disaster. Pg. 33
    Don't answer the foolish arguments of fools, or you will become as foolish as they are. Pg. 142
    Don't waste your breath on F., for they will despise the wisest advice. Pg. 126
    F. are destroyed by their lack of common sense. Pg. 34
    F. plunge ahead with reckless confidence. Pg. 66
    F. refuse to turn from evil to attain dreams. Pg. 62
    Slandering others makes you a F. Pg. 34
    The effort of F. yields only foolishness. Pg. 67
    The F. feeds on trash. Pg. 72
    The mouth of a F. belches out foolishness. Pg. 70

What they despise. Pg. 2
The best way to defeat a person who is difficult. Pg. 142

Foolishness

Fact.
    Fools don't think before they act—and even brag about their F. Pg. 61
    People ruin their lives by their own F. and then are angry at the Lord. Pg. 100
    Simpletons are clothed with F. Pg. 66

Warning.
    A hot temper shows great F. Pg. 68
    Fools broadcast their F. Pg. 53
    Get wisdom before F. gets you. Pg. 14
    The mouth of a fool belches out F. Pg. 70

Fork

In the road. Pg. 13

Forget—Forgetful

Duty.

Never F. what God has taught you. Pg. 7

Forgive—Forgiven—Forgiveness
Duty.
F. when you find a FAULT, LOVE when you would rather LASH out, and GIVE GRACE because you need it too. Pg. 88
Fact.
Love prospers when a fault is F. Pg. 88
Warning.
Dwelling on a fault separates close friends. Pg. 88

Fortress
Fact.
The name of the Lord is a strong F. Pg. 95

Foundation
Fact.
Fear of the Lord is the F. of wisdom. Pg. 30
Key to building your life on a firm F. Pg. 35

Fountain
Fact.
The instruction of the wise is like a life-giving F. Pg. 58

Frankl, Viktor E.
Quote of.
When we are no longer able to change a situation, we are challenged to change ourselves.
Pg. xi

Friend—Friends—Friendship
Duty.
Be a GOOD F. by being a GOOD LISTENER so you will be able to give GOOD ADVICE that will help your F. have a GOOD DAY. Pg. 105
Be INTENTIONAL in your ENCOURAGEMENT of your F. and build them up and resist the urge to FLATTER them and fatten up their pride and ego. Pg. 158
Be on the lookout for sharp F. who will make you sharper and not allow dull acquaintances to suck the life out of you and make you lose your edge. Pg. 146
Be the kind of F. you need to be for you. Pg. 89
Be the kind of trusted friend your intimate circle of friends needs from you. Pg. 98
Be the most LOYAL and RELIABLE F. you know. Pg. 105
Cultivate the kinds of F. that when everything hits the fan your F. will be your biggest fans. Pg. 145
Make it your goal to ADD VALUE to everyone you meet. Pg. 49
Never abandon a F.—either yours or your father's. When disaster strikes, you won't have to ask your brother for assistance. It's better to go to a neighbor than to a brother who lives far away. Pg. 146

Treat everyone you meet with impeccable fairness. Pg. 106
Fact.
> A friend is always loyal, and a brother is born to help in time of need. Pg. 89
>
> An open rebuke is better than hidden love! Wounds from a sincere F. are better than many kisses from an enemy. Pg. 145
>
> As iron sharpens iron, so a F. sharpens a F. Pg. 146
>
> Arguments separate F. like a gate locked with bars. Pg. 97
>
> A wise person wins F. Pg. 49
>
> Good to have a good friend for good. Pg. 105
>
> It's poor judgment to guarantee another person's debt or put up security for a F. Pg. 94
>
> Many will say they are loyal F., but who can find one who is truly reliable? Pg. 105
>
> The heartfelt counsel of a F. is as sweet as perfume and incense. Pg. 145

Fanclub. Pg. 145
F. qualities that matter. Pg. 105
Kind of.
> Best kind of. Pg. 89
>
> Good. Pg. 105
>
> Loyal. Pg. 105
>
> Truly reliable. Pg. 105
>
> Winning. Pg. 49

Warning.
> A gossip separates the best of F. Pg. 85
>
> An offended F. is harder to win back than a fortified city. Pg. 97
>
> Don't befriend angry people or associate with hot-tempered people, or you will learn to be like them and endanger your soul. Pg. 124
>
> Dwelling on a fault separates close F. Pg. 88
>
> Guaranteeing another's debt. Pg. 23
>
> The wicked lead their F. astray. Pg. 55
>
> There are "F." who destroy each other, but a real F. sticks closer than a brother. Pg. 98
>
> To flatter friends is to lay a trap for their feet. Pg. 158

What real F. do. Pg. 98

Fruit

Kind of.
> Abundant. Pg. 9

Full—Fulfill

Duty.
> You are to F. your ministry. Pg. 132

Future

Fact.
> My child, eat honey, for it is good, and the honeycomb is sweet to the taste. In the same way, wisdom is sweet to your soul. If you find it, you will have a bright F., and your hopes will not be cut short. Pg. 136

G

Garbage
- Warning.
  - Guard yourself from the G. Pg. 114

Give—Given—Giver

- Blessing of being a giver.
  - He will fill your barns with grain. Pg. 10
  - Your vats will overflow with good wine. Pg. 10
- Charge.
  - Honor the Lord with your W. Pg. 10
- Duty.
  - Have a BIG heart to meet the BIG needs of those who may be less fortunate than you. Pg. 101
- Fact.
  - Some people are always greedy for more, but the godly love to G.! Pg. 120
- How.
  - G. back to God what He has already given to you. Pg. 9
- Responsibility of.
  - Honor the Lord with your W. Pg. 10

Generous
- Duty.
  - Work SMARTER and HARDER so you can EARN MORE to GIVE AWAY. Pg. 57
- Fact.
  - Blessed are those who are G., because they feed the poor. Pg. 123
  - The G. will prosper. Pg. 48

Gentle
- Fact.
  - A G. answer deflects anger. Pg. 70
  - G. words are a tree of life. Pg. 70

Gift—Gifts
- Duty.
  - BE THE G. that ADDS VALUE to important people. Pg. 97
- Fact.
  - A man's G. makes room for him and brings him before great men. Pg. 148
  - Ears to hear and eyes to see—both are G. from the Lord. Pg. 106
  - Giving a G. can open doors; it gives access to important people! Pg. 97
- Power G. Pg. 97
- Warning.
  - A person who promises a G. but doesn't give it is like clouds and wind that bring no rain. Pg. 140

Give—Giver—Giving
    Duty.
        Work SMARTER and HARDER so you can EARN MORE to G. AWAY. Pg. 57

Glad
    Duty.
        Do the things that will make you G. and not SAD. Pg. 72
        Make your finest effort to help everyone you know be G. Pg. 155
    Fact.
        A G. heart makes a happy face. Pg. 72
        When the godly succeed, everyone is G. When the wicked take charge, people go into hiding. Pg. 155
    G. to be G. Pg. 155

Glory
    Fact.
        Gray hair is a crown of G.; it is gained by living a godly life. Pg. 85

Graham, Billy
    Fact.
        Not everyone has the gift of evangelism that God has granted B. G. Pg. 132
    Quote of.
        The Psalms tell us how to get along with God, and the Proverbs tell us how to get along with our fellow man. Pg. x

Goal—Goals
    To be the most loyal and kind person I know. Pg. 8

God
    Bigness Of. Pg. 161
    Duty.
        Do not MUDDLE in the MUNDANE but instead live your life always AMAZED by an AMAZING G. who delights in showing off His glory to you. Pg. 163
        Give your big problems to a BIGGER G. Pg. 161
    Fact.
        Every word of G. proves true. He is a shield to all who come to him for protection. Pg. 162
        The Lord corrects those He loves. Pg. 10
    How to know G. really loves you. Pg. 10
    Seven things He hates. Pg. 24
    Where is G. when it hurts? Pg. 108

Godly—Godliness
    Blessing of.
        Are showered with blessings. Pg. 31
        The lips of the G. speak helpful words. Pg. 37
        The words of the G. are a life-giving fountain. Pg. 32

Duty.
> As you get older, get wiser by becoming more G. Pg. 85
> Do your part to make your nation great by living a life of G. Pg. 70

Fact.
> Better to have little, with G., than to be rich and dishonest. Pg. 81
> Gray hair is a crown of glory; it is gained by living a G. life. Pg. 85
> G. makes a nation great. Pg. 70
> Only the G. will live in the land. Pg. 7
> Plans of the G. are just. Pg. 51
> Reward of the G. will last. Pg. 47
> Some people are always greedy for more, but the G. love to give! Pg. 120
> The earnings of the G. enhance their lives. Pg. 33
> The G. are directed by honesty. Pg. 38
> The G. care about the rights of the poor; the wicked don't care at all. Pg. 159
> The G. give good advice to their friends. Pg. 55
> The G. have a lasting foundation. Pg. 35
> The G. have deep roots. Pg. 50
> The G. flourish like leaves in spring. Pg. 49
> The godly may trip seven times, but they will get up again. Pg. 137
> The G. of good people rescues them. Pg. 38
> The godly run to him and are safe. Pg. 95
> The heart of the G. thinks carefully before speaking. Pg. 78
> The hopes of the G. result in happiness. Pg. 36
> The Lord loves those who pursue G. Pg. 71
> The Lord will not let the G. go hungry. Pg. 31
> The way of the G. leads to life; that path does not lead to death. Pg. 55
> The whole city celebrates when the G. succeed. Pg. 39
> The words of the G. are like sterling silver. Pg. 34
> When the G. succeed, everyone is glad. When the wicked take charge, people go into hiding. Pg. 155
> The words of the G. save lives. Pg. 51

G. gray. Pg. 85

Gold—Golden

Duty.
> Choose knowledge rather than G. Pg. 27

Fact.
> Being held in high esteem is better than silver or G. Pg. 121
> Fire tests the purity of silver and G., but the Lord tests the heart. Pg. 87
> How much better to get wisdom than G., and good judgment than silver! Pg. 82
> Timely advice is lovely, like G. apples in a silver basket. To one who listens, valid criticism is like a G. earring or other G. jewelry. Pg. 139
> Wisdom's gifts are better than G. Pg. 28
> Wisdom's wages are better than G. Pg. 11
> Wise words are more valuable than much G. and many rubies. Pg. 114

Golden Rule
    Duty.
        Set your heart to live by the G. R. and not be ruled by a poisonous plot. Pg. 143
    The benefits of living by the G.R. Pg. 143

Good
    Charge.
        Do not withhold G. from those who deserve it. Pg. 13
    Fact.
        Be a G. FRIEND by being a G. LISTENER so you will be able to give G. ADVICE that will help your friend have a G. DAY. Pg. 105
        G. to have a G. friend for G. Pg. 105
        If you plan to do G., you will receive unfailing love and faithfulness. Pg. 67
        The Lord approves of those who are G. Pg. 50

Good Deeds
    Charge.
        THINK good thoughts, do G. D., and make a good CONTRIBUTION to your community. Pg. 50
    Fact.
        The seeds of G. D. become a tree of life. Pg. 49

Good News
    Fact.
        G. N. from far away is like cold water to the thirsty. Pg. 141

Gordon, Arthur
    Quote of.
        Nothing is easier than saying words. Nothing is harder than living them day after day. Pg. 128

Gospel
    Duty.
        Preach the Word. Pg. 128
        You must be ready at any moment to share the G. Pg. 129

Gossip
    Duty.
        Make sure every word you use builds someone up and not take them down. Pg. 85
        Resist the urge to join a gossip party and instead look for ways to speak well of those who are being slandered. Pg. 143
    Fact.
        Fire goes out without wood, and quarrels disappear when G. stops. Pg. 143
    No G. zone. Pg. 85
    Warning.
        A G. goes around telling secrets. Pg. 45, 115

A G. separates the best of friends. Pg. 85
Wrongdoers eagerly listen to G. Pg. 87

GPS
God's GPS for you. Pg. 37

Grace
Duty.
Do an act of kindness for someone who could never repay you. Pg. 69
FORGIVE when you find a FAULT, LOVE when you would rather LASH out, and GIVE
Choose to give up a chance to stir up anger and instead stir up love, peace, and G. Pg. 164
G. because you need it too. Pg. 88
Give G. to those who do not deserve it. Pg. 52
REJOICE when G. has comforted you and may you have COMPASSION on those who need
His G. too. Pg. 137
Fact.
G. says that God never wastes anything in our life—even the most difficult of things.
Pg. 110
Is free. Pg. 52
Why G. and compassion matter. Pg. 137

Grain
Blessing of being a giver.
He will fill your barns with grain. Pg. 10

Gray
Fact.
G. hair is a crown of glory; it is gained by living a godly life. Pg. 85

Great
Saying yes to the G. and no to the good. Pg. 71

Greed—Greedy
Fact.
G. causes fighting; trusting the Lord leads to prosperity. Pg. 158
Some people are always G. for more, but the godly love to give! Pg. 120
Fate of those who are G. for money. Pg. 3
No G. Zone. Pg. 2

Grief
Fact.
Laughter can conceal a heavy heart, but when the laughter ends, the G. remains. Pg. 65

Grow—Growth
- Duty.
  - Create a personal G. plan. Pg. 76
  - Love yourself enough to G. yourself enough to be a blessing to others. Pg. 100
- Embrace this posture of humility: the more I know the less I know thus the need to keep learning more and more. Pg. 78
- Fact.
  - If you listen to correction, you G. in understanding. Pg. 79
- Have an open MIND to learn more, an open HEART to change more and an open LIFE to show more of God's grace at work in you. Pg. 61
- Three suggestions on how a Quality Leader can experience G. Pg. 76

Guard—Guarding
- Duty.
  - G. what your EARS hear so that toxic WORDS will not leave your MOUTH. Pg. 114
  - G. your heart so you will not LOSE your soul. Pg. 124
- G. yourself from the garbage. Pg. 114
- How to G.
  - With your own eyes. Pg. 26
  - Write God's commands deep within your heart. Pg. 26
- Reason why you are to G. your heart.
  - It determines the course of your life. Pg. 16
- Warning.
  - Be on your G. and do not become entangled with the kind of people who want to pull you down. Pg. 6
  - Guard your heart above all else. Pg. 16
- What to G.
  - His instructions as you G. your own eyes. Pg. 26

Guidance
- Fact.
  - When people do not accept divine G., they run wild. But whoever obeys the law is joyful. Pg. 160

H

Hair
- Fact.
  - Gray H. is a crown of glory; it is gained by living a godly life. Pg. 85

Hand—Hands
- That kill the innocent. The Lord hates, detests them. Pg. 24

Happy—Happiness
- Fact.
  - A glad heart makes a H. face. Pg. 72

Make the kind of choices that will produce within you a H. heart and a satisfied soul. Pg. 73

The hopes of the godly result in H. Pg. 36

Result of.

Having a deep and abiding relationship with God's wisdom. Pg. 11

Hardship

Duty.

You are to endure H. Pg. 131

Harm

Fact.

Fear of the Lord leads to life, bringing security and protection from H. Pg. 103

Harvest—Harvests

Fact.

A wise youth H. in the summer. Pg. 31

Those too lazy to plow in the right season will have no food at the H. Pg. 104

You need a strong ox for a large H. Pg. 63

Warning.

One who sleeps during H. is a disgrace. Pg. 31

Haste

Warning.

H. makes mistakes. Pg. 99

Hate—Hater—Hatred

Duty.

Be a lover not a H. Pg. 32

Warning.

Hiding H. makes you a liar. Pg. 34

Stirs up quarrels. Pg. 33

Haughty—Haughtiness

Fact.

Pride goes before destruction, and H. before a fall. Pg. 83

Warning.

H. goes before destruction. Pg. 96

Heal—Healed—Healing

Benefit of.

Letting His words penetrate deep into your heart. Pg. 15

Fact.

The words of the wise bring H. Pg. 53

How it comes.

For your body. Pg. 9

Health—Healthy
- Duty.
  - Experience a peaceful, easy feeling, and avoid making any decision that will poison your life. Pg. 69
- Fact.
  - A peaceful heart leads to a H. body. Pg. 69
  - Good news makes for good H. Pg. 78
  - Jealousy is like cancer in the bones. Pg. 69
- Secrets to H. living. Pg. 69

Heart—Hearts
- Benefit of putting God's Word in your H. Pg. 7
- Charge.
  - Be willing to check your H. and be humble. Pg. 10
- Duty.
  - Be the good medicine to those whose H. is breaking. Pg. 94
  - Bless your H. so you can bless others. Pg. 123
  - Check your H. before you trust your EYES. Pg. 117
  - Do not allow your H. to mess with your mind. Pg. 125
  - Give Him your H. so that your EYES can follow His ways and ENJOY your life. Pg. 134
  - Give Him your H. May your eyes take delight in following His ways. Pg. 134
  - Give someone a piece of your H. before you give them a piece of your MIND. Pg. 167
  - Guard your lips and protect your ears so your H. will be clear and pure. Pg. 87
  - Have a BIG H. for the people who need your COMPASSION and your CARE. Pg. 159
  - Have a BIG H. that will care for the BIG NEEDS of people who need BIG LOVE from YOU. Pg. 166
  - Have a keen awareness of the material needs of others who are not as fortunate as you and have a tender H. for them. Pg. 158
  - Have a H. of HUMILITY that will be open to ADVICE and SUCCEED. Pg. 58
  - Keep an OPEN H. to have a LEARNING H. so you will have a TRUSTING H. in the Lord. Pg. 124
  - KEEP a SMILE on your FACE and in your H. too. Pg. 78
  - Keep INTEGRITY in full view knowing that your HONESTY will give you the right to influence someone's H. Pg. 82
  - Keep the right words in your H. so you can bless the H. of another. Pg. 123
  - Listen to the words of the wise; apply your H. to my instruction. For it is good to keep these sayings in your H. and always ready on your lips. Pg. 123
  - Set your heart to live by the GOLDEN rule and not be ruled by a poisonous plot. Pg. 143
  - To store His commands in your H. Pg. 7
  - Win the battle between your EARS by what comes out of your H. and through your MOUTH. Pg. 100
  - Write God's commands deep within your H. Pg. 26
- Fact.
  - A big H. is a caring H. Pg. 159
  - A broken H. crushes the spirit. Pg. 72
  - A cheerful look brings joy to the H. Pg. 78

A cheerful H. is good medicine, but a broken spirit saps a person's strength. Pg. 94
A glad H. makes a happy face. Pg. 72
A peaceful H. leads to a healthy body. Pg. 69
Each H. knows its own bitterness, and no one else can fully share its joy. Pg. 65
Fire tests the purity of silver and gold, but the Lord tests the H. Pg. 87
For the happy H., life is a continual feast. Pg. 73
Laughter can conceal a heavy H., but when the laughter ends, the grief remains. Pg. 65
People may be right in their own eyes, but the Lord examines their H. Pg. 117
Though good advice lies deep within the H., a person with understanding will draw it out. Pg. 105

H. check. Pg. 87, 117
Kind of.
    A broken H. Pg. 72
    A discerning H. Pg. 135
    A glad H. Pg. 72
    A happy H. Pg. 73
    A peaceful H. Pg. 69
Open H., open mind, growing life. Pg. 124
Reason why you are to guard your H.
    It determines the course of your life. Pg. 16
The benefits of having a tender heart for the poor. Pg. 158
The blessing of having a humble H. Pg. 58
RX for the H. Pg. 94
Warning.
    A H. that plots evil. The Lord hates, detests it. Pg. 24
    Be careful to learn the balance between using your head and your H. Pg. 46
    Don't envy evil people or desire their company. For their H. plot violence, and their words always stir up trouble. Pg. 135
    Give your H. to only those who will PROTECT it and not POISON it. Pg. 135
    Guard your H. above all else. Pg. 16
    Guard your H. before you break your neck. Pg. 83
    GUARD your H. so you will not LOSE your soul. Pg. 124
    Hope deferred makes the H. sick. Pg. 57
    The H. of a fool has no wise advice to give. Pg. 71
    The H. of a fool is worthless. Pg. 34
    The Lord detests people with crooked H. Pg. 47
    The Lord hates, detests them. Pg. 24
Wisdom will enter your H. Pg. 5

Head
    Warning.
        Be careful to learn the balance between using your H. and your heart. Pg. 46

Health—Healthy
    Fact.
        Kind words are sweet to the soul and H. for the body. Pg. 84

Help—Helping
    Fact.
        H. the poor honors your Maker. Pg. 69

Helpless
    Duty.
        Speak up for the poor and H., and see that they get justice. Pg. 164

Hemingway, Ernest
    Quote of.
        There is nothing noble in being superior to your fellow man; true nobility is being superior to your former self. Pg. xi

High
    Experiencing a supernatural H. Pg. 36
    H. hopes. Pg. 36

High Road
    Duty.
        If your enemies are hungry, give them food to eat. If they are thirsty, give them water to drink. You will heap burning coals of shame on their heads, and the Lord will reward you. Pg. 140
        Take the H. R. no matter how LOW your adversary may GO. Pg. 140
    Why you need to take the H. R. Pg. 140

Home
    Blessing of.
        The Lord blesses the H. of the upright. Pg. 13

Honest—Honesty
    Duty.
        Be H. to others, H. to yourself, and above all, H. to God. Pg. 38
        Be H. with others, H. with yourself, and H. to God. Pg. 99
        Be on the Lord's side and treat people with H. and respect, especially the ones who are on the other side of the power relationship and cannot defend themselves. Pg. 127
        Keep INTEGRITY in full view knowing that your H. will give you the right to influence someone's HEART. Pg. 82
        Live an attractive life by being LOYAL and H. Pg. 102
        Make a commitment to earn an H. dollar by telling and living the TRUTH before others and before God. Pg. 118
        Set in your heart to be THE REAL DEAL in your character with those who are depending upon you to be H. and TRUE. Pg. 47
    Fact.
        An H. witness does not lie. Pg. 64
        Better to be poor and H. than to be dishonest and a fool. Pg. 99

Better to be poor and H. than to be dishonest and rich. Pg. 155
Better to have little, with godliness, than to be rich and dishonest. Pg. 81
H. guides good people. Pg. 38
The godly are directed by H. Pg. 38
The Lord demands accurate scales and balances; He sets the standards for fairness. Pg. 82

God grants a treasure of common sense to the H. Pg. 5

The H. legacy. Pg. 127

Warning.
Dishonesty destroys treacherous people. Pg. 38

Honey
Fact.
Kind words are like H. Pg. 84
My child, eat H., for it is good, and the honeycomb is sweet to the taste. In the same way, wisdom is sweet to your soul. If you find it, you will have a bright future, and your hopes will not be cut short. Pg. 136

Honor—Honors—Honorable
A legacy of generational H. Pg. 103

Charge.
Be a person of H. and never allow yourself to be a shameful EMBARRASSMENT and become a person of public DISGRACE. Pg. 103
H. the Lord with your wealth. Pg. 10
Set your sight on LIVING RIGHT and pursuing the kind of LOVE that never FAILS and then fully experience LIFE, RIGHTEOUSNESS, and H. Pg. 119

Duty.
Fix your mind on what is H., or honest, noble, and highly respected. 150

Fact.
Helping the poor H. your Maker. Pg. 69
H. thoughts are uplifting thoughts. Pg. 151
Humility precedes H. Pg. 79, 96
If you accept correction, you will be H. Pg. 61
Pride ends in humiliation, while humility brings H. Pg. 160
The wise inherit H. Pg. 14
True humility and fear of the Lord lead to riches, H., and long life. Pg. 122
Whoever pursues righteousness and unfailing love will find life, righteousness, and H. Pg. 119

Humility with H. Pg. 96

Result of.
Having a deep and abiding relationship with God's wisdom. Pg. 11

Warning.
Don't lose your H. because of sexual sins. Pg. 18

Hope—Hopes
    Duty.
        Gladly ACCEPT all that the Lord has provided for you and keep your H. alive. Pg. 134
        Keep your H. alive and DARE to DREAM the dreams that only God can answer. Pg. 57
    Fact.
        Don't envy sinners, but always continue to fear the Lord. You will be rewarded for this; your H. will not be disappointed. Pg. 134
        My child, eat honey, for it is good, and the honeycomb is sweet to the taste. In the same way, wisdom is sweet to your soul. If you find it, you will have a bright future, and your H. will not be cut short. Pg. 136
    H. floats your dreams. Pg. 133
    Warning.
        H. deferred makes the heart sick. Pg. 57

House
    Duty.
        Do your planning and prepare your fields before building your H. Pg. 137
    Fact.
        A H. is built by wisdom and becomes strong through good sense. Pg. 135
    Warning.
        The Lord curses the H. of the wicked. Pg. 13

Huffty, Stanley
    Quote of.
        It's not the position that makes the leader; it's the leader that makes the position. Pg. 59

Humble—Humility
    Charge.
        Be open to the Lord's loving correction. Pg. 10
        Be willing to check your heart and be H. Pg. 10
        Love H. so that you may embrace discipline and correction and LEARN. Pg. 50
    Duty.
        Be bold enough to dream but H. enough to adjust and go. Pg. 82
        Be willing to be H. when you are WRONG and be willing to be H. when you are RIGHT. Pg. 79
        Be WILLING to hear a CONSTRUCTIVE CRITIQUE from those who are WILLING to tell you the TRUTH about you. Pg. 145
        Be willing to receive CORRECTION when a CORRECTION is needed. Pg. 88
        Be willing to take some good advice that will make you an even better version of you. Pg. 139
        Don't demand an audience with the king or push for a place among the great. It's better to wait for an invitation to the head table than to be sent away in public disgrace. Pg. 139
        Have a heart of H. that will be open to ADVICE and SUCCEED. Pg. 58
        LOOK UP to the Lord before you LOOK DOWN on those who are not as fortunate as you. Pg. 87

Practice the things that make you a H. hero and not a HUMILIATED heel. Pg. 160
Embrace this posture of H: the more I know the less I know thus the need to keep learning more and more. Pg. 78
Fact.
An open rebuke is better than hidden love! Wounds from a sincere friend are better than many kisses from an enemy. Pg. 145
A single rebuke does more for a person of understanding than a hundred lashes on the back of a fool. Pg. 88
God is gracious to the H. Pg. 14
H. precedes honor. Pg. 79, 96
If you listen to constructive criticism, you will be at home among the wise. Pg. 78
It's not about you. Pg. 22
Pride ends in humiliation, while H. brings honor. Pg. 160
Seek to be the wisest, most H. person you know. Pg. 79
Timely advice is lovely, like golden apples in a silver basket. To one who listens, valid criticism is like a gold earring or other gold jewelry. Pg. 139
True H. and fear of the Lord lead to riches, honor, and long life. Pg. 122
With H. comes wisdom. Pg. 37
H. rules. Pg. 79
The blessing of having a H. heart. Pg. 58
Warning.
Duty.
Allow the Lord to PROMOTE you before you PROMOTE yourself. Pg. 139
Don't be proud of your H. Pg. 37
Guard your heart from being proud of your H. Pg. 37
Never become proud of your H. Pg. 96
Pride leads to disgrace. Pg. 37
With honor. Pg. 96

Hunger—Hungry
Duty.
Feed the people who H. for the kinds of words that produce VALIDATION for those who need to experience SATISFACTION. Pg. 97
Work like your meals depend upon it. Pg. 156
Fact.
A wise person is H. for knowledge. Pg. 72
H. works. Pg. 156
The Lord will not let the godly go H. Pg. 31
Those too lazy to plow in the right season will have no food at the harvest. Pg. 104

Hurt—Hurts
Where is God when it H.? Pg. 108

Husband
The blessing of having a godly, virtuous and capable wife.
A hard worker. Pg. 165

Her husband can trust her. Pg. 165
Her lamp burns late into the night. Pg. 166
She brings him good, not harm all the days of her life. Pg. 165
She extends a helping hand to the poor. Pg. 166
She gives instructions with kindness. Pg. 167
She goes to inspect a field and buys it. Pg. 165
She is clothed with strength and dignity. Pg. 166
She is energetic and strong. Pg. 165
She is more precious than rubies. Pg. 165
She laughs without fear of the future. Pg. 166
She makes sure her dealings are profitable. Pg. 166
She opens her arms to the needy. Pg. 166
She will greatly enrich his life. Pg. 165
When she speaks, her words are wise. Pg. 167
With her earnings she plants a vineyard. Pg. 165

I

Identity
- Fact.
  - A healthy view of your I. (who you are) empowers you to go beyond yourself and serve others. Pg. 92
  - Having clarity about our I. empowers us. Pg.92
  - Your I. matters. Pg. 90

Imitate—Imitation—Imitators
- Example of.
  - I. of "us and of the Lord." Pg. 59
- Fact.
  - The "right" kind of I. can change the world. And the wrong kind can as well. Pg. 59

Incense
- Fact.
  - The heartfelt counsel of a friend is as sweet as perfume and I. Pg. 145

Influence—Influencing
- A life of. Pg. 1
- Duty.
  - Keep INTEGRITY in full view knowing that your HONESTY will give you the right to I. someone's HEART. Pg. 82
  - Speak up for the poor and helpless, and see that they get justice. Pg. 164
  - Speak up for those who cannot speak for themselves; ensure justice for those being crushed. Pg. 164
  - Treat everyone you meet with impeccable fairness. Pg. 106
  - Use your I. to INTERCEDE for those who are INNOCENT. Pg. 164
- Fact.

All of us are I. someone else. Pg. 59
A man's gift makes room for him and brings him before great men. Pg. 148
God has called us to Intentionally I. others for good. Pg. 60
I. is a gift; it is a trust. Pg. 59
Integrity gives you the right to I. others. Pg. 82
Integrity Impacts your I. Pg. 32
Intentional I. Pg. 59
Nine strategic steps for impacting the world through your life and ministry. Pg. 128

Insight
Cry out for I. Pg. 4

Instruct—Instructed—Instruction—Instructions
Duty.
Be wise enough to listen to good I. and trusting enough to be joyful. Pg. 83
Get all the advice and I. you can, so you will be wise the rest of your life. Pg. 101
Take hold of His instructions; don't let them go. Pg. 15
I. the wise. Pg. 29
Listen to the words of the wise; apply your heart to my I. For it is good to keep these sayings in your heart and always ready on your lips. Pg. 123

Fact.
The I. of the wise is like a life-giving fountain. Pg. 58
The wise are glad to be I. Pg. 31
Those who listen to instruction will prosper. Pg. 83

Warning.
If you stop listening to I., my child, you will turn your back on knowledge. Pg. 104

Insult—Insulted
Fact.
A wise person stays calm when I. Pg. 52

Integrity
Blessing of.
Benefits of a life driven by I. Pg. 38
People with I. walk safely. Pg. 32

Duty.
Be a person of your word and be satisfied with whatever provisions God may send your way. Pg. 162
Do whatever it takes to keep your I. intact and your love for the Lord INTENSE. Pg. 65
Keep I. in full view knowing that your HONESTY will give you the right to influence someone's HEART. Pg. 82
Keep your I. in what you think and in what you say and in what you do. Pg. 87
Let YOUR PERSONAL I. be the greatest gift you give everyone you meet. Pg. 36
Let everything you do reflect the integrity and seriousness of your T. Pg. 60
Live like your PERSONAL I. is the greatest gift you will give someone else. Pg. 38

Make every business decision with a commitment to live out the teachings of Jesus with your own PERSONAL I. and WORK ETHIC. Pg. 125

Set in your heart to be THE REAL DEAL in your character with those who are depending upon you to be HONEST and TRUE. Pg. 47

Treat everyone you meet with impeccable fairness. Pg. 106

Your word is your bond. Pg. 162

Fact.
- Gives you the right to influence others. Pg. 82
- Impacts your influence. Pg. 32
- I. matters in everything you believe and practice. Pg. 60
- Only those with I. will remain in the land. Pg. 7
- The Lord delights in those with I. Pg. 47
- The way of the Lord is a stronghold to those with integrity. Pg. 36

God is a shield to those who walk with I. Pg. 5

Warning.
- Don't cheat your neighbor by moving the ancient boundary markers set up by previous generations. Pg. 125
- If you set a trap for others, you will get caught in it yourself. If you roll a boulder down on others, it will crush you instead. Pg. 143

Intelligent

Fact.
- I. people are always ready to learn. Their ears are open for knowledge. Pg. 96

Intense

Duty.
- Do whatever it takes to keep your integrity intact and your love for the Lord INTENSE. Pg. 65

Intentional—Intentionally

Charge.
- Look for those who take the baton from you and win. Pg. 22

Duty.
- Be I. and use your words for good. Pg. 34
- Be I. in experiencing a focused and fruitful life. Pg. 65
- Be I. on using wise words and working hard so you may be SUCCESSFUL. Pg. 51
- Do whatever it TAKES to get whatever you WANT to do with whatever you WISH as long as you do it for the RIGHT reasons. Pg. 56
- Make an I. decision that everything you THINK, SAY, and DO will be based upon what is TRUE. Pg. 64
- Treat everyone you meet with impeccable fairness. Pg. 106

Fact.
- God has called us to I. influence others for good. Pg. 60
- Integrity matters in everything you believe and practice. Pg. 60

Invest—Investment—Investments
- Duty.
  - Make the right kinds of LIFE I. that will pay off in dividends not only NOW but well into the FUTURE. Pg. 47
  - SPEND your life on things that really MATTER and SPEND your money to FUND the things that really MATTER. Pg. 49
- Kindness as an I. Pg. 46
- Kind of.
  - Life. Pg. 47, 49
  - In people. Pg. 29
  - Time I. Pg. 29

Iron
- Fact.
  - As I. sharpens I., so a friend sharpens a friend. Pg. 146

J

Jealous—Jealousy
- Fact.
  - J. is like cancer in the bones. Pg. 69

Jehovah Jireh
- Meaning of.
  - My Provider. Pg. 126
- Warning.
  - Don't wear yourself out trying to get rich. Be wise enough to know when to quit. In the blink of an eye wealth disappears, for it will sprout wings and fly away like an eagle. Pg. 126

Jesus
- Quote of. The value of abiding, remaining.
  - *But if you remain in me and my words remain in you, you may ask for anything you want, and it will be granted! When you produce much fruit, you are my true disciples. This brings great glory to my Father.* Pg. xi

Joy—Joyful
- Blessing of.
  - J. are those who listen to wisdom. Pg. 28
  - To experience a J. day. Pg. 28
- Consequences of being a person of J. Pg. 11
- Duty.
  - Be wise enough to listen to good instruction and trusting enough to be J. Pg. 83
- Fact.
  - A cheerful look brings J. to the heart. Pg. 78
  - Each heart knows its own bitterness, and no one else can fully share its J. Pg. 65

Those who trust the Lord will be J. Pg. 83
Person of J. Pg. 11
Wisdom will fill you with J. Pg. 5

Judge—Judgment
Charge.
Develop good J. Pg. 14
Duty.
Use good J. Pg. 26
Fact.
Knowledge of the Holy One results in good J. Pg. 30
How much better to get wisdom than gold, and good J. than silver! Pg. 82

Just
Plans of the godly are J. Pg. 51

Justice
Duty.
Speak up for the poor and helpless, and see that they get J. Pg. 164
Speak up for those who cannot speak for themselves; ensure J. for those being crushed. Pg. 164
Fact.
Evil people don't understand J., but those who follow the Lord understand completely. Pg. 154

K

Key—Keys
To a wildly successful life. Pg. 8

Kind—Kindness
As an investment. Pg. 46
Charge.
Be the KIND of person who intentionally does KIND things for people who need to experience your KINDNESS. Pg. 46
Do an act of K. for someone who could never repay you. Pg. 69
Never let loyalty and K. leave you. Pg. 8
Set your goal to be the most loyal and K. person you know. Pg. 8
Fact.
K. words are like honey. Pg. 84
K. words are sweet to the soul and healthy for the body. Pg. 84
Your K. will reward you. Pg. 46

King—Kings
Duty.

Don't demand an audience with the K. or push for a place among the great. It's better to wait for an invitation to the head table than to be sent away in public disgrace. Pg. 139

Fact.

Do you see any truly competent workers? They will serve K. rather than working for ordinary people. Pg. 125

Unfailing love and faithfulness protect the K.; his throne is made secure through love. Pg. 117

Knowledge

Duty.

Choose K. rather than gold. Pg. 27

Fact.

A wise person is hungry for K. Pg. 72

Enthusiasm without K. is no good. Pg. 99

Intelligent people are always ready to learn. Their ears are open for K. Pg. 96

K. of the Holy One results in good judgment. Pg. 30

The prudent are crowned with K. Pg. 66

The tongue of the wise makes K. appealing. Pg. 70

The wise are mightier than the strong, and those with K. grow stronger and stronger. Pg. 135

The wise don't make a show of their K. Pg. 53

Fear of the Lord is the foundation of true K. Pg. 2

Of God. Pg. 4

Warning.

If you stop listening to instruction, my child, you will turn your back on K. Pg. 104

The fool feeds on trash. Pg. 72

Will fill you with joy. Pg. 5

L

Lamp

Purpose of a L.

To give light to everyone. Pg. 60

Land

Fact.

Only the godly will live in the L. Pg. 7

Only those with integrity will remain in it. Pg. 7

Laugh—Laughter

Fact.

L. can conceal a heavy heart, but when the L. ends, the grief remains. Pg. 65

Law

Fact.

When people do not accept divine guidance, they run wild. But whoever obeys the L. is joyful. Pg. 160

Lazy—Laziness
Duty.
Be motivated to do the work TODAY that will provide for your needs TOMORROW. Pg. 104
Fact.
L. people are soon poor. Pg. 31
L. people want much but get little. Pg. 56
Qualities of.
Lazybones. Pg. 24
Warning.
A little extra sleep, a little more slumber, a little folding of the hands to rest—then poverty will pounce on you like a bandit; scarcity will attack you like an armed robber. Pg. 138
Be L. and become a slave. Pg. 54
Those too L. to plow in the right season will have no food at the harvest. Pg. 104
Too much sleep, too much rest will bring poverty. Pg. 24

Lead—Leader—Leaders—Leadership
By example. Pg. 54, 60
Duty.
Be an example by doing good works of every kind. Pg. 60
L. by example and be a good steward of your time by working harder and smarter. Pg. 54
LISTEN to the needs around you and LEARN what you can do to LEVERAGE your L. and be a blessing to the LEAST of these. Pg. 119
Live in a way in which your actions speak for themselves. Pg. 60
Make sure you put the right people on your team. Pg. 142
Pray for our L. so they may be wise in who they listen to and what they do. Pg. 45
Pray for the kind of L. in your city, state, and country who would choose to be wise and knowledgeable and that the people would enjoy stability. Pg. 147
Treat everyone you meet with impeccable fairness. Pg. 106
Example of.
John Maxwell. Pg. 22
Moses. Pg. 21
Paul. Pg. 20
Fact.
Guided experience is the best teacher. Pg. 20
Integrity matters in everything you believe and practice. Pg. 60
It's hard to let go of control and power. It takes courage to pass on the baton to others you have trained. Pg. 22
It's not the position that makes the L.; it's the L. that makes the position. Pg. 59
L. ability is always the lid on personal and organizational effectiveness. If a person's leadership is strong, the organization's lid is high. But if it's not, then the organization is limited. Pg. 148

One of the great characteristics of a Quality L. is the ability to trust the process. Pg. 75
The best L. are always the leaders who use their influence for the good of others. Pg. 59
The pessimist complains about the wind. The optimist expects it to change. The L. adjusts the sails. Pg. 59
Wise and knowledgeable L. bring stability. Pg. 147
Work hard and become a L. Pg. 54

Five key phrases for why mentorship matters. Pg. 21
How to increase your L. ability. Pg. 148
Loving to L. Pg. 147
Legacy.
    A leader's lasting value is measured by succession. Pg. 22
Power of.
Three suggestions on how a Quality L. can experience growth. Pg. 76
Three take-a-ways for the leader who desires to leave a legacy. Pg. 22
    Others may be able to experience God's peace. Pg. 20
Qualities of a secure leader. Pg. 21
Warning.
    Many impatient leaders grow weary of the process and make a rash decision, and often fail. Pg. 75
    Without wise L., a nation falls. Pg. 45
When a Quality L. has a healthy self-image.
    Is empowered to serve others. Pg. 93
    Is secure in who they are. Pg. 93
    Has not left their soul behind. Pg. 93
When L. depend upon you. Pg. 45

Leap
Before you L. Pg.61
Duty.
    Before you do anything, THINK, PRAY, LISTEN, and then ACT. Pg. 61
Fact.
    Wise people think before they act. Pg. 61

Learn—Learning
Always be in a posture of L. Pg. 1
Duty.
    Be willing to L. so you will be able to be WISE the REST of your LIFE. Pg. 101
    Get all the advice and instruction you can, so you will be wise the rest of your life. Pg. 101
    LISTEN and L. from those who LOVE you so you may live a SWEET LIFE. Pg. 145
    Live like the more you L. the less you know thus the need to keep on L. more. Pg. 103
    Make it your goal to L. more than you did yesterday and to use what you learn to add value to more people. Pg. 96
Fact.
    Intelligent people are always ready to learn. Their ears are open for knowledge. Pg. 96
    To L., you must love discipline. Pg. 50

Embrace this posture of humility: the more I know the less I know thus the need to keep learning more and more. Pg. 78

Unending. Pg. 78

Warning.
> If you stop listening to instruction, my child, you will turn your back on knowledge. Pg. 104

Legacy

A L. of generational honor. Pg. 103

Charge.
> Look for those who take the baton from you and win. Pg. 22

Duty.
> Make decisions that will add value to others and credibility to your L. Pg. 32
> Treat everyone you meet with impeccable fairness. Pg. 106

Fact.
> Is a daily decision. Pg. 20
> It's hard to let go of control and power. It takes courage to pass on the baton to others you have trained. Pg. 22

Power of.
> Others may be able to experience God's peace. Pg. 20

Three take-a-ways for the leader who desires to leave a L. Pg. 22

Lend—Lender

Fact.
> Just as the rich rule the poor, so the borrower is servant to the L. Pg. 123

Less

When L. is more. Pg. 95

Liar—Liars

Warning.
> Hiding hatred makes you a L. Pg. 34
> L. pay close attention to slander. Pg. 87

Lie—Lies—Lying

Fact.
> A false witness tells L. Pg. 52
> An honest witness does not L. Pg. 64

Kind of prayer.
> Help me never to tell a L. Pg. 162

Warning.
> A false witness breathes L. Pg. 64
> Liars pay close attention to slander. Pg. 87
> L. are soon exposed. Pg. 53
> The Lord detests L. lips. Pg. 53
> Wealth created by a L. tongue is a vanishing mist and a deadly trap. Pg. 118

Life
- Benefit of.
  - Letting His words penetrate deep into your heart. Pg. 15
- Between the ditches. Pg. 72
- Blessing of.
  - Give your L. away so you can get it back even better. Pg. 48
- Charge.
  - Live the L. you believe. Pg. 50
- Duty.
  - Be COURAGEOUSLY CAUTIOUS as you live your life. Pg. 146
  - Be intentional in experiencing a focused and fruitful life. Pg. 65
  - Keep it between the ditches and resist the urge to abandon the right path. Pg. 72
  - Keep your L. between the DITCHES and stay on the JOYFUL PATH. Pg. 160
  - LISTEN and LEARN from those who LOVE you so you may live a SWEET L. Pg. 145
  - Live an attractive L. by being LOYAL and HONEST. Pg. 102
  - PURSUE right THOUGHTS and right ACTIONS so that you may live a right L. Pg. 71
  - Set the example of living a transformed life. Pg. 60
  - Work hard like it all depended upon you and pray like it all depended upon Him. Pg. 165
- Fact.
  - Be willing to LEARN so you will be able to be WISE the REST of your L. Pg. 101
  - Fear of the Lord leads to L., bringing security and protection from harm. Pg. 103
  - Gentle words are a tree of L. Pg. 70
  - True humility and fear of the Lord lead to riches, honor, and long L. Pg. 122
  - Whoever pursues righteousness and unfailing love will find L, righteousness, and honor. Pg. 119
- Expecting an amazing L. Pg. 163
- Kind of.
  - Abundant L. Pg. 9
  - "All in" L. Pg. 165
  - Amazing L. Pg. 163
  - Attractive L. Pg. 102
  - Average L. Pg. 149
  - Be honest L. Pg. 38
  - Best kind of L. Pg. 8
  - Big hearted L. Pg. 166
  - Common sense L. Pg. 5
  - Courageous L. Pg. 146
  - Do it L. Pg. 99
  - Focused. Pg. 104, 160
  - Growing. Pg. 124
  - Happy. Pg. 11
  - Joyful. Pg. 28
  - Long. Pg. 11, 122
  - Long, good. Pg. 15
  - Mentored. Pg. 25
  - Predictable. Pg. 106

Prioritized. Pg. 122
Prize-driven. Pg. 26
Right. Pg. 71
Right kind. Pg. 119
Rich. Pg. 28
Satisfied L. Pg. 8, 11, 73
Sharp L. Pg. 146
Sweet L. Pg. 145
Stay away. Pg. 24
Transformed. Pg. 60
Wildly successful L. Pg. 8, 80
Word-driven L. Pg. 162
Living a big L. Pg. 101
Loving the sweet L. Pg. 145
Open heart, open mind, growing L. Pg. 124
Robbed of L. Pg. 3
Secret to living many years. Pg. 8
The fine art of giving away what you cannot save. Pg. 48
The sharp L. Pg. 146
The way to L.
    Embracing the life teachings of your parents. Pg. 25
The Word-driven L. Pg. 162
Warning.
    The tongue can bring death or L. Pg. 98

Light
    Duty.
        Let your little L. shine and bring an infectious joy to everyone you meet. Pg. 56
    Fact.
        The Lord's L. penetrates the human spirit, exposing every hidden motive. Pg. 116
        You are the L. of the world. Pg. 60
    Purpose of a lamp.
        To give L. to everyone. Pg. 60

Lips
    Duty.
        Guard your L. and protect your ears so your heart will be clear and pure. Pg. 87
        Listen to the words of the wise; apply your heart to my instruction. For it is good to keep these sayings in your heart and always ready on your L. Pg. 123
    Fact.
        The L. of the wise give good advice. Pg. 71
    Warning.
        The Lord detests lying L. Pg. 53

Listen—Listening—Listener
    Benefits of L. Pg. 3

Duty.
> Be a GOOD FRIEND by being a GOOD L. so you will be able to give GOOD ADVICE that will help your friend have a GOOD DAY. Pg. 105
> Be wise enough to L. to good instruction and trusting enough to be joyful. Pg. 83
> L. and LEARN from those who LOVE you so you may live a SWEET LIFE. Pg. 145
> L. to His voice to know what to do and may you SEE where He leads you to go DO what He wants. Pg. 106
> L. to the needs around you and LEARN what you can do to LEVERAGE your LEADERSHIP and be a blessing to the LEAST of these. Pg. 119

Fact.
> Ears to hear and eyes to see—both are gifts from the Lord. Pg. 106
> If you listen to constructive criticism, you will be at home among the wise. Pg. 78
> Those who L. to instruction will prosper. Pg. 83

The importance of being a good L. Pg. 106
The powerful reason why being a good listener matters. Pg. 83

Warning.
> Wrongdoers eagerly L. to gossip. Pg. 87

Live—Living

Duty.
> Do the RIGHT things in the RIGHT way to get the RIGHT results at the RIGHT time. Pg. 137
> Live like the more you learn the less you know thus the need to keep on learning more. Pg. 103
> Make a commitment to earn an HONEST dollar by telling and L. the TRUTH before others and before God. Pg. 118
> Set your sight on L. RIGHT and pursuing the kind of LOVE that never FAILS and then fully experience LIFE, RIGHTEOUSNESS, and HONOR. Pg. 119

Fact.
> Right L. can save your life. Pg. 30
> Right L. leads to a right L. Pg. 137

Kind of.
> Awesome. Pg. 2
> Fork in the road. Pg. 13
> Look up. Pg. 17
> On purpose. Pg. 17
> Right. Pg. 7

Loan—Loans

Warning.
> There's danger in putting up security for a stranger's debt. Pg. 46

Loyal—Loyalty

Duty.
> Be the most L. and RELIABLE friend you know. Pg. 105
> Live an attractive life by being L. and HONEST. Pg. 102

Fact.

A friend is always L., and a brother is born to help in time of need. Pg. 89
L. makes a person attractive. It is better to be poor than dishonest. Pg. 102
Many will say they are L. friends, but who can find one who is truly reliable? Pg. 105

Love—Loves—Lover
- Benefits of.
    - Makes up for all offenses. Pg. 33
- Duty.
    - Be a L. not a hater. Pg. 32
    - Choose to give up a chance to stir up anger and instead stir up L., peace, and grace instead. Pg. 164
    - FORGIVE when you find a FAULT, L. when you would rather LASH out, and GIVE GRACE because you need it too. Pg. 87
    - Have a BIG HEART that will care for the BIG NEEDS of people who need BIG L. from YOU. Pg. 166
    - Lead with unfailing L. in every decision you make, with every person you touch and be absolutely secure in His L. for you. Pg. 117
    - L. to grow you. Pg. 100
    - L. what matters. Pg. 50
    - L. yourself enough to grow yourself enough to be a blessing to others. Pg. 100
    - Make sure the only thing you OWE anyone is L. Pg. 123
    - Protect the relationships that are important to you by winning their L., not by winning the argument. Pg. 97
- Fact.
    - An open rebuke is better than hidden L.! Wounds from a sincere friend are better than many kisses from an enemy. Pg. 145
    - Love prospers when a fault is forgiven. Pg. 87
    - The Lord corrects those He L. Pg. 10
    - To acquire wisdom is to L. yourself. Pg. 100
    - Three things that amaze me—no, four things that I don't understand:
        - How a man loves a woman. Pg. 163
    - Unfailing L. and faithfulness protect the king; his throne is made secure through L. Pg. 117
    - Whoever pursues righteousness and unfailing L. will find life, righteousness, and honor. Pg. 119
- Of God.
- Take a deep breath when you want to lash out in anger and instead reach out in L. and be firm in your response. Pg. 68
    - How to know God really L. you. Pg. 10
- Warning.
    - Make sure the only "Payback Currency" comes out of the L account. Pg. 138
- What to L.
    - L. humility so that you may embrace discipline and correction and LEARN. Pg. 50
- When unfailing L. influences everything you do. Pg. 117

Lovely
- Duty.

Fix your mind on what is lovely, what is gracious, as in seeing images of kindness, always seeing the positive in someone else, to build them up. Pg. 152

Fact.
A L. mindset is one that always looks the good in a person and in a circumstance. Pg. 152

Loyal—Loyalty
Charge.
Never let L. and kindness leave you. Pg. 8
Set it to be your goal to be the most L. and kind person you know. Pg. 8

Lying
Warning.
A L. tongue hates its victims, and flattering words cause ruin. Pg. 143

M

Maker
Fact.
Helping the poor honors him. Pg. 69
Warning.
Those who mock the poor insult their M. Pg. 87
Those who oppress the poor insult their M. Pg. 69

Man
Fact.
Three things that amaze me—no, four things that I don't understand:
How a M. loves a woman. Pg. 163

Maxwell, John C.
Fact.
Leadership ability is always the lid on personal and organizational effectiveness. If a person's leadership is strong, the organization's lid is high. But if it's not, then the organization is limited. Pg. 148
The pessimist complains about the wind. The optimist expects it to change. The leader adjusts the sails. Pg. 59
Growth is the great separator. Pg.
Legacy.
A leader's lasting value is measured by succession. Pg. 22

Meal—Meals
Divine Dining. Pg. 74
Duty.
Be the REAL DEAL when it comes to having a MEANINGFUL M. Pg. 74
Work like your M. depended upon it. Pg. 156
Fact.

A bowl of vegetables with someone you love is better than steak with someone you hate. Pg. 74

Measure—Measures
> Warning.
>> False weights and unequal measures — the Lord detests double standards of every kind. Pg. 106

Medicine
> Duty.
>> Be the good M. to those who hearts are breaking. Pg. 94
>
> Fact.
>> A cheerful heart is good M., but a broken spirit saps a person's strength. Pg. 94

Mentor—Mentoring—Mentorship
> Blessing of.
>> Embrace the life teachings from your spiritual parents (Mentors) and live a life marked by success. Pg. 25
>
> Charge.
>> Look for those who take the baton from you and win. Pg. 22
>
> Example of.
>> John Maxwell. Pg. 22
>> Moses. Pg. 21
>> Paul. Pg. 20
>
> Fact.
>> Guided experience is the best teacher. Pg. 20
>> It's hard to let go of control and power. It takes courage to pass on the baton to others you have trained. Pg. 22
>> M. or discipling another believer involves taking upon the burdens of another and giving hope and encouragement. Pg. 42
>
> Five key phrases for why M. matters. Pg. 21
>
> Legacy.
>> A leader's lasting value is measured by succession. Pg. 22
>
> Power of.
>> Three take-a-ways for the leader who desires to leave a legacy. Pg. 22
>> Others may be able to experience God's peace. Pg. 20
>
> Purpose of.
>> To make an intentional investment in people who are serious about becoming an even better version of themselves. Pg. 29
>
> Qualities of a secure leader. Pg. 21

Mercy
> Fact.
>> People who conceal their sins will not prosper, but if they confess and turn from them, they will receive M. Pg. 156

Messenger
- Duty.
  - Be a refreshing blessing to those who are a blessing to you. Pg. 140
  - Trustworthy M. refresh like snow in summer. They revive the spirit of their employer. Pg. 140
- The refreshing M. Pg. 140

Michaels, Jillian
- Quote of.
  - *Transformation is not five minutes from now; it's a present activity. In this moment you can make a different choice, and it's these small choices and successes that build up over time to help cultivate a healthy self-image and self-esteem. Pg. xi*

Mind
- An open M. to learn more. Pg. 103
- Duty.
  - Be SPIRIT FILLED when you want to give someone a PIECE of your M., give them His PEACE instead. Pg. 159
  - Do not allow your heart to mess with your M. Pg. 125
  - Feed your M. with HEALTHY thoughts and leave the brainless JUNK FOOD of UNHEALTHY thoughts alone. Pg. 72
  - Give someone a piece of your HEART before you give them a piece of your M. Pg. 167
  - Win the battle between your EARS by what comes out of your HEART and through your MOUTH. Pg. 100
  - Keep an open M. as you ask for His. Pg. 80
- Fact.
  - From a wise M. comes wise speech. Pg. 84
- M. wars. Pg. 100
- Open heart, open M., growing life. Pg. 124
- Open M. to success. Pg. 96

Ministry
- Duty.
  - You are to fulfill your M. Pg. 132

Misfortune
- Warning.
  - Those who rejoice at the misfortune of others will be punished. Pg. 87

Mistake—Mistakes
- Warning.
  - Haste makes M. Pg. 99

Mock—Mocks—Mocker
- Kind of person.
  - The Lord M. them. Pg. 14

Warning.
- Anyone who rebukes a M. will get an insult in return. Pg. 29
- Don't bother correcting M. Pg. 29
- Those who M. the poor insult their Maker. Pg. 87

Money
- Blessing of.
  - Give freely and become more wealthy. Pg. 48
  - The earnings of the godly enhance their lives. Pg. 33
- Crazy M. Pg. 94
- Duty.
  - Make a commitment to earn an HONEST dollar by telling and living the TRUTH before others and before God. Pg. 118
  - Make good sense in every financial decision you make, and for God's glory and His purpose, make many dollars for His work. Pg. 67
  - SPEND your life on things that really MATTER and SPEND your M. to FUND the things that really MATTER. Pg. 49
  - Work SMARTER and HARDER so you can EARN MORE to GIVE AWAY. Pg. 57
- Fact.
  - Better to have little, with godliness, than to be rich and dishonest. Pg. 81
  - Evil people get rich for the moment. Pg. 47
  - It's poor judgment to guarantee another person's debt or put up security for a friend. Pg. 94
- Fate of those who are greedy for M. Pg. 3
- Losing Your Cents Will Cost You Many Dollars. Pg. 125
- M. matters in a material world. Pg. 67
- Stewardship of.
  - When it comes to stewarding the M. God entrusts to you, be careful to learn the balance between using your head and your heart. Pg. 46
- Warning.
  - Be stingy and lose everything. Pg. 48
  - Evil people squander their M. on sin. Pg. 33
  - Not allow your HEART to get ahead of your HEAD or you might lose more than your MIND. Pg. 94
  - Trust in your M. and down you go. Pg. 49

Moses
- Example of being a mentor. Pg. 21

Mother
- Blessing of having godly parents.
  - Their command is a lamp. Pg. 25
  - Their corrective discipline is the way to life. Pg. 25
  - Their instruction is a light. Pg. 25
  - When you sleep, they will protect you. Pg. 25
  - When you wake up, they will advise you. Pg. 25

When you walk, their counsel will lead you. Pg. 25
Duty.
Do not neglect your mother's instruction. Pg. 25
Keep their words always in your heart. Pg. 25
Tie their words around your neck. Pg. 25
Warning.
Children who mistreat their father or chase away their M. are an embarrassment and a public disgrace. Pg. 103

Motivate—Motivated—Motivation
Duty.
Be M. to do the work TODAY that will provide for your needs TOMORROW. Pg. 104
Motivation matters. Pg. 104

Motive—Motives
Fact.
M. matter. Pg. 80
People may be pure in their own eyes, but the Lord examines their M. Pg. 80
The Lord's light penetrates the human spirit, exposing every hidden M. Pg. 116

Mouth
Duty.
Guard your lips and protect your ears so your heart will be clear and pure. Pg. 87
GUARD what your EARS hear so that toxic WORDS will not leave your M. Pg. 114
HUSH your M. and KEEP your witness. Pg. 120
Let someone else praise you, not your own M.—a stranger, not your own lips. Pg. 144
Win the battle between your EARS by what comes out of your HEART and through your MOUTH. Pg. 100
Fact.
Sensible people control their temper; they earn respect by overlooking wrongs. Pg. 101
Watch your tongue and keep your M. shut, and you will stay out of trouble. Pg. 120
The M. of the godly person gives wise advice. Pg. 36
M. guard. Pg. 120
Warning.
Be sensible and keep your M shut. Pg. 34
Opening your M. can ruin everything. Pg. 55
The M. of the wicked overflows with evil words. Pg. 78
The M. of a fool belches out foolishness. Pg. 70
The M. of the wicked speaks perverse words. Pg. 37

Mundane
Duty.
Do not MUDDLE in the M. but instead live your life always AMAZED by an AMAZING God who delights in showing off His glory to you. Pg. 163

N

Name
Of the Lord.
> The N. of the Lord is a strong fortress. Pg. 95

Nation
Duty.
> Do your part to make your N. great by living a life of godliness. Pg. 70

Fact.
> Godliness makes a N. great. Pg. 70

Warning.
> Sin is a disgrace to any people. Pg. 70
> Without wise leadership, a N. falls. Pg. 45
> "When there is moral rot within a N., its government topples easily. Pg. 147

Need—Needs
Duty.
> TRUST GOD FOR WHAT YOU N. and then allow Him, in His way, to PROVIDE ALL OF YOUR N. Pg. 126

Negative
Wisdom of avoiding N. people. Pg. 6
Words. Pg. 6

Neighbor
Charge.
> Don't pick a fight without reason. Pg. 13
> Do not plot harm against your N. Pg. 13
> Do not withhold good from those who deserve it. Pg. 13
> Do the kinds of things that will make you the kind of N. you want your N. to be to you. Pg. 13

Duty.
> Never abandon a friend—either yours or your father's. When disaster strikes, you won't have to ask your brother for assistance. It's better to go to a N. than to a brother who lives far away. Pg. 146

Warning.
> Don't cheat your neighbor by moving the ancient boundary markers; don't take the land of defenseless orphans. For their Redeemer is strong; he himself will bring their charges against you. Pg. 127
> Don't cheat your neighbor by moving the ancient boundary markers set up by previous generations. Pg. 125
> Don't testify against your N. without cause; don't lie about them. And don't say, "Now I can pay them back for what they've done to me! I'll get even with them!" Pg. 138
> It is a sin to belittle one's N. Pg. 67

News
- Duty.
  - Be on the lookout for FAITH N. and not FAKE N.: B. Him, not them. Pg. 66
- Fact.
  - Good N. makes for good health. Pg. 78

O

Obey—Obedience
- Blessing of.
  - A long, good life. Pg. 15
  - Key to life. Pg. 15
  - O. His commands and live. Pg. 26
  - Straight paths. Pg. 15
  - Unhindered. Pg. 15
- Duty.
  - Always say YES to God's ways and NO to the things that may sound good but are foolish. Pg. 71
  - Be more intentional in giving Him your willing O. than offering Him a hollow SACRIFICE. Pg. 117
  - Do not neglect your mother's instruction. Pg. 25
  - O. your father's commands. Pg. 25
- Fact.
  - It's not your life. You belong to the Lord so whatever you do should be done in order to please Him. Pg. 60
  - The Lord is more pleased when we do what is right and just than when we offer him sacrifices. Pg. 118
- Obedience matters. Pg. 117
- Warning.
  - BE SMART and trust Him and not OUTSMART yourself and then blame the Lord when it does not work out like you thought it would. Pg. 100

Offense—Offenses—Offend—Offended
- Fact.
  - An O. friend is harder to win back than a fortified city. Pg. 97
  - Love makes up for all O. Pg. 33

Old—Older
- Duty.
  - As you get O., get wiser by becoming more godly. Pg. 85

Optimist—Optimism
- Fact.
  - The pessimist complains about the wind. The O. expects it to change. The leader adjusts the sails. Pg. 59

Oppress
- Warning.
    - Those who O. the poor insult their Maker. Pg. 69

Orphan
- Warning.
    - Don't cheat your neighbor by moving the ancient boundary markers; don't take the land of defenseless O. For their Redeemer is strong; he himself will bring their charges against you. Pg. 127

Owe
- Duty.
    - Make sure the only thing you O. anyone is LOVE. Pg. 123

Ox—Oxen
- Fact.
    - Without O. a stable stays clean. Pg. 63
    - You need a strong O. for a large harvest. Pg. 63

P

Paul, The Apostle
- Quote of. We are in process.
    - *And I am certain that God, who began the good work within you, will continue his work until it is finally finished on the day when Christ Jesus returns.* Pg. xi

Parents—Parenting
- Blessing of having godly P.
    - Their command is a lamp. Pg. 25
    - Their corrective discipline is the way to life. Pg. 25
    - Their instruction is a light. Pg. 25
    - When you sleep, they will protect you. Pg. 25
    - When you wake up, they will advise you. Pg. 25
    - When you walk, their counsel will lead you. Pg. 25
- Duty.
    - Do not neglect your mother's instruction. Pg. 25
    - Keep their words always in your heart. Pg. 25
    - Obey your father's commands. Pg. 25
    - Tie their words around your neck. Pg. 25

Passion
- Command.
    - Take a walk down the path of PROMISE, PROSPERITY, and P. so you may think right, speak right, and do right. Pg. 7
- Duty.
    - Focus your P. to keep your purity. Pg. 18

In your purpose. Pg. 63

Path—Paths
- Direction on.
    - He will show you which P. to take. Pg. 9
- Duty.
    - Don't get sidetracked. Pg. 17
    - Fix your eyes on what lies before you. Pg. 17
    - Keep it between the ditches and resist the urge to abandon the right P. Pg. 72
    - Keep your life between the DITCHES and stay on the JOYFUL P. Pg. 160
    - Keep your feet from following evil. Pg. 17
    - Look straight ahead. Pg. 17
    - Mark out a straight P. for your feet. Pg. 17
    - Make every decision a life producing P. for you and for those you love. Pg. 55
    - Make decisions that keep you on the RIGHT P. Pg. 63
    - Stay on the safe P. Pg. 17
    - The way of the godly leads to life; that P. does not lead to death. Pg. 55
- Command.
    - Stay on the P. of the righteous. Pg. 7
- Fact.
    - Those who follow the right P. fear the Lord. Pg. 63
    - We can make our own plans, but the Lord gives the right answer. Pg. 80
    - When people do not accept divine guidance, they run wild. But whoever obeys the law is joyful. Pg. 160
- Kind of.
    - Delightful. Pg. 11
- Of right living. Pg. 7
- The P. of true prosperity. Pg. 55
- Warning.
    - Those who follow crooked P. will be exposed. Pg. 32
    - Those who take the wrong P. despise the Lord. Pg. 63
    - Whoever abandons the right P. will be severely disciplined. Pg. 72

Patient—Patience—Patiently
- Duty.
    - Make it your goal to be more P. than POWERFUL, more SELF-CONTROLLED than to be OUT OF CONTROL, more SPIRIT-LED than YOU-LED. Pg. 86
- Fact.
    - Better to be P. than powerful. Pg. 86
    - David waited P. for the Lord. Pg. 109
- The power of being P. Pg. 86
- Warning.
    - Don't trap yourself by making a rash promise to God and only later counting the cost. Pg. 116
    - Many impatient leaders grow weary of the process and make a rash decision, and often fail. Pg. 75

Peace—Peaceful
- Blessing of.
    - A bold reproof promotes P. Pg. 32
- Duty.
    - Be SPIRIT FILLED when you want to give someone a PIECE of your mind, give them His P. instead. Pg. 159
    - Choose to give up a chance to stir up anger and instead stir up love, P., and grace instead. Pg. 164
    - Control your tongue so your life may be flooded with P. Pg. 89
- Fact.
    - A P. heart leads to a healthy body. Pg. 69
    - When people's lives please the Lord, even their enemies are at P. with them. Pg. 81
- How to live in P. Pg. 3
- Rest in P. to rest in life. pg. 107

People
- Duty.
    - Be on the Lord's side and treat P. with honesty and respect, especially the ones who are on the other side of the power relationship and cannot defend themselves. Pg. 127
    - BE THE GIFT that ADDS VALUE to important P. Pg. 97
    - Feed the P. who hunger for the kinds of words that produce VALIDATION for those who need to experience SATISFACTION. Pg. 97
    - Pray for the kind of LEADERSHIP in your city, state, and country who would choose to be wise and knowledgeable and that the P. would enjoy stability. Pg. 147
    - Speak words that produce life and not words that kill P. one cut at a time. Pg. 70
    - Surround yourself with the kind of P. who love you enough to tell you the truth. Pg. 157
    - Treat everyone you meet with impeccable fairness. Pg. 106
    - Use good judgment. Pg. 26
- Fact.
    - A truly wise person uses few words. Pg. 95
    - Blessing of the Lord makes a person rich. Pg. 35
    - Evil P. don't understand justice, but those who follow the Lord understand completely. Pg. 154
    - Fearing P. is a dangerous trap, but trusting the Lord means safety. Pg. 161
    - Giving a gift can open doors; it gives access to important P. Pg. 97
    - Good P. receive their reward. Pg. 65
    - Intelligent P. are always ready to learn. Their ears are open for knowledge. Pg. 96
    - The godliness of good P. rescues them. Pg. 38
    - P. may be pure in their own eyes, but the Lord examines their motives. Pg. 80
    - P. may be right in their own eyes, but the Lord examines their heart. Pg. 117
    - P. ruin their lives by their own foolishness and then are angry at the Lord. Pg. 100
    - P. who accept discipline are on the pathway to life. Pg. 34
    - P. who cherish understanding will prosper. Pg. 100
    - P. with integrity walk safely. Pg. 32

P. who conceal their sins will not prosper, but if they confess and turn from them, they will receive mercy. Pg. 156

When people's lives please the Lord, even their enemies are at peace with them. Pg. 81

P. with understanding control their anger. Pg. 68

Save your breath for the RIGHT P., at the RIGHT time, and for the RIGHT reason. Pg. 126

Sensible P. control their temper; they earn respect by overlooking wrongs. Pg. 101

Kind of.
- Evil. Pg. 135, 154
- Foolish. Pg. 26
- Hard workers. Pg. 31
- Intelligent. Pg. 96
- Lazy. Pg. 31, 138
- Mockers. The Lord mocks them. Pg. 14
- Simple. Pg. 26
- Sensible. Pg. 101
- Treacherous. Pg. 38
- Violent. Pg. 13
- Wicked. Are detestable to the Lord. Pg. 13

Learning to be a good steward of time and of people. Pg. 126

Warning.
- Dishonesty destroys treacherous P. Pg. 38
- Don't befriend angry P. or associate with hot-tempered P., or you will learn to be like them and endanger your soul. Pg. 124
- Don't envy evil P. or desire their company. For their hearts plot violence, and their words always stir up trouble. Pg. 135
- Do not envy violent P. or copy their ways. Pg. 13
- Don't envy violent P. Pg. 13
- Evil P. squander their money on sin. Pg. 33
- God detests the prayers of a person who ignores the law. Pg. 155
- P. who wink at wrong cause trouble. Pg. 32
- Sin is a disgrace to any P. Pg. 70
- The ambition of treacherous people traps them. Pg. 38

Wisdom of avoiding negative P. Pg. 6

Wisdom will save you from evil P. Pg. 6

Perch

Duty.

LOOK UP to the Lord before you LOOK DOWN on those who are not as fortunate as you. Pg. 87

Life on the P. Pg. 87

Perfume

Fact.

The heartfelt counsel of a friend is as sweet as P. and incense. Pg. 145

Person
- Duty.
  - Be a P. of your word and may you be satisfied with whatever provisions God may send your way. Pg. 162
- Fact.
  - A person with understanding is even-tempered. Pg. 95
  - A poor P. who oppresses the poor is like a pounding rain that destroys the crops. Pg. 154
  - A prudent P. foresees danger and takes precautions. Pg. 122, 146
  - A truly wise P. uses few words. Pg. 95
  - A wise P. wins friends. Pg. 49
  - Loyalty makes a P. attractive. It is better to be poor than dishonest. Pg. 102
- Of understanding.
  - A single rebuke does more for a P. of understanding than a hundred lashes on the back of a fool. Pg. 88
  - Though good advice lies deep within the heart, a P. with understanding will draw it out. Pg. 105

Persuasive
- Fact.
  - The words of the wise are P. Pg. 84

Perverse
- Warning.
  - The mouth of the wicked speaks P. words. Pg. 37

Pessimist
- Fact.
  - The P. complains about the wind. The optimist expects it to change. The leader adjusts the sails. Pg. 59

Pickowicz, Nate.
- Quote of. Pg.
  - *The beautiful thing about the wisdom of Proverbs is that it's timeless. While textbooks often need updating, Proverbs hasn't had a 2nd edition in three millennia! Pg.*

Plan—Plans—Planning
- Ask the Lord for His P. and then ask Him for the POWER and the COURAGE to live it out. Pg. 64
- Benefits from thinking wise thoughts.
  - Will help you create wise P. Pg. 28
- Duty.
  - Always be prepared to ADJUST and GO when your P. needs to align with His. Pg. 86
  - Be bold enough to dream but humble enough to adjust and go. Pg. 82
  - Be selective and only fight the battles you can win. Pg. 114
  - Do the RIGHT things in the RIGHT way to get the RIGHT results at the RIGHT time. Pg. 137
  - Do your P. and prepare your fields before building your house. Pg. 137

Give every P., every action, and every dream you have to the Lord who will bless you with the kind of success only He can give. Pg. 80

Know what you are DOING before you DO it and take your time DOING what you know to DO so you may DO it well and enjoy it too. Pg. 99

P. It. Live It. Adjust It. Pg. 102

SEEK His wisdom, not yours; His P., not yours because His WAYS are much higher than yours. Pg. 121

WORK a good P. and then WORK hard to see the P. succeed. Pg. 118

Fact.

Add value to others by how you P. and by what you SAY. Pg. 51

Commit your actions to the Lord, and your P. will succeed. Pg. 80

Good P. and hard work lead to prosperity, but hasty shortcuts lead to poverty. Pg. 118

No human wisdom or understanding or P. can stand against the Lord. Pg. 121

People ruin their lives by their own foolishness and then are angry at the Lord. Pg. 100

P. of the godly are just. Pg. 51

P. succeed through good counsel; don't go to war without wise advice. Pg. 114

The prudent understand where they are going. Pg. 64

We can make our P., but the Lord determines our steps. Pg. 82

We can make our own P., but the Lord gives the right answer. Pg. 80

You can make many P., but the Lord's purpose will prevail. Pg. 102

P. B. Pg. 82

P. like you know where you are going but be open to the idea that your P. might change. Pg. 102

P. for the worst and hoping for the best. Pg. 122

Power of.

Harnessing the power of your P. and your words

Strategic P. to win. Pg. 114

Warning.

BE SMART and trust Him and not OUTSMART yourself and then blame the Lord when it does not work out like you thought it would. Pg. 100

P. go wrong for lack of advice. Pg. 77

Working the P. to succeed. Pg. 118

Please

Duty.

Seek to P. the Lord more than you seek to P. anyone else. Pg. 81

P. who you need to P. Pg. 81

Fact.

When people's lives please the Lord, even their enemies are at peace with them. Pg. 81

Poison

Duty.

Experience a peaceful, easy feeling, and avoid making any decision that will P. your life. Pg. 69

SPEAK words of PRAISE, not words of P. Pg. 98

Poor
- Duty.
    - Have a BIG heart for the people who need your COMPASSION and your CARE. Pg. 159
    - Have a BIG heart to meet the BIG needs of those who may be less fortunate than you. Pg. 101
    - Have a keen awareness of the material needs of others who are not as fortunate as you and have a tender heart for them. Pg. 158
    - LISTEN to the needs around you and LEARN what you can do to LEVERAGE your LEADERSHIP and be a blessing to the LEAST of these. Pg. 119
    - LOOK UP to the Lord before you LOOK DOWN on those who are not as fortunate as you. Pg. 87
    - Speak up for the P. and helpless, and see that they get justice. Pg. 164
- Fact.
    - A P. person who oppresses the P. is like a pounding rain that destroys the crops. Pg. 154
    - Better to be P. and honest than to be dishonest and rich. Pg. 155
    - Blessed are those who are generous, because they feed the P. Pg. 123
    - Blessed are those who help the P. Pg. 67
    - Helping the P. honors your Maker. Pg. 69
    - Just as the rich rule the poor, so the borrower is servant to the lender. Pg. 123
    - If you help the P., you are lending to the Lord— and he will repay you! Pg. 101
    - Loyalty makes a person attractive. It is better to be P. than dishonest. Pg. 102
    - Lazy people are soon P. Pg. 31
    - The godly care about the rights of the P.; the wicked don't care at all. Pg. 159
- The benefits of having a tender heart for the P. Pg. 158
- Warning.
    - Never take advantage of anyone who is having a difficult time. Pg. 154
    - Those who shut their ears to the cries of the P. will be ignored in their own time of need. Pg. 119
    - Those who mock the poor insult their Maker. Pg. 87
    - Those who oppress the poor insult their Maker. Pg. 69
    - Those who rejoice at the misfortune of others will be punished. Pg. 87
    - Whoever gives to the P. will lack nothing, but those who close their eyes to poverty will be cursed. Pg. 158

Positive—Positively
- Fact.
    - If you want to become the very best version of you, learning how to think P. is key. Pg. 149

Poverty
- Duty.
    - Have a BIG heart to meet the BIG needs of those who may be less fortunate than you. Pg. 101
    - LISTEN to the needs around you and LEARN what you can do to LEVERAGE your LEADERSHIP and be a blessing to the LEAST of these. Pg. 119
- Fact.

Better to be poor and honest than to be dishonest and rich. Pg. 155
Blessed are those who are generous, because they feed the poor. Pg. 123
If you help the poor, you are lending to the Lord— and he will repay you! Pg. 101
Mere talk leads to P.! Pg. 67

Prayer about.
> For if I grow rich, I may deny you and say, "Who is the Lord?" And if I am too poor, I may steal and thus insult God's holy name. Pg. 162

Give me neither P. nor riches! Give me just enough to satisfy my needs. Pg. 162

Warning.
> A hard worker has plenty of food, but a person who chases fantasies ends up in P. Pg. 156
> A little extra sleep, a little more slumber, a little folding of the hands to rest—then poverty will pounce on you like a bandit; scarcity will attack you like an armed robber. Pg. 138
> Good planning and hard work lead to prosperity, but hasty shortcuts lead to P. Pg. 118
> If you ignore criticism, you will end in P. and disgrace. Pg. 61
> If you love sleep, you will end in P. Keep your eyes open, and there will be plenty to eat! Pg. 107
> Never take advantage of anyone who is having a difficult time. Pg. 154
> Those who shut their ears to the cries of the poor will be ignored in their own time of need. Pg. 119
> Whoever gives to the poor will lack nothing, but those who close their eyes to P. will be cursed. Pg. 158

Power—Powerful

Fact.
> Better to be patient than P. Pg. 86

Warning.
> Be careful how you use your P. Pg. 154
> Never take advantage of anyone who is having a difficult time. Pg. 154

Praise—Praising

Duty.
> Be okay with someone else telling you how great you really are. Pg. 144
> Let someone else P. you, not your own mouth—a stranger, not your own lips. Pg. 144
> SPEAK words of P., not words of POISON. Pg. 98

Learning how to accept P. Pg. 144
P. God when it hurts. Pg. 108

Pray—Prayer—Prayers—Praying

Duty.
> Have the kind of P. life that pleases the Lord. Pg. 155
> Keep your hope alive and DARE to DREAMS for dreams that only God can answer. Pg. 57
> THINK before you SPEAK, take a DEEP BREATH before you ACT and P. ALWAYS. Pg. 66
> P. about WHO needs a GOOD and ENCOURAGING WORD from YOU and SHARE IT. Pg. 141

P. for our leaders so they may be wise in who they listen to and what they do. Pg. 45
WORK like it all depends upon you and P. like it all depends upon Him. Pg. 121, 165

Fact.
We can make our own plans, but the Lord gives the right answer. Pg. 80

How work and P. go together. Pg. 121

Kind of.
Give me neither poverty nor riches! Give me just enough to satisfy my needs. Pg. 162
Help me never to tell a lie. Pg. 162

P. before you promise. Pg. 116

P. that please. Pg. 155

Warning.
Don't trap yourself by making a rash promise to God and only later counting the cost. Pg. 116
God detests the P. of a person who ignores the law. Pg. 155
THINK before you make a promise that only Jesus can help you KEEP. Pg. 116

Preach—Preached

Duty.
Practice what can be P. Pg. 160
P. the Word. Pg. 128
You must be ready at any moment to share the gospel. Pg. 129

Present

Duty.
Live in the P. and trust God to give you what you need for the FUTURE. Pg. 144

P. and accounted for. Pg. 144

Warning.
Don't brag about tomorrow, since you don't know what the day will bring. Pg. 144

Prepare—Preparation

Duty.
Listen to the words of the wise; apply your heart to my instruction. For it is good to keep these sayings in your heart and always ready on your lips. Pg. 123
We must be committed to do the "little things," the daily disciplines of P. Pg. 75

Pride

Charge.
Swallow it. Pg. 23

Fact.
P. goes before destruction, and haughtiness before a fall. Pg. 83

Warning.
Guard your heart before you break your neck. Pg. 83
Haughtiness goes before destruction. Pg. 96
Never become proud of your humility. Pg. 96
P. ends in humiliation, while humility brings honor. Pg. 160
P. leads to disgrace. Pg. 37

Why people trip, stumble, and fall. Pg. 83

Prioritize—Prioritized
> Duty.
>> Set yourself up with long term SUCCESS by HOW you live and WHO you live for. Pg. 122
> The P. Life. Pg. 122

Prize
> Do whatever it takes to keep my eyes on the P. Pg. 26

Process
> Duty.
>> We must be committed to do the "little things," the daily disciplines of preparation. Pg. 75
> Example of.
>> *For I am* confident of this very thing, that He who began a good work in you will perfect it until the day of Christ Jesus. Philippians 1:6. Pg. 75
> Fact.
>> One of the great characteristics of a Quality Leader is the ability to trust the P. Pg. 75
>> One of the key attributes of the successful person is their ability to embrace "The P." and see where it leads. Pg. 75
> Warning.
>> Many impatient leaders grow weary of the process and make a rash decision, and often fail. Pg. 75

Produce
> Charge.
>> Honor the Lord with your wealth and with the best part of everything you P. Pg. 10

Profit
> Fact.
>> Work brings P. Pg. 67

Promise—Promises
> Blessing of.
>> A P. made is a P. kept. Pg. 31
> Command.
>> Take a walk down the path of P., PROSPERITY, and PASSION so you may think right, speak right, and do right. Pg. 7
> Duty.
>> Seek to UNDER promise and OVER deliver on the way you serve others. Pg. 140
> Fact.
>> All of His P. are true. Pg. 108
> Pursuing the P. Pg. 108
> Warning.
>> A person who P. a gift but doesn't give it is like clouds and wind that bring no rain. Pg. 140
> Why you need to keep P. you make. Pg. 140

Promotion
- Duty.
    - Allow the Lord to PROMOTE you before you PROMOTE yourself. Pg. 139
    - Don't demand an audience with the king or push for a place among the great. It's better to wait for an invitation to the head table than to be sent away in public disgrace. Pg. 139
- Fact.
    - Promotion comes from the Lord. Pg. 139
- From the pit. Pg. 108

Prosper—Prosperity
- Command.
    - Take a walk down the path of PROMISE., P., and PASSION so you may think right, speak right, and do right. Pg. 7
- The path of true P. Pg. 55
- Fact.
    - Good planning and hard work lead to P., but hasty shortcuts lead to poverty. Pg. 118
    - Greed causes fighting; trusting the Lord leads to P. Pg. 158
    - People who cherish understanding will P. Pg. 100
    - People who conceal their sins will not P., but if they confess and turn from them, they will receive mercy. Pg. 156
    - The generous will P. Pg. 48
    - Those who listen to instruction will P. Pg. 83
    - Those who work hard will P. Pg. 56
    - Have an ATTITUDE of GRATITUDE for every blessing the Lord sends your way. Pg. 158
- Why having an attitude of gratitude leads to P. Pg. 158
- Warning.
    - A little extra sleep, a little more slumber, a little folding of the hands to rest—then poverty will pounce on you like a bandit; scarcity will attack you like an armed robber. Pg. 138

Protect—Protection
- Fact.
    - Every word of God proves true. He is a shield to all who come to him for P. Pg. 162

Proverb—Proverbs
- Purpose of. Pg. 1

Provide—Provision
- Duty.
    - TRUST GOD FOR WHAT YOU NEED and then allow Him, in His way, to PROVIDE ALL OF YOUR NEEDS. Pg. 126

Prudent
- Fact.
    - A P. person foresees danger and takes precautions. Pg. 122, 146

Poverty
    Warning.
        Too much sleep, too much rest will bring P. Pg. 24

Pride
    Warning.
        P. leads to conflict. Pg. 57

Pressure
    Duty.
        Put in the necessary WORK that will empower you to STAND when the P. is on. Pg. 136
    Warning.
        If you fail under pressure, your strength is too small. Pg. 136

Problem—Problems
    Duty.
        Give your big P. to a BIGGER God. Pg. 161
    The blessing of giving your big P. to a bigger God. Pg. 161

Promise
    Praying before you P. Pg. 116
    Warning.
        Don't trap yourself by making a rash P. to God and only later counting the cost. Pg. 116
        THINK before you make a P. that only Jesus can help you KEEP. Pg. 116

Priority—Priorities
    Duty.
        Seek to become the RICHEST person you know with the things that matter most. Pg. 82

Protect—Protection
    Fact.
        Fear of the Lord leads to life, bringing security and P. from harm. Pg. 103
    Reason why you are to P. your heart.
        It determines the course of your life. Pg. 16
    Warning.
        Guard your heart above all else. Pg. 16

Prudent
    Fact.
        Are crowned with knowledge. Pg. 66
        The P. carefully consider their steps. Pg. 66
        The P. understand where they are going. Pg. 64

Pure—Purity
    Duty.
        Fix your mind on what is P., as in undefiled, morally free from impurities. Pg. 152

Focus your passion to keep your P. Pg. 18

Fact.

Fire tests the P. of silver and gold, but the Lord tests the heart. Pg. 87

People may be pure in their own eyes, but the Lord examines their motives. Pg. 80

Purpose

Fact.

You can make many plans, but the Lord's P. will prevail. Pg. 102

Passion in your P. Pg. 63

Q

Quarrel—Quarrels—Quarreling

Duty.

Starting a Q. is like opening a floodgate, so stop before a dispute breaks out. Pg. 89

Take the HIGH road and walk over those who are UNDER the road. Pg. 104

Fact.

Avoiding a fight is a mark of honor; only fools insist on Q. Pg. 104

Fire goes out without wood, and Q. disappear when gossip stops. Pg. 143

The best way to stop an argument is not to start one. Pg. 89

Warning.

As the beating of cream yields butter and striking the nose causes bleeding, so stirring up anger causes Q. Pg. 164

Hatred stirs up Q. Pg. 33

R

Real

Duty.

Set in your heart to be THE R. DEAL in your CHARACTER with those who are depending upon you to be HONEST and TRUE. Pg. 47

The R. Deal. Pg. 47

Rebuke

Duty.

You must R. those who are playing with fire and will be burned unless they are warned. Pg. 130

Fact.

An open rebuke is better than hidden love! Wounds from a sincere friend are better than many kisses from an enemy. Pg. 145

A single R. does more for a person of understanding than a hundred lashes on the back of a fool. Pg. 88

Redeem—Redeemer

Warning.

> Don't cheat your neighbor by moving the ancient boundary markers; don't take the land of defenseless orphans. For their R. is strong; he himself will bring their charges against you. Pg. 127

Relationship—Relationships
- Duty.
    - Be the kind of friend you need to be for you. Pg. 89
    - Be the kind of trusted friend your intimate circle of friends needs from you. Pg. 98
    - Make it your goal to ADD VALUE to everyone you meet. Pg. 49
    - Protect the R. that are important to you by winning their love, not by winning the argument. Pg. 97
- Fact.
    - A friend is always loyal, and a brother is born to help in time of need. Pg. 89
    - Arguments separate friends like a gate locked with bars. Pg. 97
    - A wise person wins friends. Pg. 49
- Warning.
    - There are "friends" who destroy each other, but a real friend sticks closer than a brother. Pg. 98

Reliable
- Duty.
    - Be the most LOYAL and R. friend you know. Pg. 105
- Fact.
    - Many will say they are loyal friends, but who can find one who is truly R.? Pg. 105

Repent
- Duty.
    - You must reprove or correct those who are under the conviction of sin and lead them to confess and R. of the sin. Pg. 129

Reply
- Fact.
    - Everyone enjoys a fitting reply. Pg. 77

Refresh—Refreshed
- Fact.
    - Those who R. others will themselves be R. Pg. 48

Reproof
- Blessing of.
    - A bold R. promotes peace. Pg. 32

Reputation
- Duty.
    - Choose a good R. over great riches; being held in high esteem is better than silver or gold. Pg. 121

Have the R. of being a wise guy or wise gal. Pg. 57
How a good R. is earned. Pg. 8

Resource—Resources
Benefit of putting God's Word in your heart. Pg. 7
Kind of.
>Spiritual. Pg. 7

Length of.
>Now and for the future too. Pg. 7

Respect
Duty.
>Be on the Lord's side and treat people with honesty and R., especially the ones who are on the other side of the power relationship and cannot defend themselves. Pg. 127
>
>Have an AWESOME respect for your AWESOME God who watches after you in an AWESOME way. Pg. 103

Those who R a command will succeed. Pg. 58

Rest
Duty.
>Get enough of the right kind of R. so you will be able to enjoy the R. of your life. Pg. 107

R. In Peace To R. in Life. Pg. 107
Warning.
>If you love sleep, you will end in poverty. Keep your eyes open, and there will be plenty to eat! Pg. 107

Revenge
Duty.
>Allow the Lord to keep you on an EVEN keel and stay RIGHT so you will not fall into the vindictive trap of trying to get EVEN and wind up WRONG. Pg. 115
>
>Don't say, "I will get even for this wrong." Wait for the Lord to handle the matter. Pg. 115

No vindictive zone. Pg. 115
The best way to pay someone back. Pg. 138
Warning.
>Don't testify against your neighbors without cause; don't lie about them. And don't say, "Now I can pay them back for what they've done to me! I'll get even with them!" Pg. 138
>
>Make sure the only "Payback Currency" comes out of the love account. Pg. 138

Warning.
>If you set a trap for others, you will get caught in it yourself. If you roll a boulder down on others, it will crush you instead. Pg. 143

Reward—Rewards
Fact.
>Evil people get rich for the moment. Pg. 47

Hard work brings R. Pg. 51
Good people receive their R. Pg. 65
R. of the godly will last. Pg. 47
R. that last. Pg. 47

Rhon, Jim
Quote of.
Income seldom exceeds personal development. Pg. xi

Rich—Riches—Richest
Blessing of.
Give freely and become more wealthy. Pg. 48
Fact.
Better to be poor and honest than to be dishonest and R. Pg. 155
Better to have little, with godliness, than to be R. and dishonest. Pg. 81
Blessing of the Lord makes a person rich. Pg. 35
For if I grow R., I may deny you and say, "Who is the Lord?" And if I am too poor, I may steal and thus insult God's holy name. Pg. 162
Just as the R. rule the poor, so the borrower is servant to the lender. Pg. 123
True humility and fear of the Lord lead to R., honor, and long life. Pg. 122
Hard workers get R. Pg. 31
Duty.
Seek to become the RICHEST person you know with the things that matter most. Pg. 82
Prayer about.
Give me neither poverty nor R.! Give me just enough to satisfy my needs. Pg. 162
Result of.
Having a deep and abiding relationship with God's wisdom. Pg. 11
True R. Pg. 82
Warning.
Be stingy and lose everything. Pg. 48
Don't wear yourself out trying to get R. Be wise enough to know when to quit. In the blink of an eye wealth disappears, for it will sprout wings and fly away like an eagle. Pg. 126
The trustworthy person will get a R. reward, but a person who wants quick R. will get into trouble. Pg. 157
Too much sleep, too much rest will bring poverty. Pg. 24

Right
Charge.
Be diligent in doing the R. things in the R. way for the R. reasons, R. now. Make decisions that keep you on the R. path, connecting with the R. people, and winding up in the R. place. Pg. 63
Duty.
Be willing to be HUMBLE when you are WRONG and be willing to be HUMBLE when you are R. Pg. 79

Fix your mind on what is R., as in righteous behavior lived out before God and other people. Pg. 151

PURSUE R. THOUGHTS and R. ACTIONS so that you may live a R. LIFE. Pg. 71

Say the R. THING at the R. TIME in the R. WAY to the R. PERSON. Pg. 77

Use the R. words at the R. time in the R. way. Pg. 95

Experiencing a R. life. Pg. 71

R. on! Pg. 63

Of way. Pg. 77

Righteous—Righteousness
Blessings reward the R. Pg. 62
Command.
    Stay on the path of the R. Pg. 7
Duty.
    Set your sight on LIVING RIGHT and pursuing the kind of LOVE that never FAILS and then fully experience LIFE, R., and HONOR. Pg. 119
    Teach the R. and they will learn even more. Pg. 29
Fact.
    Whoever pursues R. and unfailing love will find life, righteousness, and honor. Pg. 119

Rob—Robbed
Of life. Pg. 3

Rod
Warning.
    Those lacking sense will be beaten with a R. Pg. 33

Root—Roots
Fact.
    The godly have deep R. Pg. 50

Rubies
Fact.
    A godly wife is more precious than R. Pg. 165
    Wisdom is more precious than R. Pg. 11, 27
    Wise words are more valuable than much gold and many R. Pg. 114

Rules
Do good R. Pg. 67
Duty.
    Treat others the way you want to be treated. Pg. 67

Run—Running
Duty.
    R. to the Lord when hell throws everything at you and by His grace may you depend upon His name when you feel unsafe. Pg. 95

Fact.
> The godly R. to him and are safe. Pg. 95

S

Sacrifice—Sacrifices
Duty.
> Be more intentional in giving Him your willing OBEDIENCE than offering Him a hollow S. Pg. 117

Fact.
> The Lord is more pleased when we do what is right and just than when we offer him S. Pg. 118

Safe—Safety
Duty.
> Run to the Lord when hell throws everything at you and by His grace may you depend upon His name when you feel unsafe. Pg. 95

Fact.
> The godly run to him and are S. Pg. 95

Hide-a-way. Pg. 95

Satisfy—Satisfaction
Duty.
> Feed the people who hunger for the kinds of words that produce VALIDATION for those who need to experience S. Pg. 97

Secure—Security
Duty.
> Run to the Lord when hell throws everything at you and by His grace may you depend upon His name when you feel unsafe. Pg. 95

Fact.
> Fear of the Lord leads to life, bringing S. and protection from harm. Pg. 103
> It's poor judgment to guarantee another person's debt or put up S. for a friend. Pg. 94
> The godly run to him and are safe. Pg. 95

Hide-a-way. Pg. 95

Sad—Sadness
Duty.
> Do the things that will make you GLAD and not S. Pg. 72

Safe—Safety
Fact.
> Fearing people is a dangerous trap, but trusting the Lord means S. Pg. 161
> There is S. in having many advisers. Pg. 45
> Understanding will keep you S. Pg. 6

Salt
- Fact.
    - You are the S. of the earth. Pg. 60
- Warning.
    - If it has lost its flavor, it will be thrown out and trampled underfoot as worthless. Pg. 60

Satisfy—Satisfied—Satisfaction
- Duty.
    - Acquire a taste for wisdom that will S. every desire for SUCCESS. Pg. 136
    - Be a person of your word and may you be S. with whatever provisions God may send your way. Pg. 162
    - Be S. with all He provides and love Him more than to have this gnawing feeling inside that is never S. Pg. 73
    - Feed the people who hunger for the kinds of words that produce VALIDATION for those who need to experience SATISFACTION. Pg. 97
- Fact.
    - Better to have little, with fear for the Lord, than to have great treasure and inner turmoil. Pg. 73
    - The right words bring S. Pg. 98
    - Wise words S. like a good meal. Pg. 98
- The power of living a S. life. Pg. 73
- Wise words that S. Pg. 97

Say—Saying
- Fact.
    - It is wonderful to S the right thing at the right time! Pg. 77
- Warning.
    - Be CAREFUL what you THINK and what you S. and what you DO. Pg. 78

Scale—Scales
- Fact.
    - The Lord delights in accurate weights. Pg. 37
    - The Lord demands accurate S. and balances; he sets the standards for fairness. Pg. 82
- Warning.
    - The Lord detests the use of dishonest scales. Pg. 37

Scarcity
- Warning.
    - S. will attack you like an armed robber. Pg. 24
    - Too much sleep, too much rest will bring poverty. Pg. 24

Schemers
- Are hated. Pg. 66

Secret—Secrets
- A safe place for S. Pg. 65

Duty.
> Assure those who trust you that they can be CONFIDENT in your COMPETENCE to keep a CONFIDENCE. Pg. 45
>
> Find a safe place to unpack the S. of your heart. Pg. 65

Fact.
> Those who are trustworthy can keep a confidence. Pg. 45

Value of keeping a S. Pg. 45

Warning.
> A gossip goes around telling S. Pg. 45, 115
>
> Don't hang around with chatterers. Pg. 115

Secure

Reason why you are to S. your heart.
> It determines the course of your life. Pg. 16

Warning.
> Guard your heart above all else. Pg. 16

Security (Financial)

Guaranteeing another's debt. Pg. 23

Warning.
> Don't agree to guarantee another person's debt or put up security for someone else. If you can't pay it, even your bed will be snatched from under you. Pg. 125
>
> There's danger in putting up S. for a stranger's debt. Pg. 46

Seed—Seeds

Warning.
> A troublemaker plants S. of strife. Pg. 85

Self-Awareness

Fact.
> One of the greatest gifts you can ever give yourself is your very own SA. Pg. 93

Kind of.
> Strategic. Pg. 90

Self-Control—Self-Controlled

Fact.
> A person without S.-C. is like a city with broken-down walls. Pg. 141
>
> Better to have SC. than to conquer a city. Pg. 86
>
> Sensible people control their temper; they earn respect by overlooking wrongs. Pg. 101

Duty.
> Make it your goal to be more PATIENT than POWERFUL, more SC. than to be OUT OF CONTROL, more SPIRIT-LED than YOU-LED. Pg. 86
>
> Take a deep breath and, before you do or say anything that you would later regret, count to ten. Pg. 141

The blessing of counting to ten. Pg. 141

Sense
- Warning.
    - Fools are destroyed by their lack of common S. Pg. 34
    - Those lacking S. will be beaten with a rod. Pg. 33

Sex—Sexual
- Consequences of S. Sin.
    - In the end you will groan in anguish. Pg. 18
    - Someone else will enjoy the fruit of your labor. Pg. 18
    - Strangers will consume your wealth. Pg. 18
    - When disease consumes your body You will say, "How I hated discipline!" Pg. 18
    - When disease consumes your body You will say, "If only I had not ignored all the warnings!" Pg. 18
    - When disease consumes your body You will say, "Oh, why didn't I listen to my teachers? Why didn't I pay attention to my instructors?" Pg. 18
    - When disease consumes your body You will say, "I have come to the brink of utter ruin, and now I must face public disgrace." Pg. 18
    - Will lose to merciless people all you have achieved. Pg. 17
    - Will lose your honor. Pg. 17
- Duty.
    - Focus your passion to keep your purity. Pg. 18
- Warning.
    - Look UP before you look DOWN and stay out of S. trouble. Pg. 17

Shame
- Fact.
    - Fools are put to S. Pg. 14

Sharp—Sharper—Sharpens—Sharpened
- Duty.
    - Be on the lookout for S. friends who will make you S. and not allow dull acquaintances to suck the life out of you and make you lose your edge. Pg. 146
- Fact.
    - As iron S. iron, so a friend S. a friend. Pg. 146

Shepherd
- Caregiver. Pg. 147
- Duty.
    - "Know the state of your flocks, and put your heart into caring for your herds," Pg. 147
    - Make it your very BEST EFFORT to take special CARE of the people God Places under your CARE. Pg. 147

Shield
- Fact.
    - Every word of God proves true. He is a S. to all who come to him for protection. Pg. 162
    - God is a S. to those who walk with integrity. Pg. 5

Shine
- Duty.
  - Let your little light S. and bring an infectious joy to everyone you meet. Pg. 56

Ship
- Fact.
  - Three things that amaze me—no, four things that I don't understand:
    - How a S. navigates the ocean. Pg. 163

Shortcuts
- Warning.
  - Good planning and hard work lead to prosperity, but hasty S. lead to poverty. Pg. 118

Simpleton—Simpletons
- Are clothed with foolishness. Pg. 66
- Warning.
  - Only S. believe everything they're told! Pg. 66
  - The S. goes blindly on and suffers the consequences. Pg. 146

Sin—Sins—Sinner—Sinners
- Duty.
  - Don't envy S., but always continue to fear the Lord. You will be rewarded for this; your hope will not be disappointed. Pg. 134
  - Keep short accounts with God and stay clean before Him and before others. Pg. 156
  - You must reprove or correct those who are under the conviction of S. and lead them to confess and repent of the S. Pg. 129
- Fact.
  - People who conceal their S. will not prosper, but if they confess and turn from them, they will receive mercy. Pg. 156
  - Trouble chases S. Pg. 62
- Warning.
  - It is a S. to belittle one's neighbor. Pg. 67
  - S. is a disgrace to any people. Pg. 70
  - Too much talk leads to S. Pg. 34

Silver
- Duty.
  - Choose God's instruction rather than S. Pg. 27
- Fact.
  - Being held in high esteem is better than S. or gold. Pg. 121
  - Fire tests the purity of S. and gold, but the Lord tests the heart. Pg. 87
  - How much better to get wisdom than gold, and good judgment than S.! Pg. 82
  - The words of the godly are like sterling S. Pg. 34
- Wisdom is more profitable than S. Pg. 11
- Wisdom's wages are better than sterling S. Pg. 28

Simpleton
- Warning.
  - A prudent person foresees danger and takes precautions. The S. goes blindly on and suffers the consequences. Pg. 122

Slander—Slandered—Slandering
- Duty.
  - Resist the urge to join a gossip party and instead look for ways to speak well of those who are being S. Pg. 143
- Warning.
  - Liars pay close attention to S. Pg. 87
  - Never S. a worker to the employer, or the person will curse you, and you will pay for it. Pg. 163
  - S. others makes you a fool. Pg. 34

Slave—Slavery
- Warning.
  - Be lazy and become a S. Pg. 54

Sleep—Sleeps—Sleepy
- Blessing of.
  - Protected by your spiritual parents
- Warning.
  - If you love S., you will end in poverty. Keep your eyes open, and there will be plenty to eat! Pg. 107
  - One who S. during harvest is a disgrace. Pg. 31
  - Too much S., too much rest will bring poverty. Pg. 24

Smart
- Duty.
  - BE S. and trust Him and not OUTSMART yourself and then blame the Lord when it does not work out like you thought it would. Pg. 100

Smile—Smiling
- Duty.
  - KEEP a SMILE on your FACE and in your HEART too. Pg. 78
- The benefits of a well-placed S. Pg. 78

Snake
- Fact.
  - Three things that amaze me—no, four things that I don't understand:
    - How a S. slithers on a rock. Pg. 163

Snare—Snared
- Avoiding the S. of death. Pg. 58

Sober—Sober Minded
- Duty.
  - You must be S., keep your head, in all things. Pg. 131
- Fact.
  - It's not about you. Pg. 22

Soul
- Duty.
  - GUARD your heart so you will not LOSE your S. Pg. 124
  - Make the kind of choices that will produce within you a happy heart and a satisfied S. Pg. 73
- S. food. Pg. 72
- Fact.
  - Kind words are sweet to the S. and healthy for the body. Pg. 84
  - My child, eat honey, for it is good, and the honeycomb is sweet to the taste. In the same way, wisdom is sweet to your S. If you find it, you will have a bright future, and your hopes will not be cut short. Pg. 136
- Warning.
  - Don't befriend angry people or associate with hot-tempered people, or you will learn to be like them and endanger your soul. Pg. 124

Speak—Speaking
- Duty.
  - S. words that produce life and not words that kill people one cut at a time. Pg. 70
- Fact.
  - The heart of the godly thinks carefully before S. Pg. 78
- Kind of.
  - Corrupt. Pg. 16
  - Perverse. Pg. 16
- Think before you S. Pg. 6
- Warning.
  - Stay away from corrupt speech. Pg. 16

Speech
- Fact.
  - From a wise mind comes wise S. Pg. 84

Spirit
- Fact.
  - A broken heart crushes the S. Pg. 72
  - A cheerful heart is good medicine, but a broken S. saps a person's strength. Pg. 94
- Warning.
  - A deceitful tongue crushes the S. Pg. 70

Spirit-Led
- Duty.

Make it your goal to be more PATIENT than POWERFUL, more SELF-CONTROLLED than to be OUT OF CONTROL, more SL. than YOU-LED. Pg. 86

Spirit-Filled
> Duty.
>> Be S. F. when you want to give someone a PIECE of your mind, give them His PEACE instead. Pg. 159

Spurgeon, Charles
> Quote of.
>> *The Proverbs appear at first sight to be thrown together without connection, but it is not so: when you come to close reading you will discover that they are threaded pearls, and that they are in proper position with regard to each other."* Pg. x

Stable—Stability
> Duty.
>> Pray for the kind of LEADERSHIP in your city, state, and country who would choose to be wise and knowledgeable and that the people would enjoy S. Pg. 147
>
> Fact.
>> Wise and knowledgeable leaders bring S. Pg. 147
>
> Warning.
>> Wickedness never brings S. Pg. 50

Steady
> Duty.
>> Remember that in any significant race of life that the TURTLE always wins, always.; so stay S., stay TRUSTWORTHY, stay out of TROUBLE. Pg. 157

Steps
> Duty.
>> Follow the S. of the good. Pg. 7
>
> Fact.
>> We can make our plans, but the Lord determines our S. Pg. 82
>> The Lord directs our S., so why try to understand everything along the way? Pg. 115
>> The prudent carefully consider their S. Pg. 66
>
> Of the good. Pg. 7

Steward—Stewardship
> Blessing of.
>> Give freely and become more wealthy. Pg. 48
>
> Duty.
>> Do not allow your heart to mess with your mind. Pg. 125
>> Don't agree to guarantee another person's debt or put up security for someone else. If you can't pay it, even your bed will be snatched from under you. Pg. 125
>> Managing what you do not own. Pg. 33

Make good sense in every financial decision you make, and for God's glory and His purpose, make many dollars for His work. Pg. 67

SPEND your life on things that really MATTER and SPEND your money to FUND the things that really MATTER. Pg. 49

Fact.

It's not your life. You belong to the Lord so whatever you do should be done in order to please Him. Pg. 60

It's safer not to guarantee another person's debt. Pg. 46

Losing Your Cents Will Cost You Many Dollars. Pg. 125

Learning to be a good steward of time and of people. Pg. 126

Warning.

Be stingy and lose everything. Pg. 48

Guaranteeing another's debt. Pg. 23

There's danger in putting up security for a stranger's debt. Pg. 46

Trust in your money and down you go. Pg. 49

Stomach

Fact.

It is good for workers to have an appetite; an empty S. drives them on. Pg. 85

Store

Duty.

To S. His commands in your heart. Pg. 7

Storm—Storms

Of life. Pg. 35

Stranger

Duty.

Let someone else praise you, not your own mouth—a S., not your own lips. Pg. 144

Strategy—Strategic

S. plans to win. Pg. 114

Strength

Fact.

A cheerful heart is good medicine, but a broken spirit saps a person's S. Pg. 94

How it comes.

For your bones. Pg. 9

Stress—Stressed

Duty.

Put in the necessary WORK that will empower you to STAND when the pressure is on. Pg. 136

Fact.

To blessed to be S. Pg. 35

S. test. Pg. 136

Strife
    Warning.
        A troublemaker plants seeds of S. Pg. 85

Stronghold
    Fact.
        The way of the Lord is a S. to those with integrity. Pg. 36

Student
    Always the S. Pg. 1

Stumble—Stumbled—Stumbling
    Duty.
        Keep yourself from S. into the pit of despair. Pg. 25

Success—Successful—Succeed
    Blessing of a S. life. Pg. 16
    Duty.
        Acquire a taste for wisdom that will SATISFY every desire for S. Pg. 136
        Be intentional on using wise words and working hard so you may be S. Pg. 51
        Give every plan, every action, and every dream you have to the Lord who will bless you with the kind of S. only He can give. Pg. 80
        Make it your goal to learn more than you did yesterday and to use what you learn to add value to more people. Pg. 96
        Set yourself up with long term S. by HOW you live and WHO you live for. Pg. 122
        WORK a good plan and then WORK hard to see the plan S. Pg. 118
    How one is S.
        Embrace the life teachings from your spiritual parents (Mentors) and live a life marked by S. Pg. 25
    Open mind to S. Pg. 96
    The key to experiencing a wildly S. life. Pg. 80
    Thinking for S. Pg. 28
    Those who respect a command will S. Pg. 58
    Fact.
        Commit your actions to the Lord, and your plans will S. Pg. 80
        Many advisers bring S. Pg. 77
        One of the key attributes of the S. person is their ability to embrace "The Process" and see where it leads. Pg. 75
        The secret of S. in life is for a man to be ready for his time when it comes. Pg. 75
        True humility and fear of the Lord lead to riches, honor, and long life. Pg. 122

Sweet
- Fact.
  - My child, eat honey, for it is good, and the honeycomb is S. to the taste. In the same way, wisdom is sweet to your soul. If you find it, you will have a bright future, and your hopes will not be cut short. Pg. 136
  - The heartfelt counsel of a friend is as S. as perfume and incense. Pg. 145

T

Talk
- Duty.
  - Make sure my walk matches my T. Pg. 15
- Kind of.
  - Perverse. Pg. 16
- Warning.
  - Be sensible and keep your mouth shut. Pg. 34
  - Mere T. leads to poverty! Pg. 67
  - Stay away from corrupt speech. Pg. 16
  - Those who love to talk will reap the consequences. Pg. 98
  - Too much T. leads to sin. Pg. 34

Taste
- Fact.
  - My child, eat honey, for it is good, and the honeycomb is sweet to the T. In the same way, wisdom is sweet to your soul. If you find it, you will have a bright future, and your hopes will not be cut short. Pg. 136
- Duty.
  - Acquire a T. for wisdom that will SATISFY every desire for SUCCESS. Pg. 136
  - T. and see for yourself. Pg. 136

Teach—Teaches—Teaching
- Duty.
  - Let everything you do reflect the integrity and seriousness of your T. Pg. 60
  - T. the truth so that your teaching can't be criticized. Pg. 60
- Fact.
  - Fear of the Lord T. wisdom. Pg. 79
- Results of.
  - I am teaching you today—yes, you—so you will trust in the Lord. Pg. 124

Team
- Being on the right T. Pg. 157
- Duty.
  - Make sure you put the right people on your T. Pg. 142
  - Surround yourself with the kind of people who love you enough to tell you the truth. Pg. 157
- Fact.

An employer who hires a fool or a bystander is like an archer who shoots at random. Pg. 142

Temper—Tempers—Tempered
Fact.
- A fool is quick-T. Pg. 52
- A person with understanding is even-T. Pg. 95
- Sensible people control their T.; they earn respect by overlooking wrongs. Pg. 101

Warning.
- A hot T. shows great foolishness. Pg. 68
- Don't befriend angry people or associate with hot-T. people, or you will learn to be like them and endanger your soul. Pg. 124
- Harsh words make T. flare. Pg. 70
- Short-tempered people do foolish things. Pg. 66

Test—Tests
Fact.
- Fire T. the purity of silver and gold, but the Lord tests the heart. Pg. 87

Thankful—Thankfulness
Duty.
- Be T. that you have the ability to help others be T. too. Pg. 120

T. to be T. Pg. 120

Fact.
- Some people are always greedy for more, but the godly love to give! Pg. 120

Theology

A solid T. of work. Pg. 138

Think—Thinks—Thinking
Challenge:
- Commit yourself to T. wise thoughts. Pg. 28

Duty.
- T. before you speak. Pg. 160
- T. before you SPEAK, take a DEEP BREATH before you ACT and PRAY ALWAYS. Pg. 66

Fact.
- If you want to become the very best version of you, learning how to T. positively is key. Pg. 149
- The heart of the godly T. carefully before speaking. Pg. 78
- There is more hope for a fool than for someone who speaks without T. Pg. 160

T. for success. Pg. 28
The benefit of thinking before you speak. Pg. 160
The wisdom of T. before you speak. Pg. 6
Warning.

Be CAREFUL what you T. and what you SAY and what you DO. Pg. 78

Thirst—Thirsty
> Fact.
>> Good news from far away is like cold water to the T. Pg. 141

Thoreau, Henry David
> Quote of.
>> *You cannot dream yourself into a character; you must hammer and forge yourself one.*
>>> Pg. xi

Thoughts
> Challenge:
>> Commit yourself to thinking wise T. Pg. 28
>
> Duty.
>> Feed your mind with HEALTHY T. and leave the brainless JUNK FOOD of UNHEALTHY T. alone. Pg. 72
>>
>> Fix your T. Pg. 150
>
> What you are to fix your T. on.
>> What is admirable. Pg. 150
>>
>> What is honorable. Pg. 150
>>
>> What is lovely. Pg. 150
>>
>> What is pure. Pg. 150
>>
>> What is right. Pg. 150
>>
>> What is true. Pg. 150

Time
> Save.
>> Save your breath for the RIGHT people, at the RIGHT T., and for the RIGHT reason. Pg. 126
>>
>> Learning to be a good steward of T. and of people. Pg. 126

Tolerant—Tolerance
> Duty.
>> FORGIVE when you find a FAULT, LOVE when you would rather LASH out, and GIVE GRACE because you need it too. Pg. 87
>>
>> When T. is spelled L-O-V-E. Pg. 87

Tomlin, Lily
> Quote.
>> *I always wanted to be somebody, but I should have been more specific. Pg. 90*

Tongue
> Fact.
>> The T. can bring death or life. Pg. 98
>>
>> Watch your T. and keep your mouth shut, and you will stay out of trouble. Pg. 120

Those who control their T. will have a long life. Pg. 55
Duty.
Control your T. so your life may be flooded with peace. Pg. 89
SPEAK words of PRAISE, not words of POISON. Pg. 98
Kind of.
Lying T.
Hates its victims. Pg. 143
The Lord hates, detests it. Pg. 24
The power of the T. Pg. 98
Warning.
A deceitful T. crushes the spirit. Pg.70
A lying T. hates its victims, and flattering words cause ruin. Pg. 143
The T. that deceives will be cut off. Pg. 36
Wealth created by a lying T. is a vanishing mist and a deadly trap. Pg. 118

Tracy, Brian
Quote of.
Personal development is a major time-saver. The better you become, the less time it takes you to achieve your goals. Pg. xi

Traitor
Fact.
A false witness is a T. Pg. 68

Transform
Duty.
Let God T. you into a new person. Pg. 60

Transparent—Transparency
Duty.
Live a T. life before the Lord and may His AGENDA become yours. Pg. 116
Fact.
The Lord's light penetrates the human spirit, exposing every hidden motive. Pg. 116
The T. life. Pg. 116

Trap
Warning.
Wealth created by a lying tongue is a vanishing mist and a deadly T. Pg. 118

Trash
Warning.
The fool feeds on T. Pg. 72

Treacherous
Warning.
Advice of the wicked is T. Pg. 51

Dishonesty destroys T. people. Pg. 38
The ambition of T. people traps them. Pg. 38

Treasure—Treasured—Treasures
Duty.
Always T. the Lord's commands. Pg. 26
Make it your T. to embrace words that add value to you and to everyone who hears you speak. Pg. 114
Commands are to be T. Pg. 4
Fact.
Better to have little, with fear for the Lord, than to have great T. and inner turmoil. Pg. 73
God grants a T. of common sense to the honest. Pg. 5
Hidden. Pg. 4
T. trove. Pg. 114

Tree
Fact.
Gentle words are a T. of life. Pg. 70
Of Life.
A dream fulfilled is a tree of life. Pg. 57
The seeds of good deeds become a T. of life. Pg. 49
Wisdom is a T. of life to those who embrace her. Pg. 11

Trouble
Duty.
Run away from T. and run to the blessings God has promised you. Pg. 62
Remember that in any significant race of life that the TURTLE always wins, always.; so stay STEADY, stay TRUSTWORTHY, stay out of T. Pg. 157
Fact.
For the despondent, every day brings T. Pg. 73
T. chases sinners. Pg. 62
Watch your tongue and keep your mouth shut, and you will stay out of T. Pg. 120
Warning.
Associate with fools and get in T. Pg. 62
Look UP before you look DOWN and stay out of sexual T. Pg. 17
People who despise advise are asking for T. Pg. 58
Stay out of sexual T. Pg. 17
The trustworthy person will get a rich reward, but a person who wants quick riches will get into T. Pg. 157

Troublemaker
Warning.
A T. plants seeds of strife. Pg. 85

True—Truth—Truthful
Duty.

Determine to make every decision you make be based upon the T., no matter how "inconvenient" it may be for you. Pg. 68

Make a commitment to earn an HONEST dollar by telling and living the T. before others and before God. Pg. 118

Make an intentional decision that everything you THINK, SAY, and DO be based upon what is T. Pg. 64

Set in your heart to be THE REAL DEAL in your character with those who are depending upon you to be HONEST and T. Pg. 47

Speak the T., the whole T., nothing but the T., so help you God. Pg. 53

Surround yourself with the kind of people who love you enough to tell you the T. Pg. 157

Teach the T. so that your teaching can't be criticized. Pg. 60

Think on what is T., as in authentic, real, genuine. Pg. 150

Fact.

An honest witness tells the T. Pg. 52

A T. witness saves lives. Pg. 68

If you want to live a set free life, then think on what is T. Pg. 150

In the end, people appreciate honest criticism far more than flattery. Pg. 157

The Lord delights in those who tell the T. Pg. 53

T. is a verb, an adjective, and a noun. Pg. 53

T. is the currency that finances how you build your life into the very best version of you. Pg. 150

Living in the land of truth. Pg. 66

Warning.

Wealth created by a lying tongue is a vanishing mist and a deadly trap. Pg. 118

Trust—Trusting

Duty.

Assure those who T. you that they can be CONFIDENT in your COMPETENCE to keep a CONFIDENCE. Pg. 45

Check your HEART before you T. your EYES. Pg. 117

Live in the PRESENT and T. God to give you what you need for the FUTURE. Pg. 144

To T. Him with everything you've got. Pg. 8

T. His will to take you where you need to go. Pg. 8

Fact.

Fearing people is a dangerous trap, but T. the Lord means safety. Pg. 161

Greed causes fighting; T. the Lord leads to prosperity. Pg. 158

The Lord directs our steps, so why try to understand everything along the way? Pg. 115

Those who trust the Lord will be joyful. Pg. 83

How.

With all your heart. Pg. 9

How T. empowers you to live a wildly successful life. Pg. 8

Warning.

Don't brag about tomorrow, since you don't know what the day will bring. Pg. 144

Do not T. you with everything you have. Pg. 8

What it means to T. the Lord. Pg. 111

Trustworthy
    Duty.
        Remember that in any significant race of life that the TURTLE always wins, always.; so stay STEADY, stay T., stay out of TROUBLE. Pg. 157
    Fact.
        Those who are T. can keep a confidence. Pg. 45
    Warning.
        The T. person will get a rich reward, but a person who wants quick riches will get into trouble. Pg. 157

Turtle
    Duty.
        Remember that in any significant race of life that the T. always wins, always.; so stay STEADY, stay TRUSTWORTHY, stay out of TROUBLE. Pg. 157
    Win like a T. Pg. 157

U

Under Advisement
    Fact.
        Always get better advice than your own. Pg. 77

Understand—Understanding
    Concentrate on U. Pg. 4
    Directions to foolish people.
        Show some U. Pg. 26
    Fact.
        A person with U. is even-tempered. Pg. 95
        If you listen to correction, you grow in U. Pg. 79
        No human wisdom or U. or plan can stand against the Lord. Pg. 121
        People with U. control their anger. Pg. 68
        People who cherish U. will prosper. Pg. 100
        The Lord directs our steps, so why try to U. everything along the way? Pg. 115
        Though good advice lies deep within the heart, a person with U. will draw it out. Pg. 105
    Warning.
        Do not depend on your own U. Pg. 9
    Will keep you safe. Pg. 6

V

Validation
    Duty.
        Feed the people who hunger for the kinds of words that produce V. for those who need to experience SATISFACTION. Pg. 97

Value—Values—Valuable
    A life of essential V. Pg. 155
    Duty.
        Add V. to those you love by intentionally using kind words that build them up. Pg. 84
        Be sure your Christian V. are the most V. possession you live out before God and others. Pg. 155
        Make decisions that will add V. to others and credibility to your legacy. Pg. 32
        Make it your goal to ADD V. to everyone you meet. Pg. 49
        Make it your goal to learn more than you did yesterday and to use what you learn to add V. to more people. Pg. 96
        Make it your treasure to embrace words that add V. to you and to everyone who hears you speak. Pg. 114
    Fact.
        Better to be poor and honest than to be dishonest and rich. Pg. 155
        Wise words are more V. than much gold and many rubies. Pg. 114

Vengeance
    Duty.
        Allow the Lord to keep you on an EVEN keel and stay RIGHT so you will not fall into the vindictive trap of trying to get EVEN and wind up WRONG. Pg. 115
        Don't say, "I will get even for this wrong." Wait for the Lord to handle the matter. Pg. 115
    No vindictive zone. Pg. 115

Victory
    Fact.
        The horse is prepared for the day of battle, but the V. belongs to the Lord. Pg. 121

Violent—Violence
    Warning.
        Don't envy V. people. Pg. 13
        Words of the wicked conceal V. intentions. Pg. 31

Voice—Voices
    Shutting out destructive V. Pg. 87

W

Wage—Wages
    Duty.
        Seek to become the RICHEST person you know with the things that matter most. Pg. 82
    Fact.
        How much better to get wisdom than gold, and good judgment than silver! Pg. 82
    Wisdom's W. are better than gold. Pg. 11

Walk
    Duty.
        Make sure my W. matches my talk. Pg. 15

War
    Fact.
        Plans succeed through good counsel; don't go to W. without wise advice. Pg. 114
    Warning.
        Don't go to W. without wise advice. Pg. 114

Wardrobe
    Duty.
        Put on the right kind of W. where you inspire confidence in everyone around you. Pg. 166
    Fact.
        The virtuous woman is clothed with strength and dignity. Pg. 166
        The right kind of W. sets you apart. Pg. 166

Warren, Rick
    Quote of.
        Transformation is a process, and as life happens there are tons of ups and downs. It's a journey of discovery. Pg. xi

Watch—Watching
    Reason why you are to W. your heart.
        It determines the course of your life. Pg. 16
    Warning.
        Guard your heart above all else. Pg. 16
    Wise choices will W. over you. Pg. 6

Wealth
    Blessing of being a giver.
        Give freely and become more wealthy. Pg. 48
        He will fill your barns with grain. Pg. 10
        Your vats will overflow with good wine. Pg. 10
    Charge.
        Honor the Lord with your W. Pg. 10
    Duty.
        Make a commitment to earn an HONEST dollar by telling and living the TRUTH before others and before God. Pg. 118
        Make good sense in every financial decision you make, and for God's glory and His purpose, make many dollars for His work. Pg. 67
        Seek to become the RICHEST person you know with the things that matter most. Pg. 82
        Work SMARTER and HARDER so you can EARN MORE to GIVE AWAY. Pg. 57
    Fact.
        Evil people get rich for the moment. Pg. 47
        How much better to get wisdom than gold, and good judgment than silver! Pg. 82

The earnings of the godly enhance their lives. Pg. 33
W. is a crown for the wise. Pg. 67
Reason for creating. Pg. 57
Responsibility of.
Honor the Lord with your W. Pg. 10
Stewardship of.
When it comes to stewarding the money God entrusts to you, be careful to learn the balance between using your head and your heart. Pg. 46
Those who love wisdom inherit W. Pg. 28
Using wisdom with your W. Pg. 46
Warning.
Be stingy and lose everything. Pg. 48
Don't wear yourself out trying to get rich. Be wise enough to know when to quit. In the blink of an eye W. disappears, for it will sprout wings and fly away like an eagle. Pg. 126
Evil people squander their money on sin. Pg. 33
Tainted W. has no lasting value. Pg. 30
W. created by a lying tongue is a vanishing mist and a deadly trap. Pg. 118
Trust in your money and down you go. Pg. 49
W., honestly speaking. Pg. 118

Weights
Warning.
False W. and unequal measures — the Lord detests double standards of every kind. Pg. 106

Who Am I
Fact.
A healthy view of your identity (who you are) empowers you to go beyond yourself and serve others. Pg. 92
Having clarity about our identity empowers us. Pg.92
Your identity matters. Pg. 90

Wicked—Wickedness
Fact.
The godly care about the rights of the poor; the W. don't care at all. Pg. 159
The Lord detests the way of the W. Pg. 71
The whole city shouts for joy when the W. die. Pg. 39
People.
Are detestable to the Lord. Pg. 13
Warning.
Advice of the W. is treacherous. Pg. 51
Anyone who corrects the W. will get hurt. Pg. 29
But one disaster is enough to overthrow the W. Don't rejoice when your enemies fall; don't be happy when they stumble. For the Lord will be displeased with you and will turn his anger away from them. Pg. 137

The expectations of the W. come to nothing. Pg. 36
The Lord condemns those who plan W. Pg. 50
The Lord curses the house of the W. Pg. 13
The talk of the wicked tears a city apart. Pg. 39
The W. fall beneath their load of sin. Pg. 38
The W. lead their friends astray. Pg. 55
When the storms of life come, the W. are whirled away. Pg. 35
When the W. take charge, people go into hiding. Pg. 155
W. never brings stability. Pg. 50
Words of the W. are like a murderous ambush. Pg. 51
Words of the W. conceal violent intentions. Pg. 31

Wife
Fact.
Charm is deceptive, and beauty does not last; but a woman who fears the Lord will be greatly praised. Pg. 167

Qualities of a godly, virtuous and capable W.
A hard worker. Pg. 165
Her husband can trust her. Pg. 165
Her lamp burns late into the night. Pg. 166
She brings him good, not harm all the days of her life. Pg. 165
She extends a helping hand to the poor. Pg. 166
She gives instructions with kindness. Pg. 167
She goes to inspect a field and buys it. Pg. 165
She is clothed with strength and dignity. Pg. 166
She is energetic and strong. Pg. 165
She is more precious than rubies. Pg. 165
She laughs without fear of the future. Pg. 166
She makes sure her dealings are profitable. Pg. 166
She opens her arms to the needy. Pg. 166
She will greatly enrich his life. Pg. 165
When she speaks, her words are wise. Pg. 167
With her earnings she plants a vineyard. Pg. 165

Will
Fact.
It's not your life. You belong to the Lord so whatever you do should be done in order to please Him. Pg. 60

Will of God
Charge.
Seek His W. in all you do. Pg. 8

Win—Winner—Winning
Duty.
Be selective and only fight the battles you can W. Pg. 114

Protect the relationships that are important to you by W. their love, not by W. the argument. Pg. 97
Fact.
    The horse is prepared for the day of battle, but the victory belongs to the Lord. Pg. 121
    The W. takes it all. Pg. 97
Strategic plans to W. Pg. 114
W. like a turtle. Pg. 157

Wine
Blessing of being a giver.
    Your vats will overflow with good wine. Pg. 10

Wink
Warning.
    People who W. at wrong cause trouble. Pg. 32

Wisdom
Benefits of.
    Don't turn your back on W., for she will protect you. Pg. 14
    Embracing God's W. Pg. 11, 28
    Embrace her, and she will honor you. Pg. 14
    Getting wisdom is the wisest thing you can do. Pg. 14
    Gifts are better than gold. Pg. 28
    If you become W. you will be the one to benefit. Pg. 30
    If you prize wisdom, she will make you great. Pg. 14
    Listen to W's. instruction and be wise. Pg. 28
    Love her, and she will guard you. Pg. 14
    Those who love W. inherit wealth. Pg. 28
    Those who search for W. will find it. Pg. 28
    Wages better than sterling silver. Pg. 28
    Whoever finds W. finds life. Pg. 28
    Whoever finds W. receives favor from the Lord. Pg. 28
    W. matters. Pg. 27
    Will add years to your life. Pg. 30
    Will multiply your days. Pg. 30
    Will place a lovely wreath on your head. Pg. 14
    Will present you with a beautiful crown. Pg. 14
    Will save you from evil people. Pg. 6
Charge.
    Cling to every bit of W. you can collect . . . and use it. Pg. 27
    Don't forget His words or turn away from them. Pg. 14
    Get it while you can. Pg. 14
    Hold it tightly. Pg. 11
    Let His words penetrate deep into your heart. Pg. 15
    Listen carefully to His words. Pg. 15

Listen to the words of the wise; apply your heart to my instruction. For it is good to keep these sayings in your heart and always ready on your lips. Pg. 123

Pay attention to what He says. Pg. 15

Compared with.
- Is a tree of life to those who embrace W. Pg. 11
- More precious than rubies. Pg. 11
- More profitable than silver. Pg. 11
- Nothing you desire can compare with W. Pg. 11
- Wages are better than gold. Pg. 11

Duty.
- Acquire a taste for W. that will SATISFY every desire for SUCCESS. Pg. 136
- Be a plentiful resource of W. that W. hunters can come and draw from you. Pg. 95
- Be WISE enough to listen to the advice of WISE people and make WISE decisions that will be a blessing to you. Pg. 58
- Listen as W. calls out. Pg. 26
- Make a focused effort to gain practical W. in your life and then have the common sense to know what to do with it. Pg. 135
- Make it your goal to make everything you THINK, SAY, and DO be anchored in W. Pg. 84
- SEEK His W., not yours; His plan, not yours because His WAYS are much higher than yours. Pg. 121
- Seek to be the wisest, most humble person you know. Pg. 79

Fact.
- A house is built by wisdom and becomes strong through good sense. Pg. 135
- A wise person wins friends. Pg. 49
- A wise youth harvests in the summer. Pg. 31
- Fear of the Lord is the foundation of W. Pg. 30
- Fear of the Lord teaches W. Pg. 79
- From a wise mind comes wise speech. Pg. 84
- How much better to get W. than gold, and good judgment than silver! Pg. 82
- Has riches and honor. Pg. 28
- Loves those who love W. Pg. 28
- My child, eat honey, for it is good, and the honeycomb is sweet to the taste. In the same way, W. is sweet to your soul. If you find it, you will have a bright future, and your hopes will not be cut short. Pg. 136
- No human W. or understanding or plan can stand against the Lord. Pg. 121
- To acquire W. is to love yourself. Pg. 100
- W. flows from the wise like a bubbling brook. Pg. 95
- W. works. Pg. 26
- With humility comes W. Pg. 37
- Wise words are more valuable than much gold and many rubies. Pg. 114

Finding W. in everything you THINK and DO. Pg. 11

How to get and use W. Pg. 79

Influence of.
- In every decision you make and in every relationship you have. Pg. 26

Kind of.
> Guiding. Pg. 3
> Heals and Strengthens. Pg. 9
> High value. Pg. 4
> Joyful. Pg. 11, 28
> That fills you with joy. Pg. 5

Of avoiding negative people. Pg. 6
Of thinking before you speak. Pg. 6
Source of.
> Comes from the Lord. Pg. 5

The filter of W. Pg. 84
The power of common sense W. Pg. 135
Using W. with your wealth. Pg. 46
Warning.
> Don't be impressed with your own W. Pg. 9
> Get W. before foolishness gets you. Pg. 14
> If you scorn wisdom, you will be the one to suffer. Pg. 30
> Protect yourself from taking your own advice and not His. Pg. 9

Why W. is a stewardship. Pg. 30
Why W. works. Pg. 58
Will enter your heart. Pg. 5

Wise—Wiser—Wisest

Duty.
> As you get older, get W. by becoming more godly. Pg. 85
> Be W. enough to listen to the advice of W. people and make W. decisions that will be a blessing to you. Pg. 58
> Be willing to LEARN so you will be able to be W. the REST of your LIFE. Pg. 101
> Correct the W. Pg. 29
> Instruct the W. Pg. 29
> Listen to the words of the W.; apply your heart to my instruction. For it is good to keep these sayings in your heart and always ready on your lips. Pg. 123
> Pray for the kind of LEADERSHIP in your city, state, and country who would choose to be W. and knowledgeable and that the people would enjoy stability. Pg. 147
> Seek to be the W., most humble person you know. Pg. 79

Fact.
> Are glad to be instructed. Pg. 31
> A truly W. person uses few words. Pg. 95
> A W. person is hungry for knowledge. Pg. 72
> A W. person stays calm when insulted. Pg. 52
> Fools vent their anger, but the W. quietly hold it back. Pg. 159
> From a W. mind comes W speech. Pg. 84
> If you listen to constructive criticism, you will be at home among the W. Pg. 78
> The lips of the W. give good advice. Pg. 71
> The instruction of the W. is like a life-giving fountain. Pg. 58
> The tongue of the W. makes knowledge appealing. Pg. 70

The W. are mightier than the strong, and those with knowledge grow stronger and stronger. Pg. 135

The wise don't make a show of their knowledge. Pg. 53

The W. are cautious and avoid danger. Pg. 66

The W. inherit honor. Pg. 14

The W. listen to others. Pg. 52

The W. person always learns. Pg. 101

The words of the W. are persuasive. Pg. 84

The words of the W. bring healing. Pg. 53

Those who take advice are W. Pg. 57

W. words are like deep waters. Pg. 95

W. words are more valuable than much gold and many rubies. Pg. 114

Wealth is a crown for the W. Pg. 67

Wisdom flows from the W. like a bubbling brook. Pg. 95

W. people treasure knowledge. Pg. 33

W. words bring many benefits. Pg. 51

How one becomes W. Pg. 3

Walk with the W. and become W. Pg. 62

Warning.

- The heart of a fool has no wise advice to give. Pg. 71
- Don't wear yourself out trying to get rich. Be W. enough to know when to quit. In the blink of an eye wealth disappears, for it will sprout wings and fly away like an eagle. Pg. 126
- Without W. leadership, a nation falls. Pg. 45

W. choices will watch over you. Pg. 6

W. words that satisfy. Pg. 97

Witness

Can I get a W.? Pg. 68

Duty.

- Determine to make every decision you make be based upon the truth, no matter how "inconvenient" it may be for you. Pg. 68
- Don't IMPRESS others by WHAT YOU KNOW but by WHAT YOU DO. Pg. 52
- HUSH your mouth and KEEP your W. Pg. 120
- Let your little light shine and bring an infectious joy to everyone you meet. Pg. 56
- Live in a way were your actions speak for themselves. Pg. 60
- Make a commitment to earn an HONEST dollar by telling and living the TRUTH before others and before God. Pg. 118
- Set the example of living a transformed life. Pg. 60

Fact.

- A false W. is a traitor. Pg. 68
- A false W. tells lies. Pg. 52
- An honest W. tells the truth. Pg. 52
- An honest W. does not lie. Pg. 64
- A truthful W. saves lives. Pg. 68
- If you plan to do good, you will receive unfailing love and faithfulness. Pg. 67

Watch your tongue and keep your mouth shut, and you will stay out of trouble. Pg. 120
Kind of.
> False. The Lord hates, detests them. Pg. 24
> Honest. Pg. 52

Warning.
> A false W. breathes lies. Pg. 64

Woman
Fact.
> Three things that amaze me—no, four things that I don't understand:
>> How a man loves a W. Pg. 163

Word—Words
Blessing of.
> A gentle answer deflects anger. Pg. 70
> An encouraging W. cheers a person up. Pg. 54
> The lips of the godly speak helpful W. Pg. 37
> The W. of the godly are a life-giving fountain. Pg. 32
> The W. of the godly encourage many. Pg. 34

Duty.
> Add value to those you love by intentionally using kind W. that build them up. Pg. 84
> Be a person of your W. and may you be satisfied with whatever provisions God may send your way. Pg. 162
> Be intentional on using wise W. and working hard so you may be SUCCESSFUL. Pg. 51
> Be intentional on using words that are TRUTHFUL, that are HEALING, and that STAND THE TEST OF TIME. Pg. 52
> Correctly explain the W. of truth. Pg. 60
> Feed the people who hunger for the kinds of W. that produce VALIDATION for those who need to experience SATISFACTION. Pg. 97
> GUARD what your EARS hear so that toxic W. will not leave your MOUTH. Pg. 114
> Give someone a piece of your HEART before you give them a piece of your MIND. Pg. 167
> Keep the right W. in your HEART so you can bless the HEART of another. Pg. 123
> KNOW the W., LIVE BY the W., and POINT others to the W. Pg. 162
> Let His W. penetrate deep into your heart. Pg. 15
> Listen to the W. of the wise; apply your heart to my instruction. For it is good to keep these sayings in your heart and always ready on your lips. Pg. 123
> Live your life and when necessary use W. Pg. 53
> Make it your treasure to embrace W. that add value to you and to everyone who hears you speak. Pg. 114
> Make sure every W. you use builds someone up and not take them down. Pg. 85
> Offer your W. as a GIFT that build up, not words that DEPLETE and DESTROY. Pg. 36
> PRAY about WHO needs a GOOD and ENCOURAGING W. from YOU and SHARE IT. Pg. 141
> Preach the W. Pg. 128
> SPEAK W. of PRAISE, not words of POISON. Pg. 98
> Speak W. that produce life and not words that kill people one cut at a time. Pg. 70
> To be laser-focused upon His W. Pg. 15

Use the RIGHT W. at the RIGHT time in the RIGHT way. Pg. 95
WATCH what you say and WHO you say it to and HOW you say it. Pg. 70
Fact.
    A truly wise person uses few W. Pg. 95
    Every W. of God proves true. He is a shield to all who come to him for protection. Pg. 162
    Gentle W. are a tree of life. Pg. 70
    Kind W. are like honey. Pg. 84
    Kind W. are sweet to the soul and healthy for the body. Pg. 84
    The right words bring satisfaction. Pg. 98
    The tongue of the wise makes knowledge appealing. Pg. 70
    The W. of the godly are like sterling silver. Pg. 34
    The W. of the godly save lives. Pg. 51
    The W. of the wise are persuasive. Pg. 84
    The W. of the wise bring healing. Pg. 53
    Truthful W. stand the test of time. Pg. 53
    Wise W. are like deep waters. Pg. 95
    Wise W. are more valuable than much gold and many rubies. Pg. 114
    Wise W. bring many benefits. Pg. 51
    Wise W. satisfy like a good meal. Pg. 98
    Your W. is your bond. Pg. 162
Kind of.
    Healing. Pg. 52
    Kind. Pg. 84
    Negative. Pg. 6
    Sweet. Pg. 84
    Timely. Pg. 141
    Toxic. Pg. 114
    Transformational. Pg. 167
    Wise. Pg. 33, 98
The W.-driven life. Pg. 162
The power of a timely W. Pg. 141
Warning.
    A deceitful tongue crushes the spirit. Pg.70
    A gossip goes around telling secrets, so don't hang around with chatterers. Pg. 115
    A lying tongue hates its victims, and flattering W. cause ruin. Pg. 143
    Opening your mouth can ruin everything. Pg. 55
    Harsh W. make tempers flare. Pg. 70
    The mouth of the wicked overflows with evil W. Pg. 78
    The mouth of the wicked speaks perverse W. Pg. 37
    Watch what you say so you will not have to eat your W. Pg. 55
    W. of the wicked are like a murderous ambush. Pg. 51
    W. of the wicked conceal violent intentions. Pg. 31, 32
Why right W. matter. Pg. 33
Wise W.
    Source of.
        From the lips of people with understanding. Pg. 33

W. diplomat. Pg. 70
W. leverage. Pg. 70
Wise W. that satisfy. Pg. 97

Word of God
Benefits of putting God's W. in your H. Pg. 7
Charge.
Don't forget His words or turn away from them. Pg. 14
Let His words penetrate deep into your heart. Pg. 15
Duty.
To be laser-focused upon His words. Pg. 15

Work—Worker—Workers
A solid theology of W. Pg. 138
Duty.
Be a good W. Pg. 60
Be motivated to do the W. TODAY that will provide for your needs TOMORROW. Pg. 104
Do enough productive W. that will be messy enough to clean up. Pg. 63
Live in a way were your actions speak for themselves. Pg. 60
Make every business decision with a commitment to live out the teachings of Jesus with your own PERSONAL INTEGRITY and W. ETHIC. Pg. 125
Seek to W. HARDER and SMARTER so you will be able to be a GIVER to the things that MATTER to the Lord. Pg. 84
W. a good plan and then W. hard to see the plan succeed. Pg. 118
W. hard and become a leader. Pg. 54
W. harder and smarter. Pg. 138
W. like it all depends upon you and PRAY like it all depends upon Him. Pg. 121, 165
W. like your meals depended upon it. Pg. 156
W. SMARTER and HARDER so you can EARN MORE to GIVE AWAY. Pg. 57
Fact.
Do you see any truly competent W.? They will serve kings rather than working for ordinary people. Pg. 125
Good planning and hard W. lead to prosperity, but hasty shortcuts lead to poverty. Pg. 118
It is good for W. to have an appetite; an empty stomach drives them on. Pg. 85
The horse is prepared for the day of battle, but the victory belongs to the Lord. Pg. 121
Those who W. hard will prosper. Pg. 56
W. brings profit. Pg. 67
Without oxen a stable stays clean. Pg. 63
You need a strong ox for a large harvest. Pg. 63
Hard W. brings rewards. Pg. 51
How W. and prayer go together. Pg. 121
The motivation of W. Pg. 84
Warning.
A hard W. has plenty of food, but a person who chases fantasies ends up in poverty. Pg. 156

A little extra sleep, a little more slumber, a little folding of the hands to rest—then poverty will pounce on you like a bandit; scarcity will attack you like an armed robber. Pg. 138

Never slander a W. to the employer, or the person will curse you, and you will pay for it. Pg. 163

Workplace
Duty.
Seek to build up your teammates when others would seek to tear them down. Pg. 163
The secret to having a great W. Pg. 163
Warning.
Never slander a worker to the employer, or the person will curse you, and you will pay for it. Pg. 163

Worry—Worried—Worrying
Duty.
Be content with the ABUNDANCE God provides and not W. about what you DO NOT HAVE. Pg. 81
Save your energy of W. about things you can't control and spend that energy building up someone who needs some encouragement. Pg. 54
Fact.
W. weighs a person down. Pg. 54

Worship
Fact.
It's not your life. You belong to the Lord so whatever you do should be done in order to please Him. Pg. 60

Wreath
Wisdom will place a lovely W. on your head. Pg. 14

Wrong
Duty.
Allow the Lord to keep you on an EVEN keel and stay RIGHT so you will not fall into the vindictive trap of trying to get EVEN and wind up W. Pg. 115
Be willing to be HUMBLE when you are W. and be willing to be HUMBLE when you are RIGHT. Pg. 79
Don't say, "I will get even for this W." Wait for the Lord to handle the matter. Pg. 115

Wrongdoers
Warning.
W. eagerly listen to gossip. Pg. 87

Y

Youth

    Fact.
        A wise Y harvests in the summer. Pg. 31

Z

Ziglar, Zig

    Quote of.
        Of course motivation is not permanent. But then, neither is bathing; but it is something you should do on a regular basis. Pg. xi

SCRIPTURE INDEX

OLD TESTAMENT

Joshua
    1:1-9. Pg. 21-22

1 Samuel
    30:6. Pg. 42

Psalms
    1:1-3. Pg. 151-152
    23:1-6. Pg. 113
    37:23. Pg. 151
    40:1-5. Pg. 108
    40:1. Pg. 108
    40:2-3. Pg. 109
    40:4. Pg. 110
    40:5. Pg. 111
    46:10. Pg. 90
    139:1-18. Pg. 112

Proverbs
    1:1-5:14. Pg. xi
    1:1-3. Pg. 1
    1:4-6. Pg. 1
    1:7. Pg. 2
    1:17-19. Pg. 2-3
    1:23. Pg. 3
    1:33. Pg. 3
    2:1-5. Pg. 4
    2:6-7. Pg. 5
    2:10. Pg. 5
    2:11. Pg. 6
    2:12-15. Pg. 6
    2:20-21. Pg. 7
    3:1-2. Pg. 7-8
    3:3-4. Pg. 8
    3:5-6. Pg. x, Pg. 9, Pg. 111
    3:7-8. Pg. 9
    3:9-10. Pg. 10
    3:11-12. Pg. 10
    3:13-15. Pg. 11
    3:16-18. Pg. 11
    3:21-26. Pg. 12
    3:27-30. Pg. 13

Proverbs (Continued)
- 3:31-35. Pg. 13-14
- 4:5-9. Pg. 14
- 4:10-13. Pg. 15
- 4:20-22. Pg. 15
- 4:23. Pg. 16
- 4:24. Pg. 16
- 4:25-27. Pg. 17
- 5:7-14. Pg. 17-18, 18-19
- 6:1-11:11. Pg. 20
- 6:1-4. Pg. 23
- 6:6-11. Pg. 23-24
- 6:16-19. Pg. 24
- 6:20-23. Pg. 25
- 7:1-3. Pg. 26
- 8:1-7. Pg. 26-27
- 8:8-11. Pg. 27
- 8:17-21. Pg. 28
- 8:32-35. Pg. 28-29
- 9:7-9. Pg. 29
- 9:10-12. Pg. 30
- 10:2. Pg. 30
- 10:3-6. Pg. 31
- 10:8. Pg. 31
- 10:9. Pg. 32
- 10:10-11. Pg. 32
- 10:12. Pg. 33
- 10:13-14. Pg. 33
- 10:16. Pg. 33
- 10:17. Pg. 34
- 10:18-22. Pg. 34
- 10:22. Pg.35
- 10:25. Pg. 35
- 10:28. Pg. 36
- 10:29. Pg. 36
- 10:31-32. Pg. 36-37
- 11:1. Pg. 37
- 11:2. Pg. 37
- 11:3. Pg. 38
- 11:5-6. Pg. 38
- 11:10-11. Pg. 39
- 11:13-13:14. Pg. 40
- 11:13. Pg. 45
- 11:14. Pg. 45
- 11:15. Pg. 46
- 11:17. Pg. 46

Proverbs (Continued)
- 11:18. Pg. 47
- 11:20. Pg. 47
- 11:24. Pg. 48
- 11:25. Pg. 48
- 11:28. Pg. 49
- 11:30. Pg. 49
- 12:1. Pg. 50
- 12:2-3. Pg. 50
- 12:5-6. Pg. 51
- 12:14. Pg. 51
- 12:15. Pg.52
- 12:16. Pg. 52
- 12:17-19. Pg. 52-53
- 12:22. Pg. 53
- 12:23. Pg. 53
- 12:24. Pg. 54
- 12:25. Pg. 54
- 12:26. Pg. 55
- 12:28. Pg. 55
- 13:3. Pg. 56
- 13:4. Pg. 56
- 13:9. Pg. 56
- 13:10. Pg. 57
- 13:11. Pg. 57
- 13:12. Pg. 57
- 13:13. Pg. 58
- 13:14. Pg. 58
- 13:16-15:17. Pg. 59
- 13:16. Pg. 61
- 13:18. Pg. 61
- 13:19. Pg. 62
- 13:20. Pg. 62
- 13:21. Pg. 62
- 14:2. Pg. 63
- 14:4. Pg. 63
- 14:5. Pg. 64
- 14:8. Pg. 64
- 14:10. Pg. 65
- 14:13. Pg. 65
- 14:14. Pg. 65
- 14:15. Pg. 66
- 14:16-18. Pg. 66
- 14:21-22. Pg. 67
- 14:23-24. Pg. 67
- 14:25. Pg. 68

Proverbs (Continued)
    14:29. Pg. 68
    14:30. Pg. 69
    14:31. Pg. 69
    14:31. Pg. 70
    15:1-2. Pg. 70
    15:4. Pg. 70
    15:7. Pg. 71
    15:9. Pg. 71
    15:10. Pg. 72
    15:13. Pg. 72
    15:14. Pg. 72
    15:15. Pg. 73
    15:16. Pg. 73
    15:17. Pg. 73
    15:22-17:17. Pg. 74
    15:22. Pg. 77
    15:23. Pg. 77
    15:28. Pg. 78
    15:30. Pg. 78
    15:31. Pg. 78
    15:32. Pg. 79
    15:33. Pg. 79
    16:1. Pg. 80
    16:2. Pg. 80
    16:3. Pg. 80
    16:7. Pg. 81
    16:8. Pg. 81
    16:9. Pg. 82
    16:11. Pg. 82
    16:16. Pg. 82
    16:18. Pg. 83
    16:20. Pg. 83
    16:23. Pg. 84
    16:24. Pg. 84
    16:26. Pg. 85
    16:28. Pg. 85
    16:31. Pg. 85
    16:32. Pg. 86
    16:33. Pg. 86
    17:3. Pg. 87
    17:4. Pg. 87
    17:5. Pg. 87
    17:9. Pg. 88
    17:10. Pg. 88
    17:14. Pg. 89

Proverbs (Continued)

Proverbs (Continued)
- 17:17. Pg. 89
- 17:18-20:13. Pg. 90
- 17:18. Pg. 94
- 17:22. Pg. 94
- 17:27. Pg. 95
- 18:4. Pg. 95
- 18:10. Pg. 95
- 18:12. Pg. 96
- 18:15. Pg. 96
- 18:16. Pg. 97, Pg. 148
- 18:19. Pg. 97
- 18:20. Pg. 98
- 18:21. Pg. 98
- 18:24. Pg. 98
- 19:1. Pg. 99
- 19:2. Pg. 99
- 19:3. Pg. 100
- 19:8. Pg. 100
- 19:11. Pg. 101
- 19:17. Pg. 101
- 19:20. Pg. 101
- 19:21. Pg. 102
- 19:22. Pg. 102
- 19:23. Pg. 103
- 19:26. Pg. 103
- 19:27. Pg. 104
- 20:3. Pg. 104
- 20:4. Pg. 104
- 20:5. Pg. 105
- 20:6. Pg. 105
- 20:10. Pg. 106
- 20:12. Pg. 106
- 20:13. Pg. 107
- 20:15-23:11. Pg. 108
- 20:15. Pg. 114
- 20:18. Pg. 114
- 20:19. Pg. 115
- 20:22. Pg. 115
- 20:24. Pg. 115
- 20:25. Pg. 116
- 20:27. Pg. 116
- 20:28. Pg. 117
- 21:2. Pg. 117
- 21:3. Pg. 118
- 21:5. Pg. 118

Proverbs (Continued)
    21:6. Pg. 118
    21:13. Pg. 119
    21:21. Pg. 119
    21:23. Pg. 120
    21:26. Pg. 120
    21:30. Pg. 121
    21:31. Pg. 121
    22:1. Pg. 121
    22:3. Pg. 122
    22:4. Pg. 122
    22:7. Pg. 123
    22:9. Pg. 123
    22:17-18. Pg. 123
    22:19. Pg. 124
    22:24-25. Pg. 124
    22:26-27. Pg. 125
    22:28-29. Pg. 125
    23:4-5. Pg. 126
    23:9. Pg. 126
    23:10-11. Pg. 127
    23:18-27:23. Pg. 127
    23:17-18. Pg. 134
    23:26. Pg. 134
    24:1-2. Pg. 135
    24:3-5. Pg. 135
    24:10. Pg. 136
    24:13-14. Pg. 136
    24:16-18. Pg. 137
    24:27. Pg. 137
    24:28-29. Pg. 138
    24:30-34. Pg. 138
    25:6-7. Pg. 139
    25:11-12. Pg. 139
    25:13. Pg. 140
    25:14. Pg. 140
    25:21-22. Pg. 140
    25:25. Pg. 141
    25:28. Pg. 141
    26:4-5. Pg. 142
    26:10. Pg. 142
    26:17. Pg. 142
    26:20. Pg. 143
    26:27-28. Pg. 143
    27:1. Pg. 144
    27:2. Pg. 144

Proverbs (Continued)
- 27:5-6. Pg. 145
- 27:9. Pg. 145
- 27:10. Pg. 146
- 27:12. Pg. 146
- 27:17. Pg. 146
- 27:23. Pg. 147
- 28:2. Pg. 147
- 28:3-31:30. Pg. 148
- 28:3. Pg. 154
- 28:5. Pg. 154
- 28:9. Pg. 155
- 28:6. Pg. 155
- 28:12. Pg. 155
- 28:13. Pg. 156
- 28:19. Pg. 156
- 28:20. Pg. 157
- 28:23. Pg. 157
- 28:25. Pg. 158
- 28:27. Pg. 158
- 29:5. Pg. 158
- 29:7. Pg. 159
- 29:11. Pg. 159
- 29:18. Pg. 160
- 29:20. Pg. 160
- 29:23. Pg. 160
- 29:25. Pg. 161
- 30:4. Pg. 161
- 30:5. Pg. 162
- 30:7-9. Pg. 162
- 30:10. Pg. 163
- 30:18-19. Pg. 163
- 30:33. Pg. 164
- 31:8-9. Pg. 164
- 31:10-12. Pg. 165
- 31:16-18. Pg. 165-166
- 31:20. Pg. 166
- 31:25. Pg. 166
- 31:26. Pg. 167
- 31:30. Pg. 167

Jeremiah
- 23:4. Pg. 133
- 18:24. Pg. ix
- 29:11. Pg. 172

Isaiah
    35:3. Pg. 42
    53:6. Pg. 172

NEW TESTAMENT

Matthew
    5:8. Pg. 152
    5:13-16. Pg. 60
    10:22. Pg. 131
    18:15-17. Pg. 130
    26:41. Pg. 131

Mark
    10:42-45. Pg. xi
    10:43-45. Pg. xi

Luke
    9:18-20. Pg. 92

John
    1:12-13. Pg. 172
    1:29. Pg. 172
    3:16. Pg. 172
    4:34. Pg. 132
    8:31-32. Pg. 150, Pg. 171
    13:1-5. Pg. 92
    13:3. Pg. 92
    13:4-5. Pg. 92
    15:9-16. Pg. 151
    15:17. Pg. 171
    17:4. Pg. 132
    17:17. Pg. 132

Acts
    1:8. Pg. 132
    4:20. Pg. 132
    4:36. Pg. 42
    4:36-37. Pg. 40
    9:26-27. Pg. 40
    11:22-26. Pg. 41
    11:23. Pg. 42
    13:2. Pg. 40
    15:25. Pg. 40
    15:31-32. Pg. 42
    15:35. Pg. 40

Acts (Continued)
16:40. Pg. 42
18:27. Pg. 43
20:24. Pg. 133
20:28. Pg. 133

Romans
3:23. Pg. 172
6:23. Pg. 172
8:28. Pg. 110, Pg. 152
12:2. Pg. 60
15:1. Pg. 41
15:2. Pg. 41
15:4. Pg. 43
15:5. Pg. 43

1 Corinthians
1:18. Pg. 129
1:21. Pg. 129
4:13. Pg. 132
8:1. Pg. 42
10:12. Pg. 131
13:4. Pg. 131
15:58. Pg. 131
16:12. Pg. 129
16:13. Pg. 131

Ephesians
3:19-20. Pg. vii
5:11. Pg. 129
4:29. Pg. 42
6:2-3. Pg. 103

Philippians
1:6. Pg. 75
1:29. Pg. 131
2:1. Pg. 43
3:10. Pg. 171
4:8. Pg. 149
4:9. Pg. 20

Colossians
2:2. Pg. 43
4:8. Pg. 43
4:11. Pg. 43

1 Thessalonians
    1:6-7. Pg. 59, Pg. 171
    3:2. Pg. 43
    4:13. Pg.
    5:11. Pg. 41, 43
    5:14. Pg. 43

1 Timothy
    1:12. Pg. 133
    5:20. Pg. 130

2 Timothy
    2:2. Pg. 171
    2:15. Pg. 60
    3:1. Pg. 129
    4:1-5. Pg. 128
    4:2. Pg. 128, 129, 130
    4:5. Pg. 131
    4:5-8. Pg. 168
    4:6-8. Pg. 133

Titus
    1:9. Pg. 130
    2:4. Pg. 43
    2:6-8. Pg. 60
    2:15. Pg. 130
    3:10. Pg. 130

Hebrews
    3:13. Pg. 43, 131
    6:18. Pg. 43
    12:1. Pg. 132

James
    1:2-4. Pg. 152
    1:12. Pg. 132

1 Peter
    1:22. Pg. 152
    3:15. Pg. 132
    5:2. Pg. 131
    5:8. Pg. 131

2 Peter
    1:3. Pg. 171

Topical Bibliography for the Quality Disciple

Spiritual Disciplines

1. Foster, Richard. 1988. *Celebration of discipline: the path to spiritual growth.* San Francisco, CA: Harper San Francisco.
2. Willard, Dallas. 1988. *The spirit of the disciplines: understanding how God changes lives.* San Francisco, CA: Harper San Francisco.

Prayer

3. Foster, Richard. 1992. P*rayer: Finding the Heart's True Home.* San Francisco, CA: Harper San Francisco.
4. Lockyer, Herbert. 1959. *All the prayers of the Bible.* Grand Rapids, MI: Zondervan.
5. Murray, Andrew. 1983, reprint. *Living a prayerful life.* Minneapolis, MN: Bethany House.
6. Duewel, Wesley L. 1986. *Touch the world through prayer.* Grand Rapids, MI: Francis Asbury Press.
7. Bounds, E. M. 2004. *The complete works of E. M. Bounds on prayer.* Grand Rapids, MI: Baker Books.
8. Sanders, J. Oswald. 1980. *Spiritual leadership.* Chicago, IL: Moody Press.

Bible Study

9. McKnight, Scot. 2008. *The blue parakeet: rethinking how you read the Bible.* Grand Rapids, MI: Zondervan.
10. McQuilkin, Robertson. 1992. *Understanding and applying the Bible*, Chicago, IL: Moody Press.
11. Peterson, Eugene H. 2006. *Eat this book: a conversation in the art of spiritual reading.* Grand Rapids, MI: Wm. B. Eerdmans Publishing Co.

Worship

12. MacDonald, James. 2006. *Downpour.* Nashville, TN: Broadman & Holdman.
13. Thomas, Gary. 2000. *Sacred Pathways: discover your soul's path to God, first Zondervan edition.* Grand Rapids, MI: Zondervan.

Grace

14. Strombeck, J. F. 1947, (2nd edition). *Disciplined by grace: studies in Christian conduct.* Moline, IL. Strombeck Agency, Inc; distributed by Van Kampen Press, Chicago, IL.
15. Swindoll, Charles, R. 2003. *The Grace Awakening.* Nashville, TN: W Publishing Group.

Community

16. Bates, Denny. 2005. *Building a Christian community of friends.* Florence, SC: Something New Christian Publishers.
17. Crabb, Larry. 1999. *The safest place on earth: where people connect and are forever changed.* Nashville, TN: Word Publishing.

Service

18. Rees, Erik. 2006. *S.H.A.P.E.: finding and fulfilling your unique purpose for life.* Grand Rapids, MI: Zondervan.

Evangelism

19. Coleman, Robert E. 1963, 1964, 1993. [New Spire edition 1994]. *The master plan of evangelism.* Grand Rapids, MI: Fleming H. Revell.
20. McQuilkin, Robertson. 1984, 2002 (rev). *The great omission.* Waynesboro, GA: Authentic Media.

21. Pippert, Rebecca Manley. 1979. *Out of the salt shaker and into the world*. Downers Grove, IL: InterVarsity Press.

Discipleship and the Christian Life

22. Allender, Dan B. 2006. *Leading with a limp: turning your struggles into strengths*. Colorado Springs, CO: Waterbrook Press.
23. Anderson, Keith R. and Reese, Randy D. 1999. *Spiritual mentoring: a guide for seeking and giving direction*. Downers Grove, IL: InterVarsity Press.
24. Arn, Win and Charles. 1998. *The master's plan for making disciples, 2nd edition*. Grand Rapids, MI: Baker Books.
25. Barna, George. 2001. *Growing true disciples: new strategies for producing genuine followers of Christ*. Colorado Springs, CO: Waterbrook Press.
26. Biehl, Bobb. 1996. *Mentoring: confidence in finding a mentor and becoming one*. Nashville, TN: Broadman and Holman Publishers.
27. Blackaby, Henry and Richard. 2001. *Spiritual leadership: moving people to God's agenda*. Nashville, TN: Broadman & Holman Publishers.
28. Boa, Kenneth. 2006. *The perfect leader: practicing the leadership traits of God*. Colorado Springs, CO: Victor (Cook Communications Ministries).
29. Burchett, Harold E. 1980. *Spiritual Life Studies*. Published by the author.
30. Campbell, James R. 2009. *Mentor like Jesus*. Nashville, TN: B & H Publishing Group.
31. Chambers, Oswald. 1985. *Christian disciplines: volumes 1 and 2*. Grand Rapids, MI: Chosen Books.
32. Chan, Simon. 1998. *Spiritual theology: a systematic theology of the Christian life*. Downers Grove, IL: InterVarsity Press.
33. Clinton, J. Robert and Richard W. 1991. *The mentor handbook*. Altadena, CA: Barnabas Publishers.
34. Cloud, Henry and Townsend, John. 2001. *How people grow: what the Bible reveals about personal growth*. Grand Rapids, MI: Zondervan.
35. Coleman, Robert E. 1987. *The Master Plan of Discipleship*. Old Tappan, NJ: Fleming H. Revell.
36. Hagberg, Janet O., and Guelich, Robert A. 2005, 1995. *The critical journey: stages in the life of faith*. Salem, WI: Sheffield Publishing Company.
37. Hanks, Billie Jr., and Shell, William A. 1982. *Discipleship: the best writings from the most experienced disciplemakers*. Grand Rapids, MI: The Zondervan Corporation.
38. Harney, Kevin. 2007. *Leadership from the inside out: examining the inner life of a healthy church leader*. Grand Rapids, MI: Zondervan.
39. Hart, Arcihbald D. 1995. *Adrenaline and Stress*. Nashville, TN: W. Publishing Group.
40. Hawkins, Greg L., Parkinson, Cally, and Arnson, Eric. 2007. *Reveal*. Barrington, IL: Willow Creek Resources.
41. Hawkins, Greg L. and Parkinson, Cally. 2008. *Follow me*. Barrington, IL: Willow Creek Resources.
42. Hendricks, Howard and William. 1995. *As iron sharpens iron*. Chicago, IL: Moody Publishers.
43. Hettinga, Jan David. 1996. *Follow me: experience the loving leadership of Jesus*. Colorado Springs, CO: NavPress.
44. Hull, Bill. 2004. *Choose the life: exploring a faith that embraces discipleship*. Grand Rapids, MI: Baker Books.
45. Hull, Bill. 1990. *The disciple-making church*. Grand Rapids, MI: Fleming H. Revell.
46. Hull, Bill. 1995. *Building high commitment in a low commitment world*. Grand Rapids, MI: Fleming H. Revell.
47. Hull, Robert W. 2006. *The complete book of discipleship*. Colorado Springs. NavPress.
48. Ingram, Chip. 2007. *Good to great in God's eyes: 10 practices great Christians have in common*.

Grand Rapids, MI: Baker Books.
49. Lovelace, Richard J. 1985. *Renewal as a way of life: a guidebook for spiritual growth*. Downers Grove, IL: InterVarsity Press.
50. MacArthur, John F. Jr. 1976. *Keys to spiritual growth*. Old Tappan, NJ: Fleming H. Revell Company.
51. Mancini, Will. 2008. *Church unique: how missional leaders cast vision, capture culture, and create movement*. San Francisco, CA: Jossey-Bass.
52. Maxwell, John C. 2005. *The 360-degree leader: developing your influence from anywhere in the organization*. Nashville, TN: Thomas Nelson, Inc.
53. McCallum, Dennis and Lowery, Jessica. 2006. *Organic disciplemaking: mentoring others into spiritual maturity and leadership*. Houston, TX: Touch Publications.
54. McIntosh, Gary L. and Rima, Samuel D., Sr. 1997. *Overcoming the dark side of leadership: the paradox of personal dysfunction*. Grand Rapids, MI: Baker Books.
55. Morley, Patrick, David Delk, and Brett Clemmer. 2006. *No man left behind: how to build a thriving disciple-making ministry for every man in your church*. Chicago, IL: Moody Publishers.
56. Nouwen, Henri J. M. 1975. *Reaching Out: the three movements of the spiritual life*. Garden City, NY: Doubleday and Company, Inc.
57. Ogden, Greg. 2003. *Transforming discipleship: making disciples a few at a time*. Downers Grove, IL: InterVarsity Press.
58. Olson, David T. 2008. *The American church in crisis*. Grand Rapids, MI: Zondervan.
59. Peterson, Jim. 1993. *Lifestyle discipleship: the challenge of following Jesus in today's world*. Colorado Springs, CO: NavPress.
60. Pue, Carson. 2005. *Mentoring leaders: wisdom for developing character, calling, and competency*. Grand Rapids, MI: Baker Books.
61. Putnam, David. 2008. *Breaking the discipleship code*. Nashville, TN: B&H Publishing Group.
62. Sanders, J. Oswald. (1994). *Spiritual discipleship*. Chicago, IL: Moody Publishers.
63. Scazzero, Peter L. (2003). *The emotionally healthy church: a strategy for discipleship that actually changes lives*. Grand Rapids, MI: Zondervan.
64. Stanford, Miles J. 1982. *The green letters: principles of spiritual growth*. Grand Rapids, MI: Zondervan Publishing House.
65. Stanley, Paul D. and Clinton, Robert J. 1992. *Connecting: the mentoring relationships you need to succeed in life*. Colorado Springs, CO: NavPress.
66. Waggoner, Brad J. 2008. *The shape of faith to come: spiritual formation and the future of discipleship*. Nashville, TN: B&H Publishing Group.
67. Willard, Dallas. 1998. *The divine conspiracy: rediscovering our hidden life in God*. San Francisco, CA: HarperSanFrancisco.
68. Willard, Dallas. 2006. *The great omission: reclaiming Jesus's essential teachings on discipleship*. San Francisco, CA: HarperSanFrancisco.
69. Warren, Rick. 1995. *The purpose-driven church*. Grand Rapids, MI: Zondervan.
70. Warren, Rick. 2002. *The purpose-driven life*. Grand Rapids, MI: Zondervan.
71. Wilkins, Michael J. 1992. *Following the Master: discipleship in the steps of Jesus*. Grand Rapids, MI: Zondervan Publishing House.

Quality Wisdom For A Modern Age

Essential Spiritual Growth Resources from Something New Christian Publishers and Quality Leadership Consultants

Websites, Newsletter, and Blogs:

www.dennybates.com and www.ReallyGoodDay4U.com is the hub for all of our teaching and coaching resources. Check out our free downloads as well as our store.

www.thequalitydisciple.com links to dennybates.com.

www.qualityleadershipconsultants.com links to dennybates.com.

www.thequalitydisciple.blogspot.com is the teaching blog for Psalms of Discipleship.

www.facebook.com/denny.bates is my portal to social networking.

Dr. Denny Bates and Quality Leadership Tips For You is my newsletter. Featured leadership articles, devotional thoughts, and a menu of coaching and book resources.

Sign up at http://www.dennybates.com You can follow me on Twitter @dennybates

Books:

Other titles from the Quality Discipleship Series:
- How To Study And Apply The Bible To Your Life (PDF Book only)
- Growing Up...Practical Bible Studies For New And Growing Christians (PDF Book only)
- Psalms of Discipleship: A One Year Journey With The Shepherd (Kindle or printed copy)
- Christmas Meditations of Worship: Four Weeks of Advent (Kindle or printed copy)
- Living Above The Fray: Learning The Seven Healthy Leadership Principles That Will Shelter You From The Destructive Effects Of Leader-I-Tis (Kindle or printed copy)
- My Spiritual Life Plan: Creating An Effective Spiritual Life Plan For The Quality Disciple (Kindle or printed copy)
- Living Above The Fray Leadership Assessment: The Coaches Guide For Leading With Quality In Mind (Kindle or printed copy)
- Building A Christian Community Of Friends: Four Practical Studies On Biblical Friendships (Kindle or printed copy)
- Changing Places: Understanding The Process Of Transition. (Kindle or printed copy)
- Life-Ol-Ogy: Mastering The Study Of Your Life, Your Team, Your Profession and Your Customers (Kindle or printed copy)
- Growing In Greatness: *31 Living Legacy Principles From the Proverbs For the Quality Leader (Proverbs 1:1-5:14), Volume 1* (Kindle or printed copy)
- Coming in 2020!!! Living Beyond The Fray: *How Bitter Busters Can Set You Free From Becoming Bitter Against Family, Friends, Career, Church and God."*

Retreat Journals:
- The Power – Broker's Guide To The Kingdom
- Four Legacies For A Life Change
- Three Commitments That Change A Life
- Growing In Grace: A Fresh Look At Biblical Discipleship

- ❖ Adding Quality To Your Life

Help Me Write My Story Books (A ghost writing and book coaching custom service)
For information connect to www.HelpMeWriteMyStory.com

- ❖ "Touched by Him: A Man Who Said Yes To Jesus" by Harry F. Lyles as told to Dr. Denny Bates (Unpublished)
- ❖ "I'm Just Rebeckah Wilhelmina And I Found A Way Out" by Rebeckah Wilhelmina (Healthy Curves Count Publishers)
- ❖ "The Blue Duck: Learning How To Discover Your Competitive Edge And Celebrate The Uniqueness Of You" by Sandra Mason (Younique Publishers)
- ❖ "Take the Soap" by Bryan Braddock, Byon "kNOw Ca$h" McCullough as told to Dr. Denny Bates (Take The Soap Publishers—Coming in 2019)

Contact us for availability and cost.
www.dennybates.com

Quality Wisdom For A Modern Age

What is your story?

Help Me Write My Story (HMWMS)
www.HelpMeWriteMyStory.com

HELP ME WRITE MY STORY is a highly relational, process-driven, professional service that empowers an aspiring author to produce a personal memoir that is shared in a self-published book (including Kindle too). HELP ME WRITE MY STORY helps you to focus on this acrostic:

H = **Heartfelt** (The best place to begin writing your story is in the HEART)

M = **Memories** (If you do not WRITE THEM DOWN you will eventually FORGET many of them)

W = **Well-spoken** (To tell your story you've got to be a CLEAR COMMUNICATOR so you will be understood)

M = **Motivational** (It's important for you not to only share with your readers how CHALLENGING your circumstances may have been but it's even more important to share how you faced your obstacles and got through them SUCCESSFULLY)

S = **Strategic** (Your story will most likely not speak to everyone, but it will speak to SOMEONE, so it's important to know WHO you are seeking to influence the most and why)

I believe that our lives are the sum of many stories filled with adventures, wonders, disappointments, successes, tragedies, victories, and mysteries. Our **STORIES**, all of them, have the necessary components for a lasting legacy.

Your story is a **GIFT** to others. Your life is a **STEWARDSHIP**. Your story matters because **YOU MATTER**. Your story needs to be **SHARED** with and **REMEMBERED** by those who need to KNOW your story.

That said, many **STORIES** never go beyond the back of our minds and fade away forever. And that is why I am writing to you. I want to help you **WRITE YOUR STORY**.

IMAGINE for a moment what you could do with **YOUR STORY** in the **FORM** of a **BOOK**:

- **YOUR STORY**, in the form of a quality published book, becomes something tangible and is in your hands.

- **YOUR STORY** can give encouragement to others, especially to your family, friends, and customers/clients, and even to people you will unlikely ever meet in this life.

- **YOUR STORY** contains your legacy and will always be there, even after you are long gone, influencing future readers.

- **YOUR STORY**, in the form of a book, will be the perfect and unique item for you to give away or sell, creating a new revenue stream.

- **YOUR STORY** can serve as a mentor to help the person who wants to learn how to apply the life lessons you experienced.

YOUR STORY matters to you and **YOUR STORY** matters to me too.

What is HELP ME WRITE MY STORY?

HELP ME WRITE MY STORY coaches the author client through each creative phase of writing a book:

- How to create the Big Story Idea
- How to create a *Write My Story Time Line*
- How to do great research
- How to create a strong outline of chapters and subchapters
- How to use creative words to paint vivid mental and emotional images
- How to tell your story in an interesting way
- How to write strong chapter summaries

- How to create of book title and subtitle that resonates with the reader
- How to create a book front and back cover that catches the reader's attention
- How to write back cover copy
- How to take an author's story to the finished product in print and in Kindle formats.
- How to use the power of social networking to promote your story

Who needs HELP ME WRITE MY STORY?

HELP ME WRITE MY STORY can be a great resource for the person who . . .

- Wants to write their story but need practical instruction, intentional coaching and accountability.
- Wants to make sure their story, their legacy, is preserved in a format so family members and friends will remember and be inspired by their story.
- Wants to use their story as a way to open doors of future opportunities for even greater influence.
- Wants a personal product to either sell or gift to others.
- Wants the rewarding satisfaction of having a professional copy of their personal story.

How does HELP ME WRITE MY STORY work?

Each writing project has its own unique set of challenges, but I've sought to present three different packages and pricing levels. All five are dependent upon the pace, progress, and extraordinary challenges of the book.

There are five Story Coaching service levels of Help Me Write My Story*:

In addition to the fees for each package, a reduced monthly payment plus a percentage of the royalties is an alternative form of payment. See me for the details.

Help Me Write My Story Books is a ghost writing and book coaching custom service. For information connect to www.HelpMeWriteMyStory.com

Daily Declarations For Positive People

QUALITY LEADERSHIP CONSULTANTS

PROFESSIONAL COACHING, CONSULTING,
AND TEACHING
Presenting Quality Ideas;
Producing Quality Leaders

Introducing Dr. Denny Bates
Professional Life, Business Coach, Teacher, Writer, Speaker And Consultant

Why is it important for you to have a professional quality life coach and leadership trainer?

It has been said, "Experience is the best guide in life." The truth is *guided experience* is the best guide! Time, money, and emotional energy can be saved by linking up with a person who already understands where you are, where you want to go and has a good grasp on how to lead you there in a positive way.

What kind of guided experience do I offer?

Seasoned in both the market place and non-profit settings, I can offer you and/or your organization Quality Leadership coaching tracks with a relational emphasis. For instance: Personal Growth, Communication Skills, Building Healthy Relationships, Career Counseling / Job Performance, Life Transitions, Organizational Health; and for faith-based individuals and/or organizations, Spiritual Growth. My practical experience in both for-profit and non-profit settings, coupled with my academic and professional training, affords me the ability to offer you unique Quality Leadership services.

My friend John Maxwell says,

"Everything rises and falls on leadership"

**As a Leadership Specialist,
I can help YOU in the marketplace!**

- ✓ With years of experience working as a manager in the marketplace, I know what it takes to create a healthy organization. I can train your leaders and employees in effective teamwork and communication.

- ✓ I know how to help business leaders practice the kind of self-care that not only benefits them personally, but also adds value to the company.

- ✓ I know how to help a management team build a culture that places great value on integrity and success.

- ✓ I can help you and your leaders set reasonable goals and show you the tools to help you reach each one.

- ✓ I can help you reproduce your values, vision and passion in the lives of others.

- ✓ I can help you sharpen your leadership skills in a group coaching setting or one to one. As a professional life coach and leadership trainer, I can offer you the finest coaching and training resources available today as a certified coach, teacher and speaker for the John Maxwell Team.

QUALITY LEADERSHIP CONSULTANTS

Email dennybates@gmail.com
www.dennybates.com

What does a Disciple-Making Ministry look like?
It looks like . . .

SOMETHING *new*

"Do not call to mind the former things, or ponder things of the past; Behold, I will do something new . . ." Isaiah 43:18, 19a

- Is a ministry that focuses upon making Quality disciples for Jesus

- Is a ministry that encourages believers to connect in community and experience the discipled life

- Is a ministry that seeks to help other body of believers to learn how to live the discipled life through seminars, workshops, keynote speaking and interactive coaching

Contact Dr. Denny Bates for more information on how you and your church can create a culture of DiscipleMakers4Jesus

www.TheQualityDisciple.com

Quality Wisdom For A Modern Age

What Others Are Saying About My Leadership Coaching And Discipleship Via DiscipleMakers4Jesus (DM4J)

I know and have worked with Denny Bates for more than a decade. Denny now serves as a leadership trainer and coach. It is my pleasure to recommend Denny as a valuable and trusted resource for leadership training and coaching. In addition to earning his doctoral degree in leadership, Denny is also an independent certified coach, teacher, and speaker for The John Maxwell Team. I believe you and your organization will benefit from his knowledge of what leaders need in order to grow as a leader. You will appreciate Denny's relational approach to leadership training and his ability to connect with people. Dr. Bates offers workshops, seminars, keynote speaking, and coaching ... aiding your personal and professional growth through study and practical application of John Maxwell's leadership methods. **(President and CEO of Regional Hospital)**

Just wanted to let you know how much our time of coaching and leadership development has meant to me. Every time I am faced with a challenge I try to walk thru the Grace tree of wisdom. You set the example every day of the man of God I want to be. Thank you! **(Corporate Manager of Medical Services)**

[I've learned] to keep the main thing the main thing!! To take care of the people that God puts in front of me everyday. **(Sales Manager of automotive dealership)**

Denny has been my friend, pastor, colleague, mentor and confidant for almost 10 years. During this time, Denny has led me through tough waters, given me wise counsel and taught me practical ways to live out my faith while falling more in love with my Savior. **(Youth Pastor)**

Other than my own father, Denny has been my most trusted friend and spiritual mentor. Denny's discipleship has been truly transforming and helped me to realize the importance of investing in others as he has invested in me. **(Medical Device Consultant)**

I treasure my relationship with Denny because we share a common heart to help people discover all that Christ wants to do in and through them. **(Disciple-Making Missionary to Eastern Europe)**

I have known Denny for many years and have had the privilege to work with him on the same pastoral staff for over 5 years. During that time I have sought Denny's counsel on many issues ranging from personal struggles to theological questions. Denny has always provided me with poignant, gracious and thoughtful counsel. They say that everyone should have a mentor and I am blessed to be able to consider Denny my mentor. He has been an invaluable asset in my life and ministry. **(Clinical Counselor)**

My relationship with Denny has been personal, honest, and Christ-centered. Denny's common sense approach to the issues of life is always soundly based on scriptural principles. I remember discussing with Denny how I felt that I needed to do so much service for the Lord because of all the times I had failed Him. Denny gently said to me, "It's all about grace". I was reminded that there is no 'payback' plan for the Lord. **(Pastor)**

Having a group of peers who candidly discuss the awesome responsibility that each carries as a servant and hearing how God has responded so richly to our needs clearly demonstrates how marvelous is our God, who works in each of our lives to do His will. **(Hospital Vice-President in a discipleship group for executives)**

Denny and I have know each other for nearly fifteen years, we bonded shortly after he had his heart attack because of an illness I had years prior – Guillain-Barre Syndrome – that made me more aware of the right priorities I should have in life. Through this episode and having children similar in age we bonded in a unique and special way rarely achieved between men. Approximately one year ago I lost my job as a senior executive at a large international company that I had been with 26 years, during the transition period of me finding another job Denny was an extreme encouragement to me. During a time when I was wrestling between accepting a position or not and I will never forget what Denny told me "You can just accept it as God's providential care". He was right! I later humbly accepted the position as President & Chief Operating Officer for a Subsea Oilfield Manufacturing company. **(Corporate Executive)**

Denny has been a teacher / mentor / discipler / encourager / prayer partner and great friend who God has used to help me keep a godly perspective on the different times & issues of life I've gone through as I've seek to follow Jesus. Once while praying with Denny through a career move, he encouraged me to think of the gifts & skills I had and then ask what I had a passion for, and then to ask God to show me how they can fit together. From this I learned to stop putting these gifts & skills in a "Box" and limiting what God could do with them, and use them for. For the first time, as I now work for a non-profit Christian organization as a warehouse manager, I feel I'm using the gifts and abilities God has given me to fulfill His purpose at something I really have a passion for! **(Former market place worker, now Missionary who is impacting the world)**

Denny met with me at 7 a.m. every Friday for a year. He came to me knowing he would receive my weekly burdens. This is not the way any of us would choose to begin our day. He does not judge nor do I ever feel judged. He is one of the most selfless and giving person I have ever met. This is easy to say because I know he is just a man. His obedience to God sets him apart. He taught me to live by grace, be long suffering, and love my wife regardless of my excuses. **(Medical Worker, Physical therapist assistant)**

Through a lifestyle of disciple making, Denny Bates has shown me what it truly means to live out Matthew 28: 19, 20. **(Educator)**

I've heard it said that on this side of eternity that there are only two things that you can be certain of: death and taxes. I'm certain of three things; the first two and that I have a friend in Denny Bates! I asked God at the beginning of my ministry to bring solid men into my life that would disciple me, teach me and hold me accountable. Denny has been an extreme answer to that prayer. **(Church-planting Pastor)**

Dr. Denny Bates opened my eyes to the power of small groups. He showed me what a true mentor really is. I will be forever grateful for his leadership, friendship, and love! **(Videographer)**

Practical application of God's teachings by normal, everyday family men such as myself; that's what DM4J means to me. Listening to and sharing the innumerable ways the Lord touches the lives of each and every man in this group is not only uplifting, but inspiring. From the greatest trials to what might seem trivial, God has a plan and a purpose for it all. The value of DM4J to me is immeasurable. **(Pharmacist)**

About Dr. Denny Bates

ABOUT THE AUTHOR: Dr. Denny Bates is Principal Consultant for Quality Leadership Consultants, Vice President of resource development at Training Churches, and a founding member of the John Maxwell Team of certified coaches, speakers, and trainers. He has earned degrees from Francis Marion College [B.S.] and Columbia Biblical Seminary and School of Missions [MDiv, DMin]. With a doctoral degree in personal and organizational leadership, he is well equipped to serve as teacher, life coach, mentor, disciplemaker, motivational speaker and writer for his own leadership and personal growth titles as well as helping others write their stories (See www.HelpMeWriteMyStory.com for this custom service). Denny has written for an international publisher of Bible commentary, served as the Discipleship Pastor in the local church, as well as being as a leader in the marketplace by creating the social networking brand #Aisle31. By God's grace, he seeks to live above the fray and "Press on!" Visit www.dennybates.com

Praise For Quality Wisdom For A Modern Age:

For me, reading from the book of Proverbs has always felt a bit like trying to drink water from a fire hydrant - too much comes at me at one time and it overwhelms me. In *Quality Living For a Modern Age*, Dr. Denny Bates has meticulously broken down this powerful, timeless Old Testament book of wise instruction into day by day "bite size" truths enabling the reader to apply each truth and get the very most out of the Scriptures. The *Prayer of Commitment* found at the end of each devotion is guaranteed to help the reader in their personal growth. This is one book you will not want to hurry through. It's great for family devotions as well.
~ Kirby King, inspirational speaker and Bible teacher; author of *Abiding in Christ: What Is it Anyway?* and *Walking Through Fire Without Getting Burned: Finding Hope In The Hard Places*

Dr. Denny Bates has a fabulous unique way to share his wealth of quality wisdom with his readers. The devotions will lift, stretch, encourage, and press you forward. Your strongest challenge may very well be the fact that you don't want to part ways and lay the book down. Just as there is a Proverbs chapter for every day of the month, this devotional will provide you with what I like to call the icing on the cake. As you begin your journey you will want to keep this book close by at all times!
~ Carol Mabe, Life Coach, Leadership Trainer, Speaker, Author of *Kick Your Own Butt: The Fine Art Of Leading Yourself Well*

Denny Bates's *Quality Wisdom for A Modern Age* is valuable for two reasons. One, it lays our Christian principles that professionals can immediately apply to their career. Two, it is an ongoing resource of daily encouragement that can be used by new and seasoned Christians alike.
~ Traci McCombs, Author and Blogger

What a wonderful daily encouragement! Dr. Denny Bates has dissected the book of Proverbs to highlight the wisdom God has provided for us in this great book of the Bible. I believe this daily devotional will help you apply Proverbs' eternal truths in a more practical and relevant way that will assist you in your everyday Christian walk. I highly recommend *Quality Wisdom for a Modern Age* for your daily study of God's Word.
~ Ron Lyles
Owner, Schofield's Hardware and Sporting Goods
Board Trustee, Leadership Ministries Worldwide

The book of Proverbs is a phenomenal book. It is such an inspiration on what, where, who God is. It helps in our daily walk. It gives you strength, wisdom, discernment for life. It gives practical ways to look at life through God's lenses. I would highly recommend *Quality Wisdom for a Modern Age.*
~ Cleo Corey, author and life coach

Denny inspires me. His thoughts captured in this book will warm your heart and challenge your mind. Get ready to consume fresh words of wisdom.
~ Kary Oberbrunner, author of *Your Secret Name, the Deeper Path, and Day Job to Dream Job*

I love the book of Proverbs. I love how you quote and simplify the meaning of each verse to give an easy understanding of this great book. Any person who reads your book will be helped by being able to apply scripture to reality. Absolutely incredible book Denny. God bless you.
~ Traceyann Pearl Brough, author of *Heaven's Got A Plan For You*

You will find that as you read this book your thoughts are transformed, and your emotions are empowered with life. God will meet you in it as you take the journey from one page into the next. I highly recommend because it is engaging, and you will gain insight to your daily life in an enjoyable way. He has presented challenges that are relatable with answers that are attainable.
~ Laura Harris, Artist, Design Director at No Other Wall

Proverbs is my favorite book in the Bible. Primarily because of its consistent message regarding wisdom. As a Christian business leader, I am responsible for leading my team and truly making a positive difference. I never want to come up short. God enables us with unique gifts/talents, but he holds us responsible to develop those talents; this book is a great place to start. I've known Denny for some time, and he has always been passionate about Christian leadership and helping those leaders do their very best in garnering the necessary wisdom to lead well.
~ Rick Saunders
President/CEO, First Reliance Bank

I remember the day I first met Denny Bates. It was his welcoming smile that made me think of Jesus. His humor and warmth put me at ease. I knew this would be someone I would collaborate with, share advice with, and enjoy as a longtime friend. With this new published work of his, *Quality Wisdom For A Modern Age*, I can see how Denny truly fathers others in the faith. He is a disciple-maker and this new book, and its easy-to-read format will help shape the next generation of believers.
~ Robin L. Lewis,
Author of *The Guts and Glory Of Forgiveness: Living Healed*, speaker, and Christ-centered life coach

I am a very simple thinker…I really enjoyed the 31 days….simple and short…to the point….easy for me to follow.
~ Wick Jackson
Envoy International, Director

In the short time I've known Denny, I have come to find him as a very dedicated man of God, who chooses daily to walk the high road, while encouraging everyone he meets to join him. Denny doesn't just offer you a kind word and send you on your way, but rather, he demonstrates a genuine interest in and concern for others ability to maneuver through the stuff of life and come out better for it on the other side. In his book, *Quality Wisdom For A Modern Age*, Denny delves into the Proverbs, unpacking the rich material contained therein, and has provided a concise and useful tool for us to apply these old Scriptural truths in todays "Modern Age." Whether you are looking for a quick reference guide or to dig deeper, I believe you have just found what you are looking for. Thank you, Denny, for sharing your love of the LORD with us, and for your desire to see others grow in His amazing Grace!
~ Leslie Rutten
Homemaker; Occupational Therapist

For anyone who desires to be obedient to the command "But prove yourselves doers of the word, and not merely hearers who delude themselves" (James 1:22 NASB) as it applies to the Book of Proverbs, then Denny's book will prove to be a well laid out tool. There are many useful resources included. The Subject Index alone makes the book worth having. It is a tremendous guide for topical searching.
Well done my friend,
~ Ron Bennett
Elder, Bible Teacher, Church at Sandhurst

Dr. Denny Bates has put together a simple, daily look at the promises of God that are declared in direction, woven to our souls in prayer. Men and women are transformed when they allow the living word of God to live in them. Each page of *Quality Wisdom For A Modern Age* is a promise of God, declared for today, brought to life in prayer. So that "Today May You" grow in the knowledge of the Greatness of God!
~ Dick Brown
Business Owner

In *Quality Wisdom For A Modern Age*, Dr. Denny Bates' commitment to make quality disciples for Jesus shines through in this collection of rich resources. If you desire to deepen your walk with Jesus and are looking for an easy to follow, systematic approach which also offers the flexibility of diving deeper, then look no more. Whether you desire a personal study or to make progress with others (QWMA) takes you on a journey through the wisdom of Proverbs, encouraging a closer walk with Jesus.
~ Lisa Ray
Retired Educator

James, the half-brother of Jesus, wrote under the inspiration of the Holy Spirit to the dispersed who were living in a world hostile to the gospel message ... "But if any of you lacks wisdom, let him ask of God, who gives to all generously and without reproach, and it will be given to him" (James 1:5). Dr. H. Dennis Bates or Denny, my spiritual brother as well as my biological sibling, has written a resource just for those that would seek God's wisdom in a world that is still hostile to His message. *Quality Wisdom for a Modern Age* is an easy to use exploration of King Solomon's masterpiece on wisdom, Proverbs. It can be used as a devotional, a small group study or a guide for wisdom on different aspects of life as the need arises. I am truly looking forward to using it in my daily life in this complicated, complex world and am thankful that Solomon had it right when he wrote that there was nothing new under the sun; Only the names and the places change. The human experience is just that, the human experience and it never changes.
~ Tamara Bates-Rhodes, RN

You know it's going to be a good day when you encounter some quality wisdom first thing, walk with it and let it guide you throughout your day. And so, it is with the daily *Declarations of Quality Wisdom* from the Proverbs-based devotional book, *Quality Wisdom for a Modern Age,* by Denny Bates. This guidebook gives you one piece of wisdom each day for you to savor and incorporate into your daily practice. In turn providing a basis for personal growth which will spill over into your professional and spiritual life. It gives you the opportunity to apply that wisdom and live it loudly. Remember, what we say is heard in what we show. So, walk with the wisdom in this devotional and grow in greatness.
~ Dennis Arnst, PhD - Audiologist

Dr. Denny Bates has created an exegesis of Proverbs that is both rich and practical, with clear encouragement about how to live wisely in a modern community of Faith. The Lord's words are like goads; spurring us on, teaching, and admonishing. Aptly applied, God's Word is alive, critical and precious, changing the trajectory of our lives. Denny's book draws a thoughtful picture of how to best glean from the Proverbs, and how to strategically do what they say. Thank you Denny for allowing yourself to be a scholar, brother, and even more so a son. When you sent this for me to read, the Lord meant it as a balm and direction for my heart. This book is dynamic and concise, Spirit led, and a daily treasure of wisdom!
~ Dee Hoehn, M.A., L.P.C. Owner and Therapist Grace Counseling, LLC

Proverbs is well known as the book of wisdom. Having the opportunity of seeing Denny's heart and service for the Lord, I know his wisdom and insight will carry his readers on a deeper dive. Get ready for the journey.
~ Dexter Godfrey, Kingdom Power Couple

'In a society where the wisdom of the Bible is continually being pushed aside, it is refreshing to see a book published that makes The Proverbs applicable. Denny's heart to see this generation embrace the Truth and direction of the Proverbs is a light to follow through Quality Wisdom for a Modern Age"
~ Debra Lynn Hayes, author *RISE....What To Do When Hell Won't Back Off*

Most won't admit that they need it, but everyone needs guidance in today's modern age. Full of wisdom and a burning desire to always help others, Denny Bates does a great job of delivering this wisdom in a simple format.
~ John Chase, Financial Advisor

Dr. Bates uses the book of Proverbs to give simple yet profound words for each daily devotional with much attention to detail giving the reader points to ponder throughout his day. A good read.
~ Pam Clemons, retired RN

"Living in this world, we need all the wisdom we can get! The Proverbs are chock full of applicable tidbits and Dr. Bates does an amazing job at breaking it down into bite-size bits that we can digest on a daily basis. I thoroughly enjoy his approach and see it as something that anyone can implement daily--over and over!"
~ Renee Vidor, speaker, and community-creator, author of *Measuring Up: How to WIN in a World of Comparison*

In *Quality Wisdom for a Modern Age*, Dr. Denny Bates has, once again, provided a million-dollar tool for followers of Christ to develop discipleship habits and to live Kingdom lives. This resource could be used in a variety of ways and is full of "high-value wisdom" about life, about living for God, about dealing with people, and about living with situations. This work is a guaranteed GRAND SLAM for every disciple of Christ!!!
Dr. David Wike, Pastor Ebenezer Baptist Church

Quality Wisdom For A Modern Age embraces the teachings of Solomon as written in Proverbs. Timely lessons that respect our schedules yet provide an in-depth challenge encouraging us to assimilate and

connect with coworkers, friends, and seekers we meet on life's road. Whether you use it as a study guide or a future reference book for all things Proverbs; check it out.
Tessy L. Baker, Ed.S School Psychologist

Quality Wisdom For A Modern Age is an insightful read that shows you how to recognize and apply the truth on a daily basis. Dr. Denny Bates provides an amazing resource that brings the wisdom and practical teaching from the book of Proverbs to life. Make it a part of your routine as you grow, lead, serve, and impact the world.
~ Jim Zugschwert, speaker, coach, and author of *Peak Perspective*

If there is a writer who can take the ancient words of the book of Proverbs and help us apply them to our present days, that writer is Dr. Denny Bates. Quality Wisdom for a Modern Age will challenge you and bless you in your professional and personal life as Dr. Bates guides you in hearing Proverbs with enlightened spirit-led ears. This book is a must-have!
~ Helen Rogers Dobbins BSN, RN Blogger for Sorrow into Dancing

Your very practical encouragement has always been a bright spot for me. Thank you for sharing this! I can't wait to see how God will continue to use you!
~ Abby Feistel, mom and blogger

Denny is a great friend and mentor of mine and has been for nearly two decades. In *Quality Wisdom for a Modern Age* you will find insight, perspective and truth that is deeply needed for life in this world. I cannot recommend this book more highly to you. It is a must use resource as you journey through life.
~ Reeves Cannon, M.A.,LPC, BCPCC, Executive Pastor, Church at Sandhurst

Quality Wisdom for a Modern Age is not book on leadership – it is a manual on how to incorporate proverbs into our daily lives to not only deal with the issues of daily life, but to anticipate them. Keep the book close to your nightstand, to use the analogy "Break glass in case of emergency", or to be inspired. Dr. Denny Bates uses daily declarations to assist individuals and leaders to help them in their daily duties. This is important as one must be able to lead themselves in order to lead others.
~ Len Clark, Ph.D. LTC Media

"Denny has a clear talent for packaging encouraging, Biblical content in a form that anyone can benefit from. *Quality Wisdom For A Modern Age* is another winner in his lineup of materials that can be used for a variety of settings and applications. I'm thankful for his contributions to the Body of Christ!"
~ Chris Honeycutt Lead Pastor, Forward /// Myrtle Beach

Dr Denny Bates is consistent in publishing *quality* resources that we can apply in our real lives. *Quality Wisdom for a Modern Age* is no different. Denny pours his mentorship onto paper again so we can turn to daily use in practical ways to become better, *quality* leaders.
~ Bo Myers: Husband, Father, Local ministry leader, Servant pastor, Deputy Coroner

www.ingramcontent.com/pod-product-compliance
Lightning Source LLC
Chambersburg PA
CBHW080411170426
43194CB00015B/2772